Focus
on Egypt

AFRICAN LITERATURE TODAY 35

Editor:	Ernest N. Emenyonu
Assistant Editor:	Patricia T. Emenyonu
Associate Editors:	Pauline Dodgson-Katiyo
	Stephanie Newell
	Chimalum Nwankwo
	Oha Obododimma
	Kwadwo Osei-Nyame, Jnr
	Kwawisi Tekpetey
	Iniobong I. Uko
Reviews Editor:	Obi Nwakanma

JC JAMES CURREY

GUIDELINES FOR SUBMISSION OF ARTICLES

The Editor invites submission of articles on the announced themes of forthcoming issues. Submissions will be acknowledged promptly and decisions communicated within six months of the receipt of the paper. Your name and institutional affiliation (with full mailing address and email) should appear on a separate sheet, plus a brief biographical profile of not more than six lines. The editor cannot undertake to return materials submitted, and contributors are advised to keep a copy of any material sent. Articles should be submitted in the English Language.

Length: Articles should not exceed 5,000 words.
Format: Articles should be double-spaced, and should use the same type face and size throughout. Italics are preferred to underlines for titles of books. Articles are reviewed blindly, so do not insert your name, institutional affiliation and contact information on the article itself. Instead, provide such information on a separate page.

Style: UK or US spellings are acceptable, but must be used consistently. Direct quotations should retain the spellings used in the original source. Check the accuracy of citations and always give the author's surname and page number in the text, and a full reference in the Works Cited list at the end of the article. Italicize titles of books, plays and journals. Use single inverted commas throughout except for quotes within quotes which are double. Avoid subtitles or subsection headings within the text.

Citations: Limit your sources to the most recent, or the most important books and journals, in English. Cite works in foreign languages only when no English-language books are available. Cite websites only if they are relatively permanent and if they add important information unavailable elsewhere.

For in-text citations, the sequence in parentheses should be (Surname: page number). No year of publication should be reflected within the text. All details should be presented in the Works Cited list at the end of the article. Consistency is advised. Examples:

Cazenave, Odile. *Rebellious Women: The New Generation of Female African Novelists.* Boulder, CO: Lynne Rienner Publishers, 2000.
Duerden, Dennis. 'The "Discovery" of the African Mask.' *Research in African Literatures.* Vol. 31, No. 4 (Winter 2000): 29-47.
Ukala, Sam. 'Tradition, Rotimi, and His Audience.' *Goatskin Bags and Wisdom: New Critical Perspectives on African Literature.* Ed. Ernest N. Emenyonu. New Jersey: Africa World Press, 2000: 91-104.

Ensure that your Works Cited list is alphabetized on a word-by-word basis, whether citations begin with the author's name or with an anonymous work's title. Please, avoid footnotes or endnotes. Do not quote directly from the Internet without properly citing the source as you would when quoting from a book. Use substantive sources for obtaining your information and depend less on general references.

Copyright: It is the responsibility of contributors to clear permissions.

All articles should be sent to the editor, Ernest N. Emenyonu, as an e-mail attachment (Word)
Email: eernest@umflint.edu
African Literature Today
Department of Africana Studies
University of Michigan-Flint
303 East Kearsley Street
Flint MI 48502 USA
Fax: 001-810-766-6719

Books for review to be sent to the Reviews Editor. Reviewers should provide full bibliographic details, including the extent, ISBN and price:
Obi Nwakanma, University of Central Florida, English Department, Colburn Hall, 12790 Aquarius Agora Drive, Orlando , FL 32816, USA
Obi.Nwakanma@ucf.edu

AFRICAN LITERATURE TODAY

Recent and forthcoming* titles
African Literature Today continues to be published as an annual volume by
James Currey (an imprint Boydell & Brewer since 2008).
North and South American distribution:
Boydell & Brewer Inc., 68 Mount Hope Avenue, Rochester, NY 14620-2731, US
UK and International distribution:
Boydell & Brewer Ltd., PO Box 9, Woodbridge IP12 3DF, GB.
Nigeria edition (ALT 24–33): HEBN Publishers Plc

*Forthcoming

Focus on Egypt

AFRICAN LITERATURE TODAY 35

James Currey is an imprint of
Boydell & Brewer Ltd
PO Box 9, Woodbridge,
Suffolk, IP12 3DF (GB)
and of
Boydell & Brewer Inc.
668 Mt Hope Avenue,
Rochester, NY 14620-2731 (US)
www.boydellandbrewer.com
www.jamescurrey.com

British Library Cataloguing in Publication Data
is available on request

ISBN 978-1-84701-171-8 (James Currey hardback)
ISBN 978-1-84701-170-1 (Africa-only paperback)

Designed and set in 12/13.5 pt Berkeley Book by
Kate Kirkwood Publishing Services, Cumbria, UK
Printed in Great Britain by
TJ International Ltd, Padstow, Cornwall

Dedication

To Nawal El Saadawi in recognition of her immense contributions to the development and appreciation of contemporary Egyptian Literature, being the spokesperson of women in the Arab world in particular for over half a century, and her relentless advocacy for human rights and social justice for women the world over.

Contents

Notes on Contributors

Khalid Abouel-lail is Associate Professor of Arabic Literature and Folklorist, Faculty of Arts, Cairo University. He is a director of the Center for Studies of Folklore at Cairo University and editor-in-chief of the folk culture series at the Egyptian Ministry of Culture.

Tomi Adeaga lectures at the Department of African Studies, University of Vienna, Austria.

Chiji Akọma is Associate Professor of African and African Diaspora Literatures and holds joint appointments in the departments of English and Global Interdisciplinary Studies at Villanova University. He is also President of the International Society for the Oral Literatures of Africa (ISOLA).

Akachi Adimora-Ezeigbo is Professor of English, Federal University Ndufu-Alike, Ikwo, Ebonyi State, Nigeria. She is a multiple-award-winning novelist, poet, dramatist, short story and children's author.

Christine Gilmore is a tutor in Islamic and Middle Eastern Studies at the University of Edinburgh.

John C. Hawley is Professor of English at Santa Clara University, California. He is past President of the US chapter of the Association for Commonwealth Literature and Language Studies.

Mona Helmy is an Egyptian writer and a poet. She has published poems, short stories and articles. Her translated collection of poems from Arabic into English, *Travelling into the Impossible*, won the 2009 Egyptian Writer's Union Prize. She received her Doctorate degree in Environmental Sciences from Ain Shams University, Cairo. She writes every week for *Rosa al Yousef Magazine*, and *Al Dostoor Journal*.

James M. Hodapp is an Assistant Professor in the Department of English at the American University of Beirut. He has published in multiple peer-reviewed journals and collections on African, world, and postcolonial literature.

Razinat T. Mohammed is Associate Professor of Feminist Literary Criticism and Theoretical Approaches at the University of Maiduguri, Nigeria. She is the award winning author of *A Love Like a Woman's and other Stories*.

F. Fiona Moolla is a Senior Lecturer in the English Department at the University of the Western Cape, South Africa. She is the author of *Reading Nuruddin Farah: The Individual, the Novel and the Idea of Home* (James Currey) and the editor of *Natures of Africa: Ecocriticism and Animal Studies in Contemporary Cultural Forms* (WITS University Press).

Deema Nasser is a PhD candidate in the Department of Comparative Literature at Brown University, Rhode Island.

Eunice Ngongkum is Associate Professor of Postcolonial African Literature and Culture, University of Yaoundé 1, Cameroon.

Temitope Abisoye Noah is a PhD candidate at New York University's Department of German. She is an interdisciplinary scholar, with particular research interests in Africana Studies, Cinema Studies and Religious Studies.

Kelvin Ngong Toh is Senior Lecturer in the Department of English at the University of Buea, Cameroon.

Mathias Iroro Orhero is a Postgraduate student in the Department of English at the University of Uyo, Nigeria.

Nduka Otiono is Assistant Professor of African Studies, Carleton University, Ottawa, Canada. He is the author of *Voices in the Rainbow* and *Love in a Time of Nightmares* (poetry collections), and *The Night Hides with a Knife* (short stories). He has been a journalist and General Secretary of the Association of Nigerian Authors.

Kalapi Sen is a part-time Lecturer in Raja Peary Mohan College, Kolkata and a guest faculty in Lady Brabourne College, Kolkata. She completed her PhD on the novels of Chinua Achebe. She is a member of the editorial board of *Perspectives: Journal of the Department of English, Raja Peary Mohan College.*

Nadia Wassef, co-founder of Diwan Bookstores, is doing her MA in Creative Writing at Birkbeck, University of London. She also holds an MA in English and Comparative Literature, and an MA in Social Anthropology from the School of Oriental and African Studies, University of London.

Foreword

NAWAL EL SAADAWI
Translated from the Arabic by Mohamed Daassa

I have travelled from my city, Cairo, to most of the world's countries before I even travelled to any country in Africa; despite the fact that the land of Egypt is located in Africa. We are born in it, we live in it, and we are buried in its ground; our material and cultural roots as well as the sources of our river (the Nile) are enshrined in the heart of its body.

But our faces and eyes have always looked towards the North, towards the ones who have tortured and oppressed us in Europe and America, and our backs have always turned to ourselves, in Africa and the South. Oppression is certainly double when one turns her or his back to herself or himself, when one is ashamed of her or his tanned or black skin and hides it with a white powder, in the same way a woman is ashamed of being a woman when she feels that her face is a flaw. She hides it with a cover. The slavery and colonial system have hurt women, the poor and Africans, when it robbed us of our economic resources and the treasures of our civilization, which extend in history, before the beginning of history. It robbed us of our material and cultural treasures which are buried in the earth's belly, and which remain on its surface until today, such as the pyramids, obelisks, statues, and the creative monuments that the peoples of the world seek to see. But the big colonial offence was that arrow that the white man has aimed at the heart of the African man. Africa has become a source of shame and his black skin a sign of slavery.

My trips to Africa have come relatively late, at the end of the seventies, when I served as a consultant with Africa's Economic Committee at the United Nations. My residence was in Addis Ababa, but my job required travel to all African countries. Some trips were long, others were short. They were not sufficient to allow me to go inside the heart of the vast and ancient continent, even though they were enough to open my heart and discover myself and that I am African.

The first manifestation of my 'Africanness' was the colour of my tanned skin, which quickly turns black after a few hours of exposure to the sun. No one notices that I am a stranger if I walk the streets of Ethiopia, Uganda or South Africa. This did not make me happy, much as I have had a deep desire (since my childhood) to be as white as cheese, as my grand-mother used to say. I have realized since my birth two certain facts: the first one is that I am 'a girl' and not 'a boy' like my brother. The second one is that my skin is 'tanned' and not 'white' like my mother. And with these two facts I have realized a more important idea: that these two attributes by themselves, unrelated to any other flaws were sufficient to doom my future to failure.

The only asset a girl had to ensure her future was to be beautiful, or to be at least white, like Turkish people. My grandmother, who was of Turkish origin, used to call me 'Ourou', the concubine at the palace of her grandfather 'the Pasha' in Istanbul.

I have realized since I was a child that my skin had the colour of the skin of slaves. I hid it with a white powder that my maternal aunt Neemat bought from the neighbouring pharmacy. She also bought liquids to whiten the skin of the face, and others to blacken the eyes with kohl. Hiding my real face became the first step towards real beauty. But, strangely enough, I realized in a dark side of my memory, buried since the beginning of history with the mother's tongue, that I was beautiful, moreover, certainly the most beautiful girl. I realized that my tanned skin, that had the colour of the sediment of the Nile, was the most beautiful skin in the universe; which is the reality I am proud of (in secret) and love. It is rather my only true love.

As I grew a little older, I have gained the courage to face the world with a washed face, a face without make up. I feel comfortable in my skin. I feel acquainted with my body, myself, and with my African friends. To my big surprise, I fell in love with a Senegalese man upon my first trip to Dakar. When I was a child, I used to run scared at the sight of a black person.

I found the coasts and the mountains of Africa fascinating. The Kilimanjaro summit has become more beautiful than the Himalayas in Nepal. The famous Swiss mountains and Lake Victoria and the sources of the Nile in Uganda have caught me in the same way mythologies, art, cinema, dance and African music touch me deeply. African literature, produced by women and men, has become my hobby. This creative and authentic literature has conquered the world today. Egypt has come back to the arms of 'Mother Africa' after it was forcibly taken away from it to be placed in an ambiguous area situated between the continents called by the colonial powers 'the Middle East'.

The first conference on African literature I was ever invited to was during the eighties of the twentieth century in New York City. Egyptian literature was not taught in the departments of African literature in most American universities. But I did not know why the committee that organized the conference invited me. Maybe because some of my writings had gone beyond the local languages, after they were translated to one of the colonial languages, which is English.

Before I went up to the podium to deliver my speech, an American college professor who happened to be seated next to me asked me: 'From which country in Africa are you, Professor?' 'I am from Egypt Sir', I answered. His blue eyes widened with surprise and asked me: 'Is Egypt in Africa, Professor?' My black eyes widened with more surprise and I asked him: 'If Egypt is not in Africa, where would it be located?' His blond eye lashes moved and said:

'Egypt is in the Middle East'. I moved my black eye lashes and asked him: 'Where is the Middle East?' He closed his eyes slightly observing me with an air of superiority and said: 'Don't you know where the Middle East is?' I looked at him with more superiority and said: 'I don't know what you mean by Middle, Sir'. He bit his rosy lips slightly and said: 'I don't understand what you say'. I smiled somewhat and said: 'The word "Middle" was coined by the British Empire. London saw Egypt and the Arab World as the Near East. The term was changed in the language of new American colonialism and became "the Middle East" in order to remove the Arab World's name from the map, to allow Israel to occupy the Biblical and Promised Land of Palestine, and to dominate the area with napalm and its military arsenal.'

The American professor bit his lips with objection and left his seat next to me silently.

Today, I celebrate with my friends from Africa and from around the world this special edition of *African Literature Today* dedicated to Egyptian literature. Egyptian literature has come back to the mother's arms. Most African countries have gained freedom from colonial domination, which continues to threaten it and to undermine it, publicly and in secret, under the name of God, development, democracy, freedom, peace, justice, human rights or women's rights.

The beauty of literary creativity, or any sort of creativity, is to be found in its ability to liberate our minds and uncover the roots of terrorism and colonial and oppressive treachery, which keeps changing its facets, shapes and language since the beginning of slavery or the class-based, patriarchal, and racist system in history.

Nawal El Saadawi
Cairo, Egypt
5 June 2017

Editorial

'Is Egypt in Africa, Professor?'

ERNEST N. EMENYONU

At the University of Michigan-Flint, I teach a First Year Experience course (UNV 100) titled, 'Sites and Sounds of Africa'. The course was designed among other things, 'to help students see the world through the eyes of another culture'. The focus is on Africa, the second-largest continent in the world, famous for its human and natural resources. Two words describe Africa perfectly – 'Diversity and Contrast'. Students 'explore' the continent's diversities and contrasts using four selected countries for illustration. The countries represent four different geographic regions of the continent: Egypt (North), Kenya (East), Nigeria (West) and South Africa (South).

Integrated into the course are various 'experiential learning components', exposing the students to real-world examples of the basic course concepts and ideas. Visits to the Detroit Institute of Arts and the Charles Wright Museum of African American History (also in Detroit) have been a field trip requirement. The focus at the Institute is on African arts and artistic productions over the centuries, while at the Museum it is on Africa as the genesis of humankind and the source of the historic transatlantic slave trade.

One year, the visit to the Detroit Institute of Arts produced an unexpected dilemma for both the students and their professor. The purpose of the visit was to study the vast array of African works of art on display at DIA. Students were to make a close study of the art works and note carefully any documentation about them. Each student would identify three favourite works of art, study and pay particular attention to them, collect information about them such as name of object, information about the artist, place of origin of both the artist and the object, description of the piece, its purpose and cultural significance ... and its journey from Africa to its present location. At the end of the visit students would write a well thought-out paper on, 'My Impressions of African Art at the Detroit Institute of Arts'.

It turned out that the exhibits of Egyptian works of art were displayed at a location separate from those of the continent of Africa! The tourist guide and the curator did not see anything unusual about that as evident in their conscious effort to 'educate' the professor and his students that Egypt was in the Middle East and not Africa! The dialogue that ensued and the professor's enthusiastic attempts to elucidate were to no avail. That visit on 6 April 2013 became the last that the professor took with the students to the Institute, and to date nothing has changed there!

The Institute however, has not been alone among individuals and agencies the world over, who preferred to 'locate' Egypt outside the continent of Africa. In their minds perhaps, the place and contributions of Egypt in world history and civilization are too spectacularly glorious to be identified or associated with Africa, a conti-nent persistently described as 'the heart of darkness', its people impenetrably barbaric consumers and never contributors to civilization. Nawal El Saadawi, the ultra-feminist Egyptian writer, in her Foreword to this volume, recounts an encounter with an American professor at a conference on African literature held in New York City about forty years ago. The said professor tried to belittle her for introducing herself as an Egyptian from Africa and patronizingly asked her: 'Is Egypt in Africa, Professor?'

To people with such mindsets, the biblical sarcastic

reference to Nazareth as a place from which nothing good could come is most often applied to Africa. Egyptian literature could not conceivably be in African literature as such world-acclaimed writers as Naguib Mahfouz, Nawal El Saadawi, Taha Hussein, Sonallah Ibrahim, Tawfiq al-Hakim, Ahdaf Soueif – to mention but a few could not possibly have had any roots in Africa at all. It is in answer to such awkward and abominable ideas and more, that continue to echo through generations in modern times, that the Editorial Board of *African Literature Today* decided to make a special issue of the series with a focus on Egypt. The 'Call for Papers' (below) drew overwhelming response:

> Egypt, a historically important and strategically located North African country, is also a leading nation in the Arab world. This special issue of *African Literature Today* will focus on Egyptian Literature and examine writers whose works have enriched African Literature through history. Of special interest are works that depict historical forces, cultural and socio-political factors that have shaped and influenced the evolution and development of contemporary Egyptian literature.
>
> Approaches include (but are not limited to) critical explorations of folklore, myths, memoirs, poetry, short stories, and novels which capture the mood of the nation and the human condition at a particular point in time. Creativity has flourished in Arabic as well as the English language, producing acclaimed national and international writers – Naguib Mahfouz, Yusuf Idris, Nawal El Saadawi, Ahdaf Soueif, Tawfiq al-Hakim, Alifa Rifaat (Fatimah Rifaat), to mention but a few – whose thematic concerns have been as versatile as they have been controversial.
>
> The Editor seeks articles that explore the diverse genres of Egyptian Literature depicting, in particular, ideas of human rights, justice and freedom; feminism against the backgrounds of intractable patriarchy; women's rights versus religious fundamentalism; socio-political transformations and the quest for a new order.

In this volume, renowned Egyptian as well as non-Egyptian scholars have contributed articles which address various aspects of Egyptian literature in the context of continental African literature. James Hodapp and Deema Nasser's article, 'The Complications of Reading Egypt as Africa…' raise some key fundamental issues, thus:

> One of the most pernicious obstacles to African literary studies incorporating the entire African continent in its purview is the persistent division between northern and southern Africa in literary scholarship. As Ziad Bentahar has recently argued, a de facto consensus exists between African literary studies and Arabic literary studies that '"Africa" now ostensibly stands for sub-Saharan Africa, whereas North Africa is considered in many academic disciplines to be part of the Middle East instead' ('Continental Drift': 1). Bentahar's appraisal is not unique; it echoes those of previous scholars, such as Farida Abu-Haidar and Anissa Talahite, in voicing frustration that African literary studies has failed to substantially incorporate North Africa despite being urged to do so for decades. In the wake of this exclusion of North African literature in our field, this article makes a case for increased inclusion, as well as highlighting barriers, by examining a particular Egyptian text in the original Arabic and in English translation, Magdy el-Shafee's مترو (*Metro*), that has been read as world literature and Arabic literature rather than African literature.

In a related discourse on boundaries and inclusions, Christine Gilmore, in her 'Narratives of the "Nubian Awakening": Reclaiming Egypt's African Identity', states:

> this paper argues that Nubian literature contests the unitary fiction of Egypt's Arab identity postulated during the heyday of Arab nationalism by highlighting the nation's marginalized African identity. As such, it can be seen as part of a broader trend in modern Egyptian writing known as 'border literature' which seeks to integrate regional and minority subjectivities into Egypt's national imaginary. (el-Refaei 'Egypt's Borders')

After an expansive discourse, the article concludes: 'Whereas the postcolonial period may have favoured a unitary conception of Egyptian identity as an Arab nation, Oddoul's writing presents Egypt itself as a site of difference by highlighting its marginalized Afro-Nubian history and civilization'.

In his article, 'African Epics: A Comparative Study…', Khalid Abouel-lail offers an extensive comparative analysis of the epic of *Sundiata* from West Africa and *Al-Sirah al-Hilaliyyah*, a North African epic, examining scrupulously their similarities and differences thus:

> This article focuses on D. T. Niane's *Sundiata: An Epic of Old Mali* and different narrations of *Al-Sirah al-Hilaliyyah* in Egypt, to investigate the similarities and differences between them in relation to the structure of the epic, represented by the stages through which the folk cultural hero passes: the prophecy, the birth of the hero, the alienation of the hero, and the final recognition of the hero. The article depends on the comparative method and the oral-formulaic theory (Finnegan *Oral Poetry*; Ong *Orality and Literacy*).

His interesting findings reveal more similarities than differences despite their settings and cultural nuances.

Earlier versions of the two articles above were originally presented as the papers 'African Epics: A Comparative Study of in Egypt *Al-Sirah al-Hilaliyyah* and *The Epic of Sundiata Keita* in West Africa' by Khalid Abouel-lail, and 'Narratives of the "Nubian Awakening": Reclaiming Egypt's African Identity' by Christine Gilmore, on panels convened by Réhab Abdelghany as part of the proceedings of the ASAUK biennial conference at the University of Sussex, 2014.

Other articles focusing on Egyptian literature in the volume are case studies of the works of specific Egyptian writers – Sonallah Ibrahim, Ahdaf Soueif, Yusuf Idris, Mohamed Salmawy and Nawal El Saadawi. They reveal works by eminent writers whose creativity and craftsmanship have enriched contemporary African writing in all genres and ramifications.

If any issues remained about the identity and heritage of Egyptian literature, they have been laid to rest by the irrepressible Nawal El Saadawi in her Foreword to this volume, part of which reads:

> The first conference on African literature I was ever invited to was during the eighties of the twentieth century in New York City. […]
>
> Before I went up to the podium to deliver my speech, an American college professor who happened to be seated next to me asked me: 'From which country in Africa are you Professor?' 'I am from Egypt Sir', I answered. His blue eyes widened with surprise and he asked me: 'Is Egypt in Africa, Professor?' My black eyes widened with more surprise and I asked him: 'If Egypt is not in Africa, where would it be located?' […]
>
> *Today, I celebrate with my friends from Africa and from around the world this special edition of* African Literature Today *dedicated to Egyptian literature. Egyptian literature has come back to the mother's arms.* (emphasis added)

In this volume too, are featured articles on other African literature topics, as well as a beautiful array of pieces of short creative writing (prose and poetry) set in Africa physically or intrinsically. Enjoy!

Coping with a Failed Revolution

Basma Abdel Aziz, Nael Eltoukhy, Mohammed Rabie &
Yasmine El Rashidi

JOHN C. HAWLEY

'In war, truth is the first casualty.' (Aeschylus)

'Now I pick up the notebook chronicling that time, starting in
the summer of 2010. On every page I take note of the question
marks. The word *truth* seems to repeat itself multiple times
on each page. My handwriting is barely legible.' (Yasmine El
Rashidi, *Chronicle of a Last Summer*, 147)

In 1992 Hilary Kilpatrick remarked that 'twenty years
ago the Arabic novel was regarded as practically synonymous with the Egyptian novel' ('The Egyptian Novel from
Zaynab to 1980': 223). Though novel production had by
1992 become firmly rooted in most Arab countries the
'relatively longer history of the genre' in Egypt 'enable[d]
its different stages of development to be distinguished and
studied more easily than is the case in countries where it
has had a life of only two or three decades'. Judging from
several recent novels, a new stage in that development is
taking place. The Democracy Spring, or 'the Arab Spring',
that stretched roughly from December 2010 to mid-2012
and seemed to cross many borders almost at the same time
has unsurprisingly become a persistent focus for Egyptian
novelists, and they are offering the most cohesive set of
responses to that startling turn in contemporary Arab
history. Their creative spectrum of reflections on the initial
hopes and ultimate disillusionment range from ongoing
defiance and hope, to a resigned acceptance, echoing
Alphonse Karr's infamous quip: '*plus ça change, plus c'est*

la même chose'. Formalistically this range of responses has expressed itself in self-deprecating wit, demonstrable in Nael Eltoukhy's *Women of Karantina*; surrealist abstraction and universalist imagery in Basma Abdel Aziz's *The Queue*; a despairing dystopic vision of a relentlessly brutal future in Mohammed Rabie's *Otared*; and a personal philosophical reflection on the nature of change and stasis, in Yasmine El Rashidi's *Chronicle of a Last Summer*. Only when such very different works are read together can one appreciate the complex psychological upheaval that is very much alive in Egyptian – and Arabic – society. For these writers, time itself becomes a central character, suggesting authors who seek in their craft a nominal agency over a series of traumas that remain beyond personal control. El Rashidi is most traditional, creating a protagonist writing as a memoirist who remembers her childhood and traces her history up to the present. Abdel Aziz blurs the reader's sense of time altogether, seeming to suggest that one monotonous day is, and always has been, much like any other. Rabie and Eltoukhy throw the reader decades into the future, rendering the present simply a precursor to a much more terrible time to come.

The events that have prompted this literary outpouring might seem to many to be amazingly short-lived, but Al-Zubaidi and others suggest:

> What we witnessed on television was only a small part of a larger struggle that didn't begin with the self-immolation of Tunisian fruitseller Mohamed Bouazizi, or end when one dictator took a plane to Saudi and another a bullet in the head. And as people took to the streets, the same media that, for so long, failed to highlight Egypt's dungeons or Bahrain's protests or Tunisia's sham elections, now covered the Arab world on its front pages. (Al-Zubaidi et al. *Diaries of an Unfinished Revolution*: vii)

In January and February of 2011 there were the protests in Tahrir Square and the surprising toppling of President

Mubarak and his government, succeeded from February 2011 until June of 2012 first by the Supreme Council of the Armed forces; this, in turn, was replaced by a government by the Muslim Brotherhood and the election of President Mohammad Morsi. That last stage lasted about one year. As Paul Amar describes those volatile days, Egyptians suddenly became 'sexy, fearless, and powerful – the model for young activists worldwide and the embodiment of surging popular sovereignty' (Amar 'Egypt': 28). 'Going full Egyptian' was a phrase that entered common parlance, meaning 'let's abandon fear, unleash solidarity, and re-occupy public space' (29). By the fall of 2011, though, that jouissance was replaced with outrage and despair as the military imposed a regime that was stricter than the one that had been overthrown. When Morsi was elected, he again dashed revolutionary hopes by seeking to extend the Brotherhood's hegemony and moving the country farther to the right.

That caused many to question whether or not a revolution had taken place, at all. Amar suggests that a *political* revolution did take place, as had a *civic* revolution, but a *social* revolution had not (38). He goes on to assert, though, that

> A revolution in consciousness (*thawra dhihniya*) had certainly taken place, as new cultures of criticism and irony – and new forms of knowledge distribution and awareness spreading – had taken root among all classes and groupings. A whole universe of new popular cultures, slang languages, political analyses, vernacular theories of power, and genres of political music, art, theater, blogs, and chants had created an utterly new set of public spheres, popular sovereignty claims, and mobilizing languages. (Amar: 38-9)

One lasting result of this fluctuating revolution in consciousness has been a broader understanding of structures undergirding the various resurgent power bases in Egypt's recent history: the structures of cronyism, the military-political economies, and the 'religionized commercial cartels'. The exposure of these mechanisms 'forced an exciting deepening and broadening of social mobilization and political consciousness among an increasingly widening set of class, gender, and cultural groupings' (39-40). These are the conclusions of social scientists. In what follows, we posit that Egyptian novelists are much less certain that anything new has actually resulted from the upheavals.

Yasmine El Rashidi's *Chronicle of a Last Summer* highlights three significant summers in the life of its protagonist in Cairo. Beginning in 1984, the six-year-old girl hears her elders worrying about the ascension of President Mubarak to power. They whisper about disappearances. The girl's father leaves the family, inexplicably. Time passes, and in 1998 the household has become impoverished. The girl, now a young woman of 20, has grown reflective: 'During the night', she records, 'inexplicable rumbles would wake me up. As a child, I had imagined these murmurs of the house to be tea parties on the roof. Now I wondered about the poetics of space, the cavities people once filled' (El Rashidi: 73). She and her mother are now the only inhabitants of the house, which had become 'like an echo chamber, most rooms permanently closed' (72-3). Her uncle, in place of her missing father, laments the changes wrought in the city: 'Everything we ever knew will be gone. Anything with traces of past histories. It was the legacy my generation would inherit, one of destruction and loss. He was sad for what we had been born into' (77). The young girl is in college, learning to be a filmmaker and a novelist, but uncertain what 'the question' is that she wishes to address (87). She thinks she might ask passers-by if they are angry. Then, if they would like to see something improved in the city. But 'people walked away. They looked at me skeptically. They asked who was asking. They said they couldn't answer such questions' (88). She hears the call to prayer and notes presciently that 'it's the most pertinent daily reminder of the increasing antagonism between the

Brotherhood and the state' (105). 'How did we land in our lives', she wonders (113).

Time passes, and now it is the summer of 2014. Tahrir Square has been opened again. The protagonist thinks of betrayal:

> Not the betrayal of my father's generation, the one of defeat, but rather the betrayal of the Brotherhood and police, colluding in clashes one November three years ago … I have to dig, consciously project myself back into an imagined past as I sit here now, writing, to recall going there with Baba … I imagine that if [Uncle] were still alive and I told him now that I wish I could preserve the older memories, erase what they have been replaced by, he would tell me that to be a witness to history is a burden for the chosen. (El Rashidi: 160)

She ends her story sitting on the balcony with her 70-year-old mother, reminiscing about earlier times. Her mother looks at her, then both women look in the direction of the Nile, the river that has been there through so many suffering generations of Cairo residents.

The novel suggests the small steps taken by individuals trying to chart a path between complicity and integrity, always confronted by institutions and more-powerful individuals who can, at a moment's notice, implicate anyone in an invented conspiracy and, in the process, force that person back to square one, or worse. Late in life, when her father comes back into the picture as mysteriously as he had gone away, she comes to understand his choices with a mature sense of forgiveness:

> I begin most days at the club with Baba now … I have a vague idea of what happened, the problems, his refusal to offer a major contract he had tendered to one of the president's sons, the corruption charges they manufactured and landed him with, case after case, unrelentingly … They had broken him … I could see all this in his face, every single day, the nervous tic that marked him … It was almost as if he were trying to blink something out of his eye, or perhaps even his memory. (El Rashidi: 150)

She can understand her father's choices more compassionately because she has come to terms with her own choices in the face of the powerful forces beyond her control. Yasmine El Rashidi writes convincingly of one individual's experience and in the process embodies an ethical dilemma common in societies under authoritarian control: must one resist, or should one remain silent. 'Activism', she writes, 'was in the genes, and if not, it came from upbringing. We are informed by the experiences and behaviors of those around us … I knew I lacked the gene. I was more interested in abstracting experience with my writing' (119). The honesty of such writing may prompt El Rashidi's readers to confront the ethics of personal choices and, like her protagonist, may prompt them to ask how they 'landed' in their particular lives, their particular place in history. By narrowing her novella's focus to the musing of one individual, she invites readers to ask questions of their obligations to those around them in society.

In *The Queue*, Basma Abdel Aziz takes several steps back from the scene of an individual's critical choice of action or passivity. Her concern, rather, is to offer her readers a striking metaphor for the absurdity of an entire city that chooses to cooperate with an arbitrary authortarian regime. She possibly draws her inspiration from the Russian writer Vladimir Sorokin, who in 1983 wrote a novel with the same name, an identical central metaphor (long, hopeless lines waiting for a response from the massive immobile bureaucracy), and a similar theme (common humanity, facing an absurd situation, concocts reasons for hope). Abdel Aziz's plot is offering something of a mock quest: a man, Yehya, runs from one office to the next, with a bullet in his belly, seeking ever-deferred permission from the elusive correct governmental office for an operation to remove the bullet before it migrates through his intestines. Days and weeks go by. The queue in which he waits grows and grows, in fact stretching miles away from The Gate, the site for the preliminary screening of 'legitimate' requests from loyal citizens. Eventually, the queue becomes so lengthy that buses are put in place to ferry supplicants to the ever-receding end of the line.

Yehya meets a seriocomic cast of characters in the line. Some strongly support the authorities against all criticism; some become paranoid; some resist, are taken in for questioning, and return deeply traumatized; others turn on their erstwhile comrades as their needs increase; others settle in and sell various needed goods to their increasingly desperate compatriots. Various readers have been reminded of Beckett's *Waiting for Godot*, with its senseless hope that soon, very soon, Godot will indeed appear; others note comparisons to Orwell's *1984*, with characters finally turning on each other and 'truth' becoming just another twisted version of Newspeak; and others think of Kafka's *The Trial*, with characters wondering how it is that they have been born into inexplicable guilt.

Although Yehya is a principal focus for the narrative, the more pressing ethical questions focus on Tarek, the examining doctor. The government wishes to destroy all records involved in the killing and maiming of citizens during the 'Disgraceful Events' that took place in the public square, and singles out physicians who oppose this obfuscation. Tarek frets over his Hippocratic oath as it comes into conflict with these all-seeing authorities, becoming sleepless as the choices one is called upon to make in such extreme situations weigh heavily on his otherwise bourgeois life. As in El Rashidi's *Chronicle of a Last Summer*, Abdel Aziz presses forward with uncomfortable questions: not only what *can* one do, but what *must* one do? If one does nothing, how does one become comfortable in the subsequent ruins? Deciding far too late to intervene, Tarek takes out Yehya's file one last time and notices that someone has written:

> 'Yehya Gad el-Rab Saeed spent one hundred and forty nights of his life in the queue'. (Abdel Aziz *The Queue*: 217)

The decision to act has, mercifully, been taken out of his hands:

> Tarek sank into thought, confused, his chest tightening. Everything that had happened swirled in his mind as if it were one long, uninterrupted scene. He sat there in silence, calm, his gaze fixed on the opposite wall … Then quickly, he added a sentence by hand to the bottom of the fifth document. He closed the file, left it on his desk, and rose. (Abdel Aziz: 217)

And thus ends both Yehya's quest (the bullet has done its job), and Tarek's responsibility to do other than comply with The Gate.

Mohammad Rabie and Nael Eltoukhy both work on a grander scale. By projecting much of their plots into some imagined dystopic future, they both look 'back' on the unnamed Arab Spring. In *Women of Karantina*, Nael Eltoukhy offers a light comic touch that provides an amoral escape hatch from despair; in *Otared*, Rabie creates a dark and menacing hell with a progressively shocking wallow in depravity. Reminiscent of Mario Puzo's *The Godfather*, *Women of Karantina* is a saga of the rise of various interlocked crime families in Alexandria. Where it differs from Puzo's book, though, is in its tone: the violence is very quick, almost whispered (though it often involves throwing victims in front of trains), and the emphasis is on the snappy dialogue. Again differing from Puzo, many of the crime bosses are women. The result is a surprisingly amorphous tone in the narrative, sometimes reflecting the hard-edged *Realpolitik* of those growing up in slums, and often inviting readers to laugh along at the self-deception and swagger that gets them through life.

On the one hand, the 'humour' of the story springs from Eltoukhy's off-beat sensibility: he tells an interviewer that the inspiration for the book came from his experience on a microbus with his girlfriend, where he allowed his imagination to run wild: 'the driver harassed her, so we both got out and killed him and then decided to go on the run and set up something new in a completely new place' (Qualey 'Discussing "Women of Karantina"': 2). On the other hand, the visceral grittiness of the ambience in Eltoukhy's created world, the bodily fluids, cussing, sewage, and dirt, are, according to its author, 'a fundamental part of the spirit of the novel. The novel is built around dirt: around a dirty, realistic tragi-comic tone' that the author describes as essential to his theme (3). He thought of the tale as a response to Naguib Mahfouz's Cairo trilogy, a similar tale of three generations – though Mahfouz's stretches over 1500 pages. Robin Moger, the English translator of *Women of Karantina*, remarks that 'you sort of are following Nael into a sewer, it's just [Eltoukhy] makes it seem like a good idea. Or maybe Nael is pointing out that, bad luck, you already are in a sewer, but it's all right because he's holding your hand' (3).

The book is populated by many strongly characterized women, and the author notes that he wanted to portray women 'who are capable of imposing their point of view, particularly those from the very poorest and deprived areas ... and specifically its Egyptian manifestation: the *hagga* or *miallima*, the woman with a powerful personality who's able to dominate men' (Qualey 'Discussing "Women of Karantina"': 6). He's also interested in portraying what he sees as the typical Alexandrian's inflated sense of his/her distinction from those from Cairo. 'Alexandria', he writes, 'is the only Egyptian city to have evolved a clear communal identity of its own and to have developed rites for the veneration of this identity – and rites for rage, should this identity be harmed' (Eltoukhy *Women of Karantina*: 32). Eltoukhy describes Alexandria as

a cosmopolitan city. At least, that is what it was before the revolution of 1952, which was followed by the systematic expulsion of foreigners from Egypt, and thus from Alexandria, in which were concentrated the country's largest European communities. From that moment on, one felt a sense of loss in Alexandria, a sense of glories past and dissatisfaction at the wretched present. (29-30)

He notes that 'the free-born Alexandrian knows that truth is worthless without the strength to protect it', but then laments that 'all their victories have been spin or symbolism: dramatic, stirring scenes rather than actual victories' (31). Gradually, the sense of sophistication had been replaced by the veneration of crime bosses over the years – and that is the 'truth' that the novel mocks.

At the same time, he is quick to remind readers that 'in those days, Alexandria was the brightest chapter in the chronicle of Egyptian resistance' (Eltoukhy: 32). *Women of Karantina* involves some of the political events of 2010-2011, particularly what happened to Alexandria's Khaled Said, a 28-year-old who was brutally beaten and disfigured by the police. That prompted the formation of Egypt's biggest dissident Facebook page on 6 June 2010, with nearly one hundred thousand subscribers joining the first day, and swelling to half a million on the eve of the 2011 revolution. ABC News broadcast the photo Khaled Said's family took of him in the morgue, calling it 'The Face that Launched a Revolution'.

Eltoukhy includes actual historical details and imagines others, and projects trends into an uncomfortable future. Grim as that brave new world may be, though, he objects to those who have characterized the book as sarcastic (Qualey 'Women of Karantina, Egypt's Female Crime Bosses': 1) – though the adjective seems quite appropriate. The story begins, for example, with an allegory of two mangy dogs in a dystopic 2064. Oddly comparable to the central wounded character in *The Queue*, the male dog is hit with a bullet and wanders aimlessly until he dies alone and is thrown in a trench by an annoyed passer-by. The 'bitch' whom he has impregnated looks for him, sniffs his decomposing body, and leaps into the pit to die there with him. The author then sets this aside and launches into the real tale of the women crime bosses. But from this allegory he draws several strikingly sarcastic conclusions:

> The tale of the dog and the bitch began three months back, on a patch of wasteland. He saw her rump wiggling in front of him and jumped her. They started rubbing their bodies against each other and the fleas made their way from his pelt to hers and vice versa. Her hide was full of sores, and his too, but that did not prevent them taking their pleasure. They fell in love and resolved to devote themselves to one another, unto death … The tale here is a tale of a nation taking shape … Many tales God does not wish to see completed. (Eltoukhy: 4-6)

The chapter is titled: 'The sweetest newlyweds, two characters set in their proper place by fate.'

Publishing the book when he did, it is hard not to read this allegory as a harsh ridicule of misplaced idealism and hopeless dreams of national healing and common cause. Yet Eltoukhy writes, no doubt with tongue in cheek, that 'should it fall to us to derive a lesson from this tale, then it would be that nothing is impossible; that provided his intentions are sound, then man – by the grace of his Lord, exalted and gloried be His name before and above all things – is capable of anything' (4). That 'anything' of which he is capable is not, in the tale that follows, anything glorious: it is a tale of several generations of corruption and self-serving violence. The fact that the tone of the tale is light-hearted and occasionally funny does not change its undergirding cynicism. After this brief dog-story prelude set in the future, we move sixty years back to 2004, when 'everything was wonderful in Egypt. Or that was how Egyptians felt about their country. The truth is what people feel, not objective, physical facts' (7). Those emotions, taking the place of 'truth', boil down quickly to '*taar* – a debt of honor to be avenged … from which Egypt has suffered greatly' (11). The tale of the dogs, therefore, serves as something of an Aria da Capo, alerting the reader to the sad trajectory of Alexandria's pride in resistance, leading to betrayal and death.

But the sense of loss and disillusionment of these three novels pales in comparison to *Otared*, set in 2025 but stretching back to 2011 and very briefly to 455 After Hijra (AH). That brief chapter in 455 AH seems to serve as proof that what is happening today and in 2025 has been going on for a very long time. That ancient narrator writes: 'And I saw that I had lived eight lives in hell, moving from torment to torment, and never knowing that I was in torment, and I knew that I was in the fire forevermore' (Rabie *Otared*: 212). The chapter ends ominously with the phrase, 'All that I possess is patience and all that I fear is hope' (214). And then begins the chapter called AD 2011 – surely intended as the latest ridiculous 'hope'.

The book is named after a mercenary sharp shooter who perches above Cairo in 2025 and picks off targets. This goes on for two years. He is a member of a group of former military officers who are the resistance to the Knights of Malta. His next assignment is to attempt to instigate a mass insurrection in the home territory of the Knights. He is to accomplish this by senselessly slaughtering as many people as he can, pushing the inhabitants beyond the point of passivity. Most people live in a doped-up state, trying to avoid offending anyone and literally wearing masks to remain anonymous and uncommitted. What might be reprehensible avoidance of social responsibility seems completely acceptable in this horrific novel, which depicts atrocities in the recent past or near future: the Battle of Rabaa that crushed the Brotherhood with the support of the majority of the people; a massacre of 4,000 people in Alexandria in 2018 without any explicit order; a dispersal of a sit-in at Ain Shams University in 2019 that resulted in 2,000 deaths: This was 'followed up by some truly heroic work by the prosecutor. Sure, we used live rounds, but no one stepped forward to point the finger … That day, we achieved everything we set out to do and we managed to tame the people forever' (Rabie: 71). Finally, there is a campaign in 2025 to bring police back to power. Gearing up to get back into power, the police laugh about the romantic niceties of prosecuting soldiers after the 2011 Uprising, and about how no one was put in that awkward position again.

These large social happenings are peppered with individual mind-numbing crudities: the death of a baby from a genetic disease that begins with the loss of ears, sight and mouth; a homeless man publicly masturbates then commits suicide; the protagonist hires a prostitute whose glass eye comes out during sex, and who menstruates all over him. Cannibalism is not far behind, and in fact the lengthy book is a depressing enactment of one human degradation after another. Not surprisingly, the idealism of the Arab Uprising becomes a point of (despairing) ridicule among the soldiers, who somehow cling to the notion that they are the good guys. But there are, obviously, no heroes in this novel. The notion of heroism is such a setting comes across as quaint, if not ridiculous.

The public execution of a woman closes the book, and it provides pornographic stimulation for an audience that masturbates while the woman squirms; her hands are tossed to the excited crowd, then an arm, then her breasts, then her legs. The frenzied crowd carries what is left of her down the street, and yet she does not die. They turn on each other, biting each other in the neck, gouging out eyeballs. When the book ends, the reader is grateful:

> And I saw that hell was eternal and unbroken, changeless and undying; and that in the end, all other things would pass away and nothing besides remain. And I knew that I was in hell forevermore, and that I belonged here. (Rabie: 341)

Even this apparent denouement is a mock revelation, since it repeats the 'insight' that his character has revealed to the reader many times earlier in this aggressive novel. What he finds most intoxicating is their unquenchable hope – something like that of the characters in *The Queue* – which keeps them from simply ending it all:

> People here were born afraid, lived afraid, and died in terror, and hope only appeared toward the end ... How could they not see what was happening? How was it not one of them had looked closely at what had been happening all these years and centuries? These ones were yet to realize that they were in hell. These ones would be tormented by hope ... Madness was a complete deliverance, a way out of hell – although no one truly left. (Rabie: 245-6)

And yet, despite the horror, from a purely aesthetic point of view the writing in this novel is the most poetic of the four under discussion in this essay. Lyrical in its technique, it renders recent events in Egypt imminent, and without any gossamer membrane between the description of physical dismemberment and the reference to discarded high political ideals. Gone are the speeches about human rights that lead ordinary citizens to imagine they might resist an authoritarian regime, of whatever stripe.

As grotesque as Rabie's response to 2011 undeniably is, it is necessary, as suggested in the opening to this essay, to consider it as only one part of the overall response of Egyptian novelists. Other writers suggest a happier prospect. Walid Phares, someone who was happy to see the Muslim Brotherhood's regime overthrown, writes that 'Egypt was, significantly, saved not by outsiders or by a foreign army, but by its own people who, while at the cliff's edge, had an opportunity to look into the abyss' (Phares *The Lost Spring*: 216). Paul Amar argues that changes in society have undeniably taken place and that, once the genie had been released, it now cannot be put back into the bottle. He sees new facts on the ground: alternative movements for local self-rule, innovative electoral mobilizations, imaginative labour actions, and boundary-challenging gender solidarities ('Egypt': 40-41) – residue, as it were, of the heady days of revolution. 'By 2013', he writes, 'a deeply exhausted, but deeply changed, wiser public sphere and popular consciousness had emerged. And bold alternatives could start to be imagined' (56). So far, though, Egyptian novelists are demanding Truth and imagining a future that is far from such hopeful dreams.

WORKS CITED

Abdel Aziz, Basma, *The Queue*, trans. Elisabeth Jaquette, Brooklyn and London: Melville House, 2016 [2013].

Al-Zubaidi, Layla, Matthew Cassel and Nemonie Craven Roderick, eds, *Diaries of an Unfinished Revolution: Voices from Tunis to Damascus*, trans. Robin Moger and Georgina Collins, New York: Penguin, 2013.

Amar, Paul, 'Egypt'. In Paul Amar and Vijay Prashad, eds, *Dispatches from the Arab Spring: Understanding the New Middle East*, Minneapolis and London: University of Minnesota Press, 2013: 24-62.

El Rashidi, Yasmine, *Chronicle of a Last Summer*, New York: Tim Duggan Books, 2016.

Eltoukhy, Nael, *Women of Karantina*, Cairo: American University of Cairo Press, 2014.

Kilpatrick, Hilary, 'The Egyptian Novel from Zaynab to 1980'. In Badawi, M. M., ed., *Modern Arabic Literature*, Cambridge: Cambridge University Press, 1992: 223-69.

Phares, Walid, *The Lost Spring: U.S. Policy in the Middle East and Catastrophes to Avoid*, New York: Palgrave Macmillan, 2014.

Qualey, Marcia Lynx, 'Women of Karantina, Egypt's Female Crime Bosses', *The New Arab* 14 February 2015, www.alaraby.co.uk/english/artsandculture/2015/2/14/women-of-karantina-egypts-female-crime-bosses

——'Discussing "Women of Karantina": A Savage Comic Epic, Relentlessly Ironic, Uncompromisingly Rude, Profoundly Moral, Totally True', *Arabic Literature* 13 October 2014, https://arablit.org/2014/10/13/discussing-women-of-karantina-a-savage-comic-epic-relentlessly-ironic-uncompromisingly-rude-profoundly-moral-totally-true

Rabie, Mohammed, *Otared*, trans. Robin Moger, New York: Hoopoe, 2016 (copyright as *Utarid*, by Dar al-Tanweer, 2014).

Sorokin, Vladimir. *The Queue*, trans. Sally Laird, New York: NYRB Classics, 2008.

The Complications of Reading Egypt as Africa

Translation and Magdy el-Shafee's مترو (Metro)

JAMES HODAPP & DEEMA NASSER

One of the most pernicious obstacles to African literary studies incorporating the entire African continent in its purview is the persistent division between northern and southern Africa in literary scholarship. As Ziad Bentahar has recently argued, a de facto consensus exists between African literary studies and Arabic literary studies that '"Africa" now ostensibly stands for sub-Saharan Africa, whereas North Africa is considered in many academic disciplines to be part of the Middle East instead' ('Continental Drift: The Disjunction of North and Sub-Saharan Africa': 1). Bentahar's appraisal is not unique; it echoes those of previous scholars, such as Farida Abu-Haidar ('Arabic Writing in Africa') and Anissa Talahite ('North African Writing'), in voicing frustration that African literary studies has failed to substantially incorporate North Africa despite being urged to do so for decades.[1] In the wake of this exclusion of North African literature in our field, this article makes a case for increased inclusion, as well as highlighting barriers, by examining a particular Egyptian text in the original Arabic and in English translation, Magdy el-Shafee's مترو (Metro), that has been read as World literature and Arabic literature rather than African literature.

Although the northern/southern African studies division elides the contribution of many African literatures (principally those in Arabic and Berber) to African literature writ large, Egyptian literature in particular has been problematically overlooked. For centuries, Cairo has

22

stood out as an intellectual hub, and beginning in the early twentieth century it cemented its status in the print era as the publishing capital of North Africa.[2] With Cairo as one of the richest production and distribution points in Africa, Egyptian literature flourished in the twentieth century with little recognition within African literary studies. This division has narrowed the scope of what the field considers its purview to largely exclude Egyptian literature despite its impressive quantity and quality, reproducing disciplinary oversight by labelling only sub-Saharan works as African literature in global circuits.

Popular African texts that circulate outside of individual African locales and the continent as a whole have been aptly termed by Rebecca Walkowitz as 'born translated', i.e. imagining a global audience from its inception and therefore written in European languages with embedded didactic cultural exposition for audiences with minimal local knowledge. Beyond being linguistically and culturally accessible to Western readers, 'born translated' works often shift much of the action of African novels to the West to circumvent the difficulty of 'translating' Africa for Western readers. Prominent examples include some of the most praised, award-winning, and widely read African novels of the past decade such as *Americanah* (2013), *Open City* (2011), *We Need New Names* (2013), *Ghana Must Go* (2013), *Behold the Dreamers* (2016), *The Beautiful Things that Heaven Bears* (2007), and *Foreign Gods Inc.* (2014). While African literature is, and has been for some time, a *world* literature whose influences beyond its borders represent an important project within African literary studies, various critics and authors, such as Ben Okri, Binyavanga Wainaina and Helon Habila, have voiced legitimate concerns that this movement is not oriented towards the entire world but rather towards producing African literature for Western tastes in the US and the UK. By contrast, we wonder here not whether Africa and specific locales within it are legible to powerful publishing concerns in the West, but how an African text whose Africanness has been passed over by global circulatory machinations makes meaning differently within Africa.

Overall, Egyptian literature has not circulated widely and has not benefitted from, nor depended on, the non-Egyptian and non-Arab worlds to validate and sustain itself either in terms of cultural value or financial viability. As a result, it has been largely self-referential, not ignoring the rest of the world, but also not shifting its registers for a non-Egyptian readership (Jankowski and Gershoni *Egypt, Islam, and the Arabs*: 270). This self-referentialism has also made it inscrutable to much of Africa and the effect has been that few Egyptian authors have gained traction in African literary studies. A cadre of well-known authors from the twentieth century such as Naguib Mahfouz, Yusuf Idris, Nawal El Saadawi, Ahdaf Soueif, Tawfiq al-Hakim, and Alifa Rifaat (Fatimah Rifaat) have dominated the scant space afforded Egyptian writers within African literary studies, meaning that several generations of Egyptian writers have been largely unrecognized as African writers. A few authors such as Basma Abdel Aziz, Ahmed Alaidy, Mona Prince, and Alaa al-Aswany occasionally feature, but by and large contemporary Egyptian literature is not brought into conversation with contemporary African writers such as Taiye Selasi, Chimamanda Adichie and Teju Cole, whose works travel the globe under the moniker of African literature.[3]

Given the above status quo of Egyptian literature in African literary studies, this article intervenes by highlighting an overlooked contemporary author, Magdy el-Shafee, who is neither 'born translated' in the way the above Anglophone authors are, nor entirely inscrutable because he writes in colloquial Arabic and has been translated into English. By turning to the original Arabic version of *Metro* and reading it comparatively with its English variant, this article ultimately seeks to explore the graphic novel's points of access for African readerships, addresses blockages (mainly a problematic translation) and strives to overcome them, intervening to argue that *Metro* is a graphic novel with an inherent African reading public. Reading Egypt as Africa in *Metro* is an attempt to suture the somewhat arbitrary division of northern and southern Africa, problematizing the notion that sub-Saharan Africa is the centre of African literature and northern Africa is marginal, while also asserting the importance of Egyptian writers beyond a rigid and limiting canon.

First published in 2008 in a localized colloquial Arabic, rather than Modern Standard Arabic, by Malameh Publishing House in Cairo, *Metro* was originally banned in Egypt under the Mubarak regime even before it was released. Malameh's offices were raided by the police and all known extant copies of the book were removed from circulation. El-Shafee and his publisher were arrested and fined for their daring portrayal of social and political corruption in Egypt under Mubarak. If the Mubarak regime intended to limit *Metro's* circulation by banning it in Egypt, the graphic novel's translation into English in 2012 by Chip Rossetti, published by Metropolitan Books (and subsequently by others into Italian, French and German) represents a spectacular failure for Egyptian censorship. Moreover, *Metro* in Arabic re-entered the Egyptian market in 2013, having gained prominence from its international variants, although not without some resistance from the Muslim Brotherhood government of Mohamed Morsi.[4]

Metro tells the story of a young software engineer and hacker, Shehab, whose plan to establish a software firm is dashed under mysterious circumstances, leaving him in significant debt to his mobster financier, Hagg Ghareeb. As the latter demands repayment under threats of violence, Shehab and his business partner and friend, Mustafa, decide to rob a bank. They successfully pull off the job, getting away with five million dollars that were earmarked as a bribe for a top official. Thus, the robbery goes unreported and Shehab and Mustafa appear to be in the clear. However, witnessing the murder of Hagg Misbah, a contractor who specializes in covering up the malfeasances of Egyptian elites, forces the pair to go into hiding. Meanwhile, Shehab and his girlfriend, Dina, are drawn into the politically charged Kefaya protests cropping up at different landmarks in central Cairo.[5] As movement within the city becomes more perilous, Shehab and Mustafa arrange to secretly meet with the attorney general to report Hagg Misbah's murder. Mustafa, however, skips the meeting, takes the stolen money and calls Shehab from the airport, telling him that escape is the only way to get around the corrupt strictures of Egypt's kleptocracy. *Metro* ends with Shehab and Dina stranded at a metro station.

This plot outline, however, does not do the graphic novel justice as the fairly trite bank robbery caper masks the purposefully oblique social commentary with which the novel cannot directly engage without risking severe reprisals – those the author and publisher sustained even for this indirect look at corruption attest to the impossibility of publishing an explicitly political critique in Egypt. With straightforward address of the ordeals of daily life out of the question, Cairo retrogressively asserts itself in an anamorphic manner as the actual subject of the novel – it cannot be viewed directly, let alone critiqued, but nonetheless stands not merely as the novel's setting but its primary subject.

Metro's ability to travel, given its specific cultural milieu, has been the subject of considerable attention, particularly in the light of the internationally publicized and protracted court proceedings against el-Shafee that threatened him with several years in prison. The most noteworthy work on the novel has been done by Brian Edwards in his 'Jumping Publics: Magdy El Shafee's Cairo Comics' in which he argues that Metro 'jumps publics' between a local Cairene audience and a Western one. As Africanists though, we wonder why the rest of Africa is an unacknowledged audience, or a 'jumped over public' to use Edwards' parlance. By focusing on the circulation of an Egyptian graphic novel in Africa, and the mechanisms put into motion to prevent circulation, this essay eschews Edwards' invocation of the conventional practice of reading non-Western texts with/ against their Western reception as their primary mode of meaning making outside their local contexts. Rather than consider how well *Metro* is understood and circulated in far-flung American or European locales, we question the fact that less remote African publics have been passed over for *Metro* and many similar texts, ultimately providing a reading that illustrates the value of the text for such geopolitically proximal publics.

In his analysis, Edwards notes that el-Shafee 'tends to leave his American reader behind' in favour of an exclusively Egyptian audience.[6] The question of audience is central to Edwards' thesis of jumping publics but two critical counter-points persist to this reading of *Metro*, both important as scholarship on Egyptian and North African texts so often follow similar critical trajectories. Edwards contends that we must imagine American readers and how they are either endeared to or alienated from the text, but if we acknowledge that both the original text in Arabic, however idiosyncratic to Egypt, and the English translation are in African languages, then the assumption of Western readers as the primary, non-Egyptian public begins to be unravelled.[7] Secondly, if we are concerned with how *Metro* manages to jump publics, which is to say its inherent ability to be legible, could we and should we consider the consequences of an African public, particularly given how the text's translation attempts to exclude African audiences? In other words, this text that is 'about a Cairo in which state corruption is generalized to the local, daily level' as insightfully summarized by Edwards, ultimately addresses the inability of ordinary people to move outside of the influence of openly corrupt private and public sector elites in ways all too familiar to millions of Africans in various cities around Africa. *Metro* is set in an overcrowded, dirty, developing African city that chokes its inhabitants, both literally via ever-present automotive exhaust and figuratively via strict confines of upward social and economic mobility. Such a precarious and fraught existence resonates not with the lives of readers in Paris, London and New York but rather with those in Lagos, Nairobi and Addis Ababa. If what we mean by the text's ability to jump publics is that *Metro* retains its almost inscrutable and untranslatable idiosyncratic 'Egyptianness' while also maintaining the ability to signify beyond Egypt – despite its original hyper-localized audience – then this jumping ability would apply as much, if not more, to locations in the developing world where readers would not need to make creative leaps to imagine state mechanisms which ensure that an elite few live in absurd wealth while the average person struggles for dignity.

Metro in its original form is not 'born translated' for Western publics, either linguistically or culturally, a fact made clear in the English translation's elision of specificity.[8] The translator and the publisher imagine a Western reader and compensate accordingly. The linguistic origins in Arabic and the setting in the developing world of North Africa make it more legible to African publics if we remain faithful to the original text. What we are doing in large part here, then, is pushing back against the limitations placed on the novel's ability to signify to African readers by the English translation that is set on empowering Western readers. In other words, *Metro's* original context of production, subject matter, and language make Edwards' 'jump' more manageable in Arabic for African publics than American ones; and a more faithful English translation, not slanted towards American readers, would also enable such an African jump. While much of *Metro's* contextual makeup is relatable to a postcolonial African sensibility, its exclusion of readers beyond Western publics is arguably a product of ideological and political considerations that frame its translation in a post-2011 moment. Publicity for the book has focused on its 'prescient portrait of ... Egypt's coming eruption', a.k.a. the Arab Spring (*Metro: A Story of Cairo*). Because of this focus on elements that ultimately sustain popular Western media claims that the ousting of Mubarak was enabled by 'the Facebook revolution', a close comparative reading of how specific moments unfold on the textual and pictorial levels between the original Arabic and the English translation retrieves a sense of cultural specificity that is lost in a Western-oriented translation (Taylor 'Why Not Call it a Facebook Revolution?'). Rather than marginalizing African audiences, such a reading highlights an affable relationship between the Cairo of the text and many African experiences with sociopolitical corruption and stasis.

A signal indicating the ideological *modus operandi* of the translation of *Metro* comes in an early scene in the narrative when Shehab finds Wannas, an old Sa'idi[9] shoe-shiner, begging for money on the street in the Maadi district of Cairo. Wannas says to Shehab, 'I don't have a penny to my name ... Not a penny' (*Metro*: 20). While this communicates general feelings of discontent and poverty available to Western and non-Western audiences, the original Arabic intimates a sociopolitical comment on the pervasiveness of corruption in the daily lives of Cairenes, stemming from 'big men' who have a stranglehold on the lives of the average people. The original Arabic reads:

"ما ليّاش عازة في الدنيا دي يا ولدي.. ما ليّاش مكان في الدنيا دي"

(24 – literally translated as: 'There's no use for me in this world, my son ... There's no place for me in this world').

The shift from a comment on the 'world' of Cairo as not accommodating the presence of an elderly man who worked an honest job his entire life to a simple comment on not having enough money may universalize Wannas' plight, allowing for an easier transition for the text to Western audiences. However, the original necessarily subtle insinuation, given the context of production, gestures to the ramifications of life in an unequal society overrun with corruption. The issue for Wannas, and millions like him, is not general poverty but the invasion of mundane daily life by an overwhelming kleptocracy that creates and controls the poor. A way of being in the world is at stake that includes, but is not limited to, concerns about money.

Unfortunately, concerns about how to manoeuver systems rife with corruption have been pervasive in several parts of Africa. By every measurable indicator, corruption in Egypt is more similar to most African publics than that in the publics that Edwards assumes for *Metro*. Transparency International, a German non-government organization, produces the 'Corruption Perceptions Index', the most cited yearly corruption index which ranks countries from 1 (best) to 174 (worst). Egypt has wavered between 88 and 118 in the last five years while Denmark ranks number 1, the UK number 10, the US number 16 and Somalia 174. In short, the top of the list is filled with countries from the global north while those at the bottom are in the global south, with African countries filling many of the bottom positions. Only Botswana breaks the top 30 and sub-Saharan African countries fill 18 of the bottom 32 positions (*The Economist* 'The Scale of Corruption in Africa').[10] This is simply to say that the relationships that many Africans, especially sub-Saharan ones, have with their governments vis-a-vis corruption is strikingly similar to the one in *Metro*'s Cairo. If we take the pervasiveness of corruption, in its anamorphic and retrogressive literary form in the novel as its subject, and are interested in who the most fitting publics are, then African publics stand as viable publics alongside American or European ones. Furthermore, we must also contend with the English translation, attempting to elide this shared sensibility of corruption.

The most controversial scene of the novel is the bank robbery, which according to the author is one of the scenes that prompted the novel's banning by the Mubarak regime in 2008. After Shehab and Mustafa take the money, they take a top official at the bank about to receive a bribe and toss him out into the street. The duo draw a crowd's attention and people rush to beat him, unleashing pent-up rage towards an entire class of elite power brokers. This official is depicted as morbidly obese and brings to mind the often repeated saying in several African countries regarding bribery: 'While a good appetite is normal, gluttony is deplorable' (Blundo et al. *Everyday Corruption and the State*: 133). In other words, some corruption is expected and even acceptable, but when corruption becomes obscene, as represented by the man's girth and his five-million-dollar bribe, decency, even among thieves, has been violated. The toleration of petty corruption that inundates everyday life, that nonetheless has limits, is decidedly not an American or European sensibility. In the scene, Shehab calls out to people on the street saying, 'All of you! You're on top now! This guy here has been robbing you, ripping you off and leaving you starving! He's all yours' (*Metro*: 34). Rossetti's translation captures the main point of the affect to demonstrate why the crowd attacks the man but neglects to render a key word that would have politicized Shehab's sentiment in a different sense 'الحكومة', or 'the government' that occurs in the Arabic version: دلوقتي.. إنتو الحكومة. وآدي العالم اللي سارقينكم واخذين فلوسكم ومجوعينكم قدامكم زي الفرخة اهه (مترو: 38).

By contrast, an earlier translation by Humphrey Davies published on the website *Words without Borders*, renders this very scene as, 'Now you're the government ... and here are the guys who've been robbing you, taking your money, and making you go hungry. Here he is, trussed like chicken' ('The Graphic World').[11] In Davies' version, the grotesque fat cat is a representative of the government, not just a wealthy businessman. The boldfaced attack on the man in broad daylight in the street is also an attack on the government by proxy in Davies, whereas Rossetti's adaptation neutralizes the association between government and financial corruption in Egypt. Once again, a pointed demonstration of the specificity of frustrations of life in a corrupt society is glossed over with a banal scene that is almost a non-sequitur about how passionately the poor despise the rich. A powerful scene that imagines in fantastic fashion a cathartic power shift from elite cronies affiliated with Mubarak's government apparatuses and the national bank to the people is defused and flattened to general class envy that ultimately provincializes Cairenes rather than empowers them.

Beyond flattening experiences in the narrative that would resonate with African publics, the Rossetti translation also reorients political elements to support the claim by *Metro*'s American publisher that it presages the 2011 Tahrir Square demonstrations often characterized as part of the 'Arab Spring'. President Hosni Mubarak, the target of the 2011 demonstrations, is not mentioned in the original Arabic version. However, in Rossetti's translation Mubarak is quoted: 'There's so many of you. What am I supposed to do with you all?' (*Metro*: 83). The quote appears near the end of the narrative as Shehab and Dina become increasingly paranoid that they are in danger whenever they step outside, the implication seemingly being that Mubarak's regime frequently strikes against its enemies, but cannot manage to suppress all dissent. This connotation leaves the narrative, in the English version, open-ended in that we see the Mubarak regime struggling to maintain its grip on power and know retrospectively that it indeed loses power. However, the original quote, 'ما انتو كتير اعمل لكم ايه', is much more extradiegetic as a disembodied comment concerning the state's struggle to fulfil its obligations, which is not attributed to Mubarak. Rossetti inserts Mubarak into the plot where he was previously absent. A breakdown of the passage in Arabic can help elucidate the tension between the different versions of the two passages and perhaps explain why Mubarak was inserted. The translation from the prepositional phrase 'لكم' in Arabic to 'with you' in English changes the sentence meaning in a subtle yet significant

way considering its publication context. The phrase 'لكم'
is technically the semantic equivalent of 'for you'. Had it
been translated more directly as 'There's so many of you.
What am I supposed to do for you all?' the connotation
would have shifted from a despotic ruler speaking to his
citizens with a menacing undertone to a feckless one who
is incapable of sustaining his subjects even if he wants
to. This linguistic manipulation is very much in line with
mainstream narratives of the 2011 Egyptian revolution in
Western media as a democratic revolution against a despot.
Furthermore, the quote is not attributable to Mubarak
as there is no evidence that Mubarak ever said those
words. With an interest in depicting popular movements
culminating in the Tahrir revolution as a secular and
youthful initiative fighting a long-held dictatorship for
democracy, Rossetti's translation, which circulates widely
at least among readers in America and Western Europe, is
invested in demonizing Mubarak and making victims of
young, liberal subjects like Shehab and Dina. And while
it might be cathartic to twist an unsourced quote against
a brutal dictator, fidelity to Arabic requires us to point
out that the text does not align with the facile narrative
of a fight for freedom against a dictator, but rather with
sentiments more salient in northern and southern Africa
that even the dictator's hands are tied at times, and that
the presence of the dictator is ubiquitous even when he is
absent; so mentioning him at all is redundant.

This cultural manipulation of the text also occurs on
the pictorial level. The most obvious example of this is the
replacement of the various maps in the Arabic narrative
with an image of a train station map in the English that is
repositioned and resized each time it is used to replace the
original Arabic map. Rather than preserving the original
maps, this modification is politically implicated in effacing
nuances specific to Egyptian history. On the full-page map
following the bank robbery scene, the roads leading to
Tahrir Square are portrayed and labelled by a mix of English

and French place-names (Le Nil; 6th October Bridge; Kasr El Nil Bridge; Rue Al Bustan). The road map is headed by an Arabic title 'محطة أنور السادات' and carries another extradiegetic statement against a bold black background: 'دي مش انتفاضة شعبية ... دي انتفاضة حرامية'. Not only is the format of the visual translation radically different, it does not depict the same geographical spaces that are in the original. Instead, the translation represents the map of train stations in Cairo with a central focus on Sadat station as the translated title indicates. Gone are the specific road names that bear historical significance.[12] More shockingly, the aforementioned commentary, which translates into: 'This isn't a popular uprising … This is a thieves' uprising' is entirely absent. The statement is significant in light of the original context as it detaches itself from inciting sentiments of popular revolt and instead insinuates that those demonstrating are not innocent but rather those who want to take as much power as they can for themselves. The irony is that the subsequent governments of Morsi and el-Sisi have proven just as 'thieving' as Mubarak's; thus the English translation's desperation to interject in presidential politics is missed by not including this quote that at first glance appears problematic.

The insertion of Mubarak where he was not and the erasure of the characterization of the protests in the novel veer the translation towards a narrative that reinforces a revolutionary resolution. *Metro* is not about revolution though and ends bleakly with one character betraying another to escape and two others finding no solution to their predicament. The system is not swayed and the individuals within it gain no agency. Ostensibly, the narrative ends where it begins: in corrupt stagnation with no hope. It is this sense of being overwhelmed, rather than optimistic, that imbues the novel, gesturing away from Western, particularly American, narratives of meritocracy towards more historically prevalent African ways of living in the corrupted ruins of empire.

None of the above is to say that reading *Metro* from an African perspective is easy; in fact the English translation actively works against African reading publics. We have highlighted the fact that *Metro* is 'born translated' neither for Western nor African audiences but that the English translation attempts to make the adoption of the text in Western contexts more comfortable, and one can certainly imagine a translation that facilitates, rather than hinders, that jump. As an Arabic text, though, *Metro* resonates much more fully in African contexts, and we must consider how and why that resonance is elided in translation, especially in reference to governments and corruption. If we do hope to suture the disparate cultures and geographies of North Africa with the rest of Africa under the rubric of African literary studies, then tracking and characterizing the mechanisms that exacerbate that rift is essential work. Unpacking *Metro*, then, is both a revelation of these global mechanisms of elision in a particular African context, as well as a small act of resistance against them.

NOTES

1 Some of the longest-published journals in the field rarely include articles on North African subjects. For example, less than four per cent of articles in *Research in African Literatures* (founded 1970), *English in Africa* (founded 1974) and *African Literature Today* (founded 1968) have been on literature from North Africa.

2 The publishing of what is considered to be the first Arabic novel, زينب: أخلاق ومناظر ريفيّة (*Zaynab: Country Scenes and Morals*), in 1913 in Cairo is a particularly seminal moment in Egypt's modern publishing history that initiated a surge in publishing fiction.

3 Adichie is an academic industry alone in this regard. By our count, 14 articles have appeared in *Research in African Literatures* since 2008 featuring her work, three in *English in Africa* and five in *African Literature Today*. By comparison, *Research in African Literatures* has published about 65 articles on North African literature since 1970, *English in Africa* three since 1974 and *African Literature Today* also only three since 1968. Adichie's

work is rightly a topic of scholarly discussion but the fact that scholarship on her three novels and one collection of short stories is remotely comparable to that on over a hundred years of printed literature from North Africa is symptomatic of the marginalization of the region's literature in African literary studies.

4 See Ghaibeh 'Telling Graphic Stories of the Region': 326.

5 The Kefaya coalition (moniker for The Egyptian Movement for Change or *Enough!*) was officially born in 2004 and cross-cut ideological currents by including members with different political and religious affiliations (nationalists, leftists, Islamists, Nasserists, communists, etc.). Its initial agenda was to protest Mubarak's fifth term as President, refuse hereditary rule, change the authoritarian political regime, revoke the state of emergency and long-term staying power Mubarak had by amending the constitution, and generally introduce internal reforms in Egypt. It has been active in major Egyptian cities (Cairo, Alexandria and Mansoura) and has received both praise and criticism for being the first openly transparent movement that mobilized Egyptians across social classes, age groups, professions, religions, and gender, in a peaceful manner on the street and through a heavy online presence on audio-visual platforms like YouTube, blogs, and their own website. For more detailed information on Kefaya's origins, successes and reasons for its decline, see Oweidat et al. 'The Kefaya Movement: A Case Study of a Grassroots Reform Initiative' and Bisgaard-Church's detailed chronology, 'Kefaya protests Mubarak's referendum and re-election, Egypt, 2005'.

6 Edwards also calls this an 'international, non-Egyptian public' but often returns to the West as the other, non-local audience and does not gesture to readerships in the global south ('Jumping Publics': 81).

7 The three largest officially Arabic-speaking populations in the world are in fact located in Africa (Egypt, Algeria, and Sudan) totalling over 150 million, and other officially Arabic-speaking countries in Africa include Morocco, Tunisia, Mauritania, and Libya, totalling 55 million, while Arabic is a co-official language in Chad, Djibouti, Somalia, South Sudan, and Eritrea with over 35 million inhabitants. English is spoken by over 150 million people in Africa, including tens of millions in officially Arabic-speaking nations. This is all to say that *Metro*, as an originally Arabic text first translated into English, does not need translation to be seen as a more suitable text to 'jump publics' to other places in Africa. In fact, ready-made

Arabic-speaking audiences exist in Africa for the original version as well as an English-reading audience for the first translation.

8 At times the translation nearly conflates the Kefaya protests of 2005 with the sensationalized 2011 Tahrir Square protests by removing street signs and references to places central to the 2005 protests but not the 2011 ones.

9 Refers to Upper Egypt and retains a classed/socioeconomic connotation of being more conservative than urban people.

10 According to *The Economist*, the best data on corruption indicates that '22% of Africans who had contact with public services admit to having paid a bribe in the past year. In Liberia, the figure was 69%. In Kenya and Nigeria, two of the most important African economies, it was 37% and 43% respectively' ('The Scale of Corruption in Africa').

11 In personal correspondence, Davies has confirmed that an entire second version of the translation exists in which the elided political elements of Rossetti's text largely remain.

12 6th October Bridge commemorates a military victory on the eponymous date in 1973 when the Egyptian army (under Sadat) crossed the Bar-Lev line to take back the Sinai Peninsula which had been under Israeli occupation since the 1967 June War. It also marks the beginning of the October War (Yom Kippur War).

WORKS CITED

Abu-Haidar, Farida. 'Arabic Writing in Africa'. *Research in African Literature* Vol. 28, No. 3 (1997): 1-4.

Bentahar, Ziad. 'Continental Drift: The Disjunction of North and Sub-Saharan Africa'. *Research in African Literatures* Vol. 42, No. 1 (2011): 1-13.

Bisgaard-Church, Elliana. 'Kefaya Protests Mubarak's Referendum and Re-election, Egypt, 2005'. *Global Nonviolent Action Database*. 8 October 2011. http://nvdatabase.swarthmore.edu/content/kefaya-protests-mubaraks-referendum-and-re-election-egypt-2005 (accessed 7 November 2015).

Blundo, Giorgio, Jean-Pierre Olivier de Sardan, N.B. Arifari and M.T. Alou. *Everyday Corruption and the State: Citizens and Public Officials in Africa*. London: Zed Books, 2006.

Davies, Humphrey. 'The Graphic World: (Worth) Ten Thousand Words, Part II'. *Words Without Borders*, February 2008. www.words without borders.org/issue/february-2008 (accessed December 2016).

Edwards, Brian. 'Jumping Publics: Magdy El Shafee's Cairo Comics'. *Novel: A Forum on Fiction* Vol. 47, No. 1 (2014): 67-89.

El-Shafee, Magdy. *Metro*. Alexandria: Fabrika, 2015 [2008].

——*Metro: A Story of Cairo*. Trans. Chip Rossetti. New York: Metropolitan Books, 2012. http://us.macmillan.com/books/978080 5094886 (accessed 14 December 2016).

Ghaibeh, Lina. 'Telling Graphic Stories of the Region: Arabic Comics after the Revolution'. *IEMed Mediterranean Yearbook 2015*. 25 June 2015. www.iemed.org/observatori/arees-danalisi/arxius-adjunts/ anuari/med.2015/IEMed%20Yearbook%202015_Panorama_ ComicsAfterRevolution_LinaGhaibeh.pdf (accessed 31 August 2017).

Jankowski, James P. and Israel Gershoni (eds). *Egypt, Islam, and the Arabs*. Oxford University Press, 1987.

Oweidat, Nadia, Cheryl Benard, Dale Stahl, Walid Kildani, Edward O'Connell and Audra K. Grant. 'The Kefaya Movement: A Case Study of a Grassroots Reform Initiative'. *RAND National Defense Research Institute*. Santa Monica, CA: RAND Corporation, 2008.

Talahite, Anissa. 'North African Writing'. In *Writing and Africa*, Misiska Mpalive-Hangson and Paul Hyland (eds). London: Longman, 1997:13-23.

Taylor, Chris. 'Why Not Call it a Facebook Revolution?' *CNN* special 24 February 2011. http://edition.cnn.com/2011/TECH/social. media/02/24/facebook.revolution (accessed 12 December 2016).

The Economist. 'The Scale of Corruption in Africa'. 3 December 2015. www.economist.com/news/middle-east-and-africa/21679473-gloomy-news-transparency-international-scale-corruption-africa (accessed 31 August 2017).

Transparency International. 'Corruption Perceptions Index 2015'. n.d. www.transparency.org/cpi2015 (accessed 14 December 2016).

Walkowitz, Rebecca. *Born Translated: The Contemporary Novel in an Age of World Literature*. New York: Columbia University Press, 2015.

Narratives of the 'Nubian Awakening'

Reclaiming Egypt's African Identity

CHRISTINE GILMORE

Since the late 1980s, authors associated with the revivalist cultural and political movement known as the *Ṣaḥwa Nubiyya* or 'Nubian Awakening' have created a new and hybrid form of Egyptian literary expression. Inspired by Nubia's distinct language, culture, history, mythology and geography, their writing makes legible a distinctively Nubian subjectivity that plays a mediating role in countering the 'layered invisibility' (Nixon *Slow Violence and the Environmentalism of the Poor*: 16) of the Nubian people in postcolonial Egypt after they were forcibly displaced from their homeland to make way for the Aswan High Dam in 1964. Taking *Nights of Musk: Stories from Old Nubia* (*Layāli al-Misk al-ʿAtiqa*), a collection of short stories by the prominent Nubian writer and activist Haggag Hassan Oddoul as a case study, this paper argues that Nubian literature contests the unitary fiction of Egypt's Arab identity postulated during the heyday of Arab nationalism by highlighting the nation's marginalized African identity. As such, it can be seen as part of a broader trend in modern Egyptian writing known as 'border literature' which seeks to integrate regional and minority subjectivities into Egypt's national imaginary (El-Refaei 'Egypt's Borders and the Crisis of Identity in the Literature of Nubia and Sinai').

In 1964 the building of the Aswan High Dam forcibly displaced some fifty thousand Egyptian Nubians from their ancient homeland to the area of Kom Ombo, around seventy kilometres north of Aswan (Dafalla *The Nubian*

Exodus; Fahim *Dams, People and Development*). All that remained of Nubia, a land traditionally falling along the Nile between the first and sixth cataracts south of Aswan and north of Khartoum, was submerged under the dam's reservoir which became known as Lake Nasser – a 'potent symbol of postcolonial power etched onto the landscape' (Dimeo 'Unimaginable Community': 80). The High Dam's redemptive symbolism as a reflection of the power, prosperity and progress of the postcolonial state proved highly popular amongst the Egyptian public who, in 1964, flocked *en masse* to the parliament crying 'Nasser, Nasser, we come to salute you: after the Dam our land will be paradise!' (Nixon: 116). However, this support was accompanied by a willed amnesia at national level about its long-term impact on Nubian culture and society, such as ongoing injustices surrounding compensation for lost land and property; non-recognition of the Nubians as a national minority by the state; and the denial of cultural and linguistic rights.

As a result of dam-induced displacement and resettlement, Egyptian Nubians have been relegated to the status of what Rob Nixon terms a 'ghost community' whose distinctive language, culture and way of life were systematically 'uncoupled from the idea of both a national future and a national memory' (151) through processes of physical and imaginative displacement which erased Nubian culture and civilization from the Egyptian national imaginary just as Lake Nasser erased Nubia from the map. Not only were the Nubian people resettled away from the river Nile in dry savannah regions which shared little, in terms of physical or human ecology, with the land they left behind (Dafalla: 278–300) but there were few, if any, attempts made by the authorities to preserve or accommodate Nubian language or culture. Instead, in keeping with the doctrine of *al-qawmiyya al-'arabiyya* (Arab nationalism), the Nubian language was refused recognition as an official language of the state, and Nubian children were schooled exclusively in Arabic, while policies of sedentarization, assimilation and Arabization aimed at weakening their distinct cultural identity (Hägg *Nubian Culture Past and Present*: 411).

This may be in large part due to nation-building considerations on the part of successive postcolonial nationalist regimes from Nasser to Mubarak. As James Scott argues, large dam projects have often been perceived by postcolonial administrations as a means of furthering the nation-building project and refashioning the physical and social environment from scratch according to 'state maps of legibility' (*Seeing Like a State*: 3). Central to this approach is the idea that the cultures of 'backward' peoples who stand in the way of development projects can be sacrificed in the name of progress, both for the 'greater good' of the nation and that of their own communities. The resettlement of unassimilated minority groups like the Nubians thus serves two purposes: it allows the state to extend its sovereignty over all the territory under its jurisdiction and to accelerate processes of assimilation and integration aimed at replacing the 'welter of incommensurable small communities, familiar to their inhabitants but mystifying to outsiders ... with a single national society perfectly legible from the centre' (Ibid.: 32).

Despite its geographical location on the African continent and the longstanding presence of communities such as the Nubians and Berbers who speak languages other than Arabic, the idea that the 'Egyptian people are part of the Arab nation', which constitutes Article 1 of the 1971 Constitution, reflected a widespread popular understanding of Egypt as an Arab nation culturally and civilizationally distinct from Sub-Saharan Africa. Within such a context, racialized discourses linking black skin with Africa operate as a 'boundary marker' differentiating Nubians from their fellow Egyptians in the popular imagination. Indeed, Nubians are widely perceived as African 'others' or, at best, second-class citizens, by their fellow Egyptians due to dominant historical stereotypes of Nubians as servants and slaves (Smith 'Place, Class and Race in the Barabra Cafe', 2006: 400–1). Consequently, the integration and Arabization of minorities pursued by the Egyptian state has not resulted in full assimilation of the Nubian people into wider Egyptian society. Rather, Nubians tend to be accorded a subordinate social position or misrecognized as African 'others' (399–413).

Ironically, it is precisely the symbolic violence of non-recognition and exclusion which contributed to the growth of Nubian identity politics in the latter half of the twentieth century. From the 1980s onwards, the 'Nubian Awakening' has advocated greater Nubian political, economic and cultural rights, producing a new generation of engaged Nubian writers and intellectuals such as Yahya Mukhtar, Ibrahim Fahmi, Hassan Nur, Haggag Hassan Oddoul and Idris 'Ali who deploy distinctly Nubian linguistic, cultural, mythological and geographic tropes to contest the unitary fiction of Egypt's Arab identity and carve out a place for Egypt's marginalized African heritage within the national imaginary.

Haggag Hassan Oddoul was born in Alexandria in 1944 and was employed as a construction worker at the Aswan High Dam from 1963–67 before starting to write at the age of forty after witnessing first-hand the impact of dam-building on the Nubian community over the course of the twentieth century. He is the author of fifteen short stories, novels and plays, including *Nights of Musk: Stories From Old Nubia* which won the State Prize for Short Stories in 1990 and the novel *Ma'tūq al-Kheyr* which won the Sawiris Cultural Award for best novel in 2005. Arguing that a broad category was required under which all literature sharing the 'various unique particularities of Nubian society' could fall (Aboul-Ela 'Haggag Hassan Adoul'), Oddoul, like other writers associated with the 'Nubian Awakening' movement, rejected dominant classifications of Nubian writing as a sub-field of Egyptian literature, coining the term 'Nubian literature' in 1990.

Defining Nubian literature as a body of work based on ethnicity rather than language or nationality has proven highly incendiary with the Egyptian literary establishment, leading to allegations by the renowned literary critic Ahmed Abdel Muti Hegazi that Oddoul was linked to a 'separatist' or 'racist' agenda aimed at weakening the unity of the Egyptian state (Aboul-Ela; Naaman *Urban Space in Contemporary Egyptian Literature*: 111–16). In response, Oddoul openly castigated Egyptian intellectuals for their exclusion of Nubian writers, artists and intellectuals in the name of what he calls a 'racist national ideal' present both in the Egyptian popular imagination and at the heart of the establishment, sparking 'a long-overdue debate about racial identity and the plight of the Nubians in Egypt' (Naaman: 111–12). Arguing that 'to embrace blackness as an essential part of Egyptianness requires acknowledgement that Egypt is a part of Africa and not just the Middle East' (113), Oddoul maintains that 'there is no conflict between being Nubian and Egyptian' (Aboul-Ela) so long as Egypt opens up to a more pluralist vision of national culture that embraces rather than elides minority identities (El-Refaei).

Driven to write by a desire to 'turn the world's attention to Nubian culture and to provoke the world to recognise and promote its renaissance' (Aboul-Ela), Oddoul's fiction reclaims Nubia's marginalized cultural heritage as an essential component of Egyptian civilization through an aesthetics of restoration that 'asserts a cultural alternative' (Meyer *The Experimental Arabic Novel*: 72) to the racially inflected claims of Arab nationalism that, since the *nahḍa* (nineteenth-century Arab renaissance), had linked Egyptian nationality with Arab ethnicity. As such, it can be considered an example of a recent trend within modern Egyptian writing known as 'border literature', whereby the marginalization of Sinai, Nubia and Siwa within the Egyptian national imaginary is given centre stage, creating 'counter-cartographies' that foreground these liminal identities as essential components of what it means to 'be' Egyptian (El-Refaei). In the case of Oddoul's writing, as Naaman observes, 'here it is the subaltern Nubian who is writing the national narrative, and doing so as a revision to the primarily urban, pro-nationalist and postcolonial fictions, where the notion of an essential (or unproblematised) "Egyptian people" is left unquestioned' (110).

Although *Nights of Musk: Stories from Old Nubia* is made up of four discrete short stories, set in different times and places, ranging from the contemporary challenges facing the Nubian people in the resettlement site at Kom Ombo to the villages of Old Nubia and even Nubia's mythical past, it 'may also be seen as a novella composed of texts' connected by common symbolic threads that present a collective vision of Nubia's history, geography, culture and language that acquire 'additional grafts of meaning when read in conjunction with each other' (Halim 'Nubian Salvage, Textualized'). Moving between Nubia's past and its present and drawing on indigenous Nubian cultural forms such as myths, folktales, poems and ballads, the four tales reinforce the deep connection between 'Old' and 'New' Nubia which continues to endure despite a century of dam-induced displacement and resettlement, and attendant policies of assimilation and Arabization which threaten Nubian culture, language and identity with extinction.

The first story, 'Adila, Grandmother', is set in the present and reflects on the condition of the Nubian community stuck, as Oddoul argues, 'between the hammer of the majority that surrounds them and commits itself to dissolving their uniqueness, and the anvil of the inner brokenness as a result of the loss of the land of origin' (Aboul-Ela). The 'barren poverty of their lives in a strange land' (Oddoul *Nights of Musk: Stories from Old Nubia*: 12) is not restricted to the material and physical challenges of living in the impoverished resettlement villages of 'New Nubia' – known colloquially as 'the exile's villages' (12) – which are described as uncultivable wastelands that 'yielded only rocks and stones' (11). It is also manifested in forms of social breakdown, notably the dislocation experienced by Nubian youth as they are faced with the challenge of negotiating their Nubian identity in a context where it is marginalized and denigrated by the majority culture and the schizophrenia (*infiṣām*) experienced by elderly characters like the grandmother, who, although physically resident in the resettlement villages, feel so alienated from that environment that they psychologically inhabit the old Nubian 'Nile World' of their memories, imagined nostalgically as the repository of all that is 'good' (25).

The cultural and psychological brokenness of the inhabitants of 'New Nubia' is portrayed as a direct consequence of the denigration and marginalization of Nubians in wider Egyptian society and the processes of Arabization and assimilation that threaten to engulf them. This is illustrated in an episode when the grandmother, upon learning that her grand-daughter is to marry a *gorbati* (northern Egyptian man), starts to perform the dance of the bereaved on the train to Alexandria. As she screams *ibiyuuuu, ibiyu* (woe is me) and beats a monotonous rhythm on the floor of the carriage with her feet while smearing her face with dirt and waving her black headscarf in the air, some of the passengers mock her, while others cower terrified in their seats, convinced that she is mad (16). By contrast, in 'Zeinab Uburty', we learn that this dance performed vital symbolic and sacred functions in Old Nubia, where women would dance it to ward off disaster, smearing their faces and heads with the *uburty* (ashes) that represented 'everything that was evil and wicked and awful' (50).

Gorbati/ya is a Nubian word that recurs repeatedly throughout these texts. Although it literally means foreigner, it is used almost exclusively to refer to northern Egyptians who are blamed for many of the Nubian community's current difficulties. As the grandmother laments:

[they have] pulled us up by our roots, and we've become brushwood. Our sons went off all over the place to work as servants in the land of plenty. They feed our grandchildren leftovers from foreigners and beys. And we here, they have thrown us into the valley of the demons. They gave us this land. Nothing grows on it but evil plants with bitter fruits that even the animals loathe. They've killed us, my son, the *gorbatis* have killed us! (13–14)

In this context, Nubians are reframed as a colonized people who suffer from an internalized inferiority complex which manifests itself in derision towards their culture and language of origin.

This is suggested in an episode in 'The River People' when the returning Mahjoub disembarks from the steamer from Cairo having swapped his traditional Nubian clothes for 'a northern suit' (106) and proceeds to address the assembled villagers in Arabic rather than their native Nubian. Since, according to Fanon's logic, lack of recognition and reciprocity on the part of the dominant culture ties all action to imitation of the 'other' (Gibson *Fanon: The Postcolonial Imagination*: 30), Mahjoub's attempt to 'turn white' by adopting northern Egyptian language, dress and customs signifies a form of totalizing cultural submission to Egypt's Arab identity. However, despite his best efforts to embody an Egyptian gentleman, Mahjoub appears a 'ridiculous sight' to the crowd who perceive him as 'neither a southerner nor a northerner, neither one of us nor one of them' (Oddoul *Nights of Musk*: 106), since, on account of the colour of his skin, he can no more abandon his Nubian identity than pass for a northern Egyptian.

By contrast, in 'Adila, Grandmother', we learn that the narrator's sister (who 'had taken none of my father's colour') regards her Nubian relatives with contempt and derision, refusing even to acknowledge her own grandmother, and marries an Arab-Egyptian in the hope of casting off her Nubian identity (17). Her desire to marry a *gorbati* can be read as evidence of a 'clear wish to be white', or at least to ensure that her children can 'pass' as such and thus avoid many of the structural disadvantages such as poverty, racism and unemployment facing the Nubian community (Fanon *Black Skin, White Masks*: 6), with 'white' glossed in these stories to refer specifically to northern Egyptians. However, whatever material advantages intermarriage between *gorbatis* and Nubians may confer upon the individual, it is considered disastrous by the community at large because of the very real threat of assimilation and Arabization that accompanies it, particularly in a context where the new generation of Nubians is being born and brought up in the cities of the north.

Products of this generation, like the boy narrator Mohamed whose father is Nubian and whose mother is a northern Egyptian, do not speak the Nubian language or practise its traditions growing up, a factor which threatens the continued viability of Nubian culture in the diaspora. A sense of alienation and shame towards his cultural origins explains Mohamed's self-hatred when he visits his father's ancestral village for the first time and feels like 'an outsider … actually frightened by the dark faces' (Oddoul *Nights of Musk*: 1). Echoing the unspoken prejudices of Egyptian society, he considers the Nubian village dirty, its way of life backward, and its dark-skinned inhabitants 'ugly' and 'stupid', reserving a particular hatred for his grandmother whom he 'detested' and whose wrinkled and shrivelled appearance makes him feel 'sick' (2–6).

However, unlike his assimilated sister who attempts to avoid 'slipping back' into blackness by renouncing all connections with her Nubian heritage, Mohamed gradually comes to embrace his Nubian identity by learning the Nubian language and adopting village dress and customs out of 'love for everything that was southern' (22). Whereas his understanding of Nubian culture had come mainly from his grandmother's tales, told in pidgin Arabic, learning the Nubian language proves a vital step towards conquering the self-alienation that afflicts him and integrating into village life since, as Fanon has argued, 'to speak a language is to take on a world, a culture' (25). At this defining point in the story, Mohamed stops referring to the village and its inhabitants in the third person, talking instead about '*our new land that spewed stones and choked palm shoots*' and how to improve it (Oddoul *Nights of Musk*: 22; emphasis added).

He eventually seals his Nubian identity by marrying Zeinab, a Nubian girl from the village, in order to 'bring forth a flood of life after Awada [who symbolizes the suffering of the displaced generation] had grown old and barren and endured an arid age' (23). The act of passing Nubia's distinctive language, identity and traditions on to a new generation, like the rituals surrounding the birth of a baby in 'Nights of Musk' where the father tells his daughter to name her own future daughter after her mother as a way of preserving intergenerational links with the past, suggests that the cyclical nature of Nubian life, which had appeared fatally undermined by the destruction of their lands and the scattering of their people, may one day be re-established.

Although the stories in this volume 'are born out of a tragedy that can never be undone' (Oddoul *Nights of Musk*: viii), clues within the text indicate that Nubian culture and history have not 'disappeared for ever under the water behind the dam', as literary critics such as Noha Radwan have argued ('Review: *Nights of Musk*': 119). Rather, the slow yet constant renewal observed in 'Adila, Grandmother' suggests that the violent legacy of dam-building is not chronic or irreparable and that the dream of return – be it a physical return to the homeland, as desired by the grandmother in 'Adila, Grandmother', a return to community and tradition as in 'Nights of Musk', or a return to the natural balance between humans and nature, as in 'Zeinab Uburty' and 'The River People' – is simply deferred until a future generation (Radwan: 120).

As such, Oddoul's writing does not simply recreate the lost Nubian 'Nile World' as a literary form of 'salvage ethnography' (Halim). Rather, Nubian myths, folktales, poems and ballads as well as dialect expressions such as *adila* (farewell) *gorbati/ya* (northern Egyptian man/ woman) and *ibiyu* (*ya wayli*, or 'woe is me') are used to evoke a distinctively Nubian worldview that relegates the Arabic language to the margins of the text. For example, in 'Zeinab Uburty' the characters greet each other with the words '*maskagru*' instead of the Arabic '*marḥaban*', while the narrator refers to a woman called '*Hajija* (that is to say, Khadija as you pronounce it nowadays with your queer way of speaking)' (Oddoul *Nights of Musk*: 51). The first of these represents the Nubian pronunciation of the name while the second is the more widely recognized standard Arabic version, thus privileging the Nubian mother tongue over Arabic, the 'major voice' of Egyptian high culture (Miller 'Theories of Africans': 133).

Oddoul's writing also reflects a change in the formal characteristics of Nubian literature in the late 1980s from a realist to a more experimental, modernist aesthetic characterized by a 'disjointed and chaotic narrative structure and frequent time lapsing between past and present' (*Oddoul Udabā' Nūbiyūn Wa-Nuqqād 'unṣuriyūn*: 36). Whereas realist texts tend to privilege a linear narrative structure and an omniscient first person narrator whose subjectivity and interpretative authority dominates, popular folk narratives of the sort found in 'Nights of Musk' and 'Zeinab Uburty' are rooted in the oral tradition of collective performance whereby 'the narrator situates himself as a physically present interlocutor between the narrative and the audience, who participate in turn in the unfolding of the narrative through their comments and interjections' – as if the story was being performed in their physical presence by a *hakawāti* or storyteller (Selim 'The Narrative Craft: Realism and Fiction in the Arabic Canon': 117).

Thus, in 'Nights of Musk' the narrator's use of onomato-poeia, repetition and vivid exclamations such as *waaah waaah* to signify the sounds made by a baby and *duum-taka dum-tak duum-taka dum-tak* for the beat of the drum, give the impression that the story is being performed in the physical presence of an audience of listeners rather than readers, as if the words have been 'freed from the written page and spoken into the air', to be responded to and repeated back (Oddoul *Nights of Musk*: viii). Here, the narrator performs the dual role common to many folk narratives of both speaking to and for the group he claims to represent, as suggested by the repeated use of the plural pronouns 'we', 'us' and 'our'. Statements such as 'there isn't a Nubian on earth who would miss a wedding' (35) and 'dancing and singing are in our blood' (38) evoke a social reality common to all members of 'one harmonious group' (33) with little evidence of individual consciousness or character development in the story. Artificial and homogenizing as this may seem, the collective voice has been widely identified as a key feature of testimonial styles of writing adopted by marginalized groups to express an emergent racial, ethnic and gender consciousness (Moore-Gilbert *Postcolonial Life-Writing*: xi–xxvi; Ostle et al. *Writing the Self: Autobiographical Writing in Modern Arabic Literature*: 18–23).

The narrator's role in these stories lies in acting as an embedded witness to the events he is recording and as an amanuensis who gathers and transcribes the oral testimonies of other members of his community. For example, the tale of 'Zeinab Uburty' is narrated by an old man called Hulla who is 'one hundred and ten floods old' (Oddoul *Nights of Musk*: 43) and claims that the mysterious and seemingly mythical events he describes, with its cast of witches and demons, are matters of historical fact which he witnessed as a boy during the last days of Ottoman rule (42). The fact that this is logically impossible requires a redefinition of what it means to 'write history' that privileges the mythic mode and traditional forms of historical narrative over empirical Western scholarly practices.

This is illustrated in the second story in the volume 'The River People' which employs myth and symbolism to suggest that all hubristic attempts to tame the mighty Nile will prove futile in the context of deeper, geological time and that one day the river will break through the High Dam's walls and flood the plains below, re-establishing its dominance over the valley. The symbiotic relationship between the natural and supernatural realms is evident in Oddoul's symbolic economy, where river water is associated with Nubia and tradition while sea water is associated with northern Egypt and the corrosive effects of modernity on Nubian's ecology, culture and society. Thus, the salty waters of the Mediterranean cities where many Nubian men are temporarily 'anchored' in their search for work, are contrasted with the sweet, pure river water of the Nile in the south, with the implication that the women of the north 'cannot quench their thirst' and will ultimately poison them, transforming erstwhile strong and resolute Nubian men into sickly and dependent creatures, weakening Nubian society as a whole (97).

Similarly, we learn that northern Egyptian interference with the Nile has polluted it, as sea water would fresh water. As Asha, the protagonist of the tale, observes, 'the river is good like the people but the dam confined the water in a huge lake. The water swelled up like boiling milk, and as it rose it swallowed up half the green valley and destroyed it. It drowned lines of palm trees and polluted the sweet water. It ruined the time of peace and purity' (96). Thus, whereas the floodwaters at the time before the barrage was built are described as life-giving and enriching, 'pouring gently into the sprawling water course ... full of fertile silt, seeping into the life-giving earth' and causing the valley to 'bring forth billions of tiny green shoots' (100), the man-made flood caused by the rising waters of the dam is associated instead with death and disease, suggesting the long-term dangers of disturbing the fine balance between humans and nature. Not only do its waters, devoid of life-giving silt, cause the crops to wither but they are also associated with several uncanny effects, causing the fish to propel themselves onto land where they 'writhed and suffocated' (99).

However, although the immediate future predicted for the Nubian community is bleak, the text suggests that the majestic, sacred Nile blessed by God and inhabited by the River People of Nubian mythology is both more powerful and resilient than the human schemes devised to tame it. Thus, although Asha perceives the Aswan barrage as having destroyed her own life and that of the river Nile by blocking and contaminating 'the life-flow of water' and disrupting its 'solemn timeless melody', the river is depicted as bruised, rather than broken, by the dam hurled into its midst (96). The story ends with the suggestion that the River People of Nubian mythology will 'flex your muscles in anger [and] bring forth an invincible flood, not around the sides but headlong into the high [dam] wall', thereby exacting retribution against the northerners who have destroyed Nubia and its way of life (106).

Mixing the fantastical with the real, the text illustrates how the natural and the supernatural worlds existed side by side as part of normal life in Nubia just as they do in many contemporary African societies whose cultural systems, beliefs, rituals and narratives are considered no less 'real' than the materialist approach to reality privileged in realist narratives (Zamora and Faris *Magical Realism: Theory, History, Community*: 3; Osore 'Magical Transformations and the Subjugation of Nature': 132). Similarly, in 'Nights of Musk' we learn that everyone in the village is present to witness the narrator's wedding including the souls of the ancestors watching from the cemetery and the mythical River People who inhabit the Nile and 'emerge dripping alone and in groups' to sit amongst the branches and fronds of the palm trees and partake of the celebrations while their young sit in the ears of corn making them dance (Oddoul *Nights of Musk*: 35). While the rustling of the palm fronds and corn stalks clearly have a more rational, natural explanation like the wind, the fact that they are acknowledged as real beings and anthropomorphized by the wedding party indicates the extent to which the living and the dead, the natural and supernatural, exist side by side and influence each other.

That the stories in *Nights of Musk* move back and forth between historical and mythic modes suggests a debt to the techniques of international magical realism, a form which influenced several Middle Eastern writers of Oddoul's generation such as the Syrian-Kurdish writer Salim Barakat and the Palestinian novelist Emile Habibi (Meyer: 60, 87). As Lois Parkinson Zamora and Wendy B. Faris have argued, magical realist narratives operate as 'enabling catalysts for the development of new national and regional literatures' (2) that allow authors to reconnect with the autochthonous folk traditions. Whereas Richard Jacquemond has interpreted the mythic character of the short stories in *Nights of Musk* as evidence that Oddoul 'tended to separate his political views from his literary work' (*Conscience of the Nation*: 183), I would disagree. In keeping with the tradition of magical realism as a form of social critique (Zamora and Faris: 6), 'Zeinab Uburty' and 'The River People' employ mythic and magical modes not just as a means of expressing a distinctly Nubian sensibility but of articulating dissenting ideas in a symbolic and allegorical manner.

The normalization of the supernatural in Oddoul's writing is ontologically disruptive precisely because it encourages the reader to discern alternative ways of viewing 'reality' that stand in opposition to the logic of scientific rationalism that underpinned Egyptian nationalist discourses celebrating large dams as engines of economic and social progress. For example, 'Zeinab Uburty' articulates a specifically Nubian historical perspective grounded in mythic and magical modes to suggest that it is ultimately wiser to maintain the traditional balance between the human and non-human worlds than to pursue human mastery over nature. The story recounts how in Old Nubia all living things are divided into three: the *adamir*, or mankind; the inhabitants of the river bottom known as *amon nutto* (River People) and *amon dugur* (river trolls); and the People of the Current, whom we learn are 'truly evil' and whose 'malice towards the *adamir* is terrifying' (Oddoul *Nights of Musk*: 41).

Crucially, all three categories of being coexist harmoniously as long as the boundaries between their kingdoms are respected. However, when Zeinab Uburty disrupts this fine balance by summoning the People of the Current, the villagers are struck by a series of disasters including plague, famine, poverty, disease, drought and communal discord (42). Although the natural balance is finally restored when Zeinab Uburty rips up her contract with the devil, the narrator implies that the moral of the story is universal – a reading reinforced by the observation that once 'a naïve human' crosses the barrier between the natural and the supernatural in the hope of gain 'the end is always the same' (42), be it in Oddoul's mythical text or the 'real world'. Although not wishing to reduce this story to a straightforward political critique of Nasser's hydropolitical agenda, tropes such as the social and ecological disaster brought about by tampering with the natural order in 'Zeinab Uburty' can nevertheless be read as attempts to demystify the High Dam as a symbol of Egypt's social and economic progress and to expose instead the unequal power relations that determine whose version of history and forms of knowledge are considered legitimate.

As I have attempted to show in this paper, the writing of Nubian author and activist Haggag Hassan Oddoul exemplifies a wider trend within modern Egyptian writing known as 'border literature' whereby peripheral regions and minority cultures are given centre stage. Whereas the postcolonial period may have favoured a unitary conception of Egyptian identity as an Arab nation, Oddoul's writing presents Egypt itself as a site of difference by highlighting its marginalized Afro-Nubian history and civilization – a factor which necessarily means 'calling into question the entire rhetorical architecture of the nationalist movement, which is predicated on unity and the eliding of difference' (Naaman: 110). Although his fiction underscores the fissures in Egyptian national identity by drawing attention to the marginalization and exclusion of the Nubian population, it also gestures towards the prospect of a more inclusive and progressive form of Egyptian national culture grounded in a recognition of the plurality of Egypt's ethnic, religious and social identities.

NOTE

1 I would like to acknowledge the support of the Leeds Humanities Research Institute at the University of Leeds, UK where I was based while writing this article.

WORKS CITED

Aboul-Ela, Hosam. 'Haggag Hassan Adoul: Nubia's Human Aspirations'. *The Nubian* 23 January 2005. thenubian.net/haggag/interview.doc (accessed 5 April 2012).

Dafalla, Hassan. *The Nubian Exodus*. London: C. Hurst in association with the Scandinavian Institute of African Studies, 1975.

Dimeo, David. 'Unimaginable Community: The Failure of Nubian Nationalism in Idris Ali's Dongola'. *Research in African Literatures* Vol. 46, No. 1, 2015: 72-89.

El-Refaei, Pervine. 'Egypt's Borders and the Crisis of Identity in the Literature of Nubia and Sinai'. Paper presented at the Spaces of (Dis)location conference. University of Glasgow. 24-25 May 2012.

Fahim, Hussein M. *Dams, People and Development: The Aswan High Dam Case*. New York: Pergamon Press, 1980.

Fanon, Frantz. *Black Skin, White Masks*. London: Pluto Press, 2008.

Gibson, Nigel C. *Fanon: The Postcolonial Imagination*. Cambridge:

Polity Press, 2003.

Hägg, Tomas, ed. *Nubian Culture Past and Present. Main Papers Presented at the Sixth International Conference for Nubian Studies in Uppsala, 11-16 August, 1986.* Stockholm: Almquist & Wiksell, 1987.

Halim, Hala. 'Nubian Salvage, Textualized'. *Al-Ahram Weekly Online* 20-26 October 2005. http://weekly.ahram.org.eg/Archive/ 2005/765/ bo12.htm (accessed 4 September 2017).

Jacquemond, Richard. *Conscience of the Nation: Writers, State, and Society in Modern Egypt.* Cairo: American University in Cairo Press, 2008.

Meyer, Stefan G. *The Experimental Arabic Novel: Postcolonial Literary Modernism in the Levant.* Albany: State University of New York Press, 2001.

Miller, Christopher. 'Theories of Africans: The Question of Literary Anthropology'. *Critical Inquiry* Vol.13, No. 1, 1986: 120-39.

Moore-Gilbert, B.J. *Postcolonial Life-Writing: Culture, Politics and Self-Representation.* London: Routledge, 2009.

Naaman, Mara. *Urban Space in Contemporary Egyptian Literature: Portraits of Cairo.* New York: Palgrave Macmillan, 2011.

Nixon, Rob. *Slow Violence and the Environmentalism of the Poor.* Cambridge, MA: Harvard University Press, 2011.

Oddoul, Haggag Hassan. *Udabā' Nūbiyūn Wa-Nuqqād 'unṣuriyūn.* Cairo Centre for the Study of Human Rights, 2006.

——*Nights of Musk: Stories from Old Nubia.* Translated by Anthony Calderbank. Cairo: American University in Cairo Press, 2008.

Osore, Miriam. 'Magical Transformations and the Subjugation of Nature in Said Ahed Mohamed's *Babu Alipofufuka*'. *International Journal of Humanities and Social Science.* Vol. 3, No. 10, 2013: 132-6.

Ostle, Robin, Ed de Moor and Stefan Wild. *Writing the Self: Auto-biographical Writing in Modern Arabic Literature.* London: Saqi Books, 1998.

Radwan, Noha. 'Review: *Nights of Musk: Stories from Old Nubia* by Haggag Hassan Oddoul, translated by Anthony Calderbank'. *The Arab Studies Journal* Vol. 15, No. 1, 2007: 118-20.

Scott, James C. *Seeing Like a State: How Certain Schemes to Improve the Human Condition Have Failed.* New Haven, CT: Yale University Press, 1998.

Selim, Samah. 'The Narrative Craft: Realism and Fiction in the Arabic Canon'. *Edebiyat: Journal of M.E. Literatures* Vol. 14, Nos 1-2,

2010: 109-28.

Smith, Elizabeth. 'Place, Class and Race in the Barabra Cafe'. In *Cairo Cosmopolitan: Politics, Culture, and Urban Space in the New Globalized Middle East*. Eds Diane Singerman and Paul Amar. Cairo: American University in Cairo Press, 2006: 399-413.

Zamora, Lois Parkinson and Wendy B. Faris, eds, *Magical Realism: Theory, History, Community*. Durham, NC: Duke University Press, 1995.

Frantz Fanon's Conceptualization of Decolonization in Sonallah Ibrahim's The Committee

TEMITOPE ABISOYE NOAH

In his October Paper of 1974, Egyptian president Anwar Sadat announced *Infitah*, an open door economic policy aimed at encouraging foreign investments in Egypt's private sector. 'Codified in Law 43/1974, *Infitah* stripped away state intervention, provided major tax exemptions for foreign companies, and lifted the requirement that foreign companies be partly Egyptian-owned' (Brownlee 'Peace Before Freedom': 649). *Infitah* ended up enriching the bourgeoisie and the foreign companies who made investments in Egypt. The populace, however, were not so fortunate: '*Infitah* had unleashed "consumption liberalization" without alleviating the strain on Egyptian families' (Brownlee: 650). The cost of living rose by 20 per cent, crime rates skyrocketed, along with unemployment, and other forms of maladies.

Following the outcome of *Infitah*, Egypt's intellectuals began to view the foreign exploitation of their country as a new form of colonialization. With the arrival of the foreign companies came not only economic exploitation, but cultural infiltration by the West. It was a painful reminder of the mid-1960s when Coca-Cola and other American multinational companies in Egypt 'played an integral role in buttressing Israeli militarism, Zionist settler colonialism, and Western imperialism' (Labelle 'De-Coca-Colonizing Egypt': 124). The intellectuals viewed this new combination of economic, cultural and political manipulation of Egypt as a major threat to their country's prosperity. Together with the Egyptian masses, they began to campaign against *Infitah* and the overall permissiveness of their country's leaders with the Western politicians and businessmen. In January 1975, thousands protested on the streets of Cairo, and in March of that same year, 40,000 workers in the town of Mahalla went on strike. In January 1977, thousands rioted in cities throughout Egypt, leaving eighty people killed, and hundreds wounded. Many intellectuals who galvanized the masses suffered frequent raids and imprisonments by the regime.

This historical moment in Egypt is the focus of Sonallah Ibrahim's *The Committee* (1981). Ibrahim, one of Egypt's most influential novelists, had been imprisoned in 1959 for alleged communist ties. He spent five years out of a seven-year sentence behind bars and was released in 1964. My discussion of Ibrahim's *The Committee* suggests that Ibrahim's novel is shot through with motifs from Frantz Fanon's *The Wretched of the Earth* (1961), and that its narrative allegorically presents several major components of Fanon's decolonization structure.

In *The Wretched of the Earth* Fanon argues that colonialism, at its most fundamental level, is the systematic destruction of a country's national culture. 'This cultural obliteration is made possible by the negation of national reality, by new legal relations introduced by the occupying power, by the banishment of the natives and their customs to outlying districts by colonial society, by expropriation, and by the systematic enslaving of men and women' (236). Fanon theorized that, in crises like these arises an intelligentsia that fashions a system to resist the workings of the colonial power. They embark on a 'passionate search for a national culture' in order 'to shrink away from that Western culture in which they all risk being swamped' (Fanon: 209). Such search for culture begins as a backlash against the colonial powers, but it crystallizes into its own culture: 'The intelligentsia, which during the period of repression was essentially a consuming public, now themselves become producers' (139). The path intellectuals take to produce this new culture is a three-step process: the period of 'unqualified assimilation', the period of 'creative work', and the 'fighting phase' (222). In Sonallah Ibrahim's *The Committee*, the unnamed narrator-protagonist, an Egyptian intellectual, evolves through these three Fanonian steps to counteract the colonial forces that close in on him, and he creates a new national culture. In the spirit of Fanon, he fights to transform his society from a population of consumers to producers.

In the beginning of *The Committee*, our narrator complains of suffering from a sense of meaninglessness and despair, and he describes himself as being a nervous wreck. Plagued by an 'aching emptiness' that makes him feel like a 'drowning man', the narrator decides to take a break from his job and seeks help; he consults an influential group he calls 'the Committee' in hopes of earning their approval to 'change my life completely' (Ibrahim: 83, 11). The tension between the Committee and the narrator during this meeting evinces a colonizer-colonized dynamic, and it sets the tone for the rest of the narrative.

When the narrator meets the Committee, he sweats profusely, and he shudders under their imposing gazes. He nervously offers them his personal documents to convince them of his talents and intellectual abilities, but they remain aloof. They do not speak Arabic, and choose only to speak in their own tongue. The narrator, on the other hand, is exceedingly eager to communicate with them: 'I spent the past year … devot[ing] myself to studying the language the Committee uses in its interviews' (Ibrahim: 6). In line with its tradition of 'set[ting] clever traps for everyone it interviews', the Committee asks him: 'By which momentous event among the wars, revolutions, or inventions will our country be remembered in the future?' (7, 16). The narrator does not completely comprehend their question, and is quite apprehensive about answering incorrectly, but he tries his luck with Coca-Cola. Coca-

Cola, he explains, 'embodies the civilization of this century' because '[w]hile the words used for God and love and happiness vary from one country to another, "Coca-Cola" means the same thing in all paces and all tongues' (19). Consequently, it 'played a decisive role in the choice of our mode of life, the inclinations of our tastes, the presidents and kings of our countries, the wars we participated in, and the treaties we entered into' (23).

The narrator's spiel about Coca-Cola is deliberate. In emphasizing the power of Coca-Cola he symbolically underscores the colonial-like power of the Committee. Like colonialists, both Coca-Cola and the Committee are involved in many global affairs: they claim to strive for 'that old dream of global unity', and to 'expand the democratic process' (Ibrahim: 113,115). Like colonialists, they instead end up associated with 'political coups d'état, sectarian massacres, and limited conflicts happening now in the Arab world'; they believe 'the end justify the means', and they are often charged with 'sadism and sometimes ... demagoguery' (115, 132, 115). Though the narrator is unaware about the Committee's secret dealings at this point in the story, he is cognizant of their enormous power, which he parallels with Coca-Cola culture. He praises Coca-Cola in order to flatter them and win their favour.

In kowtowing to the colonial power of the Committee, the narrator substantiates the symptoms of the initial stage of the native intellectual who will evolve to create a new national culture: the assimilation period. Fanon stated that, convinced of the inferiority of his culture, 'the intellectual throws himself in frenzied fashion into the frantic acquisition of the culture of the occupying power' (237). Exemplifying Fanon's statement that, in this phase, the colonial power makes the native recognize 'the imperfect character of his own biological structure', the Committee humiliates the narrator (237). They make him strip naked and dance before them and they call him 'impotent' and proceed to examine his private parts and anus (15).

According to Fanon, this phase of assimilation is a trying period for the native because, unlike his native culture, the colonial culture is dehumanizing. The colonial mother 'acts like a mother who unceasingly restrains her fundamentally perverse offspring from managing to commit suicide and from giving free rein to its evil instincts. The colonial mother protects her child from itself, from its ego, and from its physiology, its biology, and its own unhappiness which is its very essence' (211). Hence, the mother damages her child psychologically. The native is cognizant of this abuse. Yet, rather than rending himself from the colonial mother, he paradoxically attempts to win her favour by assimilating himself to her world. This malady is thoroughly devastating, but the intellectual one day awakens to the reality of his neurosis, and begins to refuse to assimilate.

The narrator begins to evolve from his assimilation phase after he leaves the interview, and the Committee assigns him a 'study on the greatest contemporary Arab luminary' (Ibrahim: 31). Discovering that 'luminary', in Arabic, bares the double meaning of 'brilliant' and 'theft', the narrator finds that a certain famous individual by the title of 'the Doctor' embodies just that (33). The Doctor is a local personality often featured in Cairo's newspapers who commits crimes against the Egyptian people in myriad ways, including manufacturing and selling them his own ersatz Coca-Cola at high cost while vowing to deliver them from consumerist exploitation. This Doctor's tendency to 'carry the torch of progress, peace, and stability for the region', while he 'manipulates from behind the scenes', is of particular curiosity to the narrator because it stirs up memories (61-2). The Doctor's fall from a once noble quixotism to exploitation of the masses, in particular, recalls the pattern of several African leaders the narrator has read about. The narrator thus decides to plunge himself into the world of the Doctor and examine the workings of his behaviour.

In investigating the Doctor, the narrator is investigating what Fanon calls 'the national bourgeoisie'. The national bourgeoisie is a class from the native group that 'steps into the shoes of the former European settlement: doctors, barristers, traders, commercial travelers, general agents, and transport agents' (Fanon: 152). This tight-fisted group makes sure Western companies pass though their hands only, and it does not distribute the ensuing funds to the rest of the natives. The national bourgeoisie is not interested in transforming the nation; it exists merely to serve as 'the transmission line between the nation and a capitalism' (152).

The Doctor is emblematic of the national bourgeoisie for several reasons. His luxurious lifestyle reflects Fanon's description that the bourgeoisie 'acquires foreign securities in the European markets, and goes off to spend the weekend in Paris or Hamburg' (173). The Doctor's clandestine dealings match Fanon's description that '[t]he behavior of the national bourgeoisie … is reminiscent of the members of a gang, who after every holdup hide their share in the loot from the other members … and prudently start thinking about their retirement' (173-4). The fall from quixotism the Doctor experiences substantiates Fanon's statement that the national bourgeoisie 'turns its back more and more on the interior and on the real facts of its undeveloped country, and tends to look toward the former mother country and the foreign capitalists who count on its obliging compliance' (165).

Not long into his research on the Doctor, the narrator is paid a house visit by the Committee. The members rush into his apartment and begin to ransack his bookshelves, his kitchen drawers, his box of index cards, and every possible nook of the dwelling. The commotion comes to a still when one of their leaders, Stubby, spots a collage the narrator had made depicting the national bourgeoisie. The collage showcases Arab leaders bowing in submission to American president Jimmy Carter. Stubby finds the depiction unsettling; the narrator's investigation into the bourgeoisie, apparently, is in direct conflict with the Committee's objectives. The Committee is interested in maintaining secrecy rather than 'offer[ing] a solution to some of the mysteries and puzzles that have baffled most people until now', as the narrator strives to accomplish (Ibrahim: 75). Because the narrator finds himself and the Committee in opposition, this marks the end of his first step toward creating a new national culture. He is no longer interested in assimilating the Committee's colonial culture, but founding his own.

The Committee eventually leaves the narrator's apartment while Stubby remains behind to steer the narrator into changing his mind about the Doctor: 'We suggested you substitute another personality. The Committee will not oppose any alternative whatsoever' (Ibrahim: 79). The narrator, however, would hear none of such suggestions. Consequently, Stubby proceeds to pester the narrator. He trails him throughout his apartment, invading his privacy at every turn. He vows that if the narrator wishes to '[w]ave other peoples' dirty laundry in public' he will make sure the narrator will not 'wash your own in private' (Ibrahim: 92). Stubby even taunts the narrator as he uses the toilet, gloating about the rectal examination he put the narrator through during his first interview with the Committee: 'I saw your bare backside under conditions less dignified than answering a call of nature' (92).

Stubby is aggressive towards the narrator because, in unravelling the truth about the national bourgeoisie (the Doctor), the narrator is unravelling the truth about the Committee with which they are in cahoots. Fanon states that the truth of the bourgeoisie 'hurries on the break-up of the colonialist regime; it is that which promotes the emergence of the nation; it is all that protects the natives, and ruins the foreigners' (Fanon: 50). As members of the colonial regime, Stubby and the national bourgeoisie run the risk of being dismantled through the narrator's investigations. He thus demoralizes the narrator so as to curtail such doom.

In an attempt to protect himself from Stubby, the narrator decides to retire for the night. But he notices that he is still perplexed:

> [A] familiar wave of doubt swamped me ... It was difficult for me to sleep with the problems on my mind. Whenever I tried thinking of something else, I would open the Pandora's box I had been trying to lock. Images and memories that had been waiting popped right into my head. Immediately my weaknesses and flaws stood out plainly. My emotions ran wild at the thought of my insignificance, of the moments when I had permitted myself to be the laughing stock of others and a plaything in their hands, of how I allowed myself to be sidetracked, and of the small pleasures I had indulged in and allowed to dominate me. (Ibrahim: 88-9)

The narrator's devastating memories and feelings of doubt typify the native's second stage towards creating a national culture: the period of creative work. Fanon describes this creative phase of the native as a 'period of distress and difficulty' where '[p]ast happenings of the bygone days of his childhood will be brought up out of the depths of his memory' (Fanon: 222). Such bygone days continue to swarm the narrator's mind:

> I closed my eyes and reviewed my past. The ideas I had believed in while growing up surfaced ... I had struggled to reevaluate them every so often and to develop them to accommodate the continual changes in the modern world, avoiding as many pitfalls and labyrinths as possible, although throughout all this I was exposed to a great deal of harm and innumerable dangers. (Ibrahim: 105)

As the narrator reviews his past, he complains about 'feeling deeply depressed and frustrated' (Ibrahim: 93). Fanon says that, in this period, the tug of war between the native's culture and that of the colonial power become so frenzied that 'we find the native is disturbed; he decides to remember what he is' (Fanon: 222).

Stubby is the personification of the colonial force that tugs on the narrator's psyche. In the narrator's apartment, not only is Stubby exceedingly obtrusive, but he also seems to trigger signifiers that substantiate his symbolic identity as colonizer. For instance, when Stubby monitors the narrator in his bath tub, the colour of the tap water turns from clear to brown, evoking Coca-Cola's infiltration into Egypt to 'leav[e] tap water as its only rival' (Ibrahim: 125). Stubby also crawls into the narrator's bed and repeatedly shoves his gun into the narrator's back, evoking the military occupation and harassment by colonial powers. Echoing the thorough infiltration and siege of Egypt by the colonial powers, the narrator remarks that he has securely locked all of his windows and doors, meanwhile the real danger is inside his home.

The particular component of colonialism that Stubby represents is the settler. Fanon states that the colonial settler is the foil of the colonial power that works with the national bourgeoisie to torment the natives and jostle them into submission: 'The appearance of the settler' implies 'the death of the aboriginal society, cultural lethargy, and the petrification of individuals' (Fanon: 93). Consistent with Stubby's attempts to psychologically break the narrator into accepting the Committee's suggestion, Fanon states that, 'in the colonial context the settler only ends his work of breaking in the native when the latter admits loudly and intelligibly the supremacy of the white man's values' (43).

Fanon theorizes that, to save himself from the destructive force of the settler, the native fervidly fights back: 'For the native, life can only spring up again out of the rotting corpse of the settler' (Fanon: 93). In the settler-native combat, '[t]he settler's work is to make even dreams of liberty impossible for the native. The native's work is to imagine all possible methods for destroying the settler' (93). This consists not only of armed struggle but ideological struggle: 'To the theory of the "absolute evil of the native" the theory of the "absolute evil of the settler" replies' (93). Such heated tension, which Stubby and the narrator interaction exudes, typifies the native's phase of creative work.

Fanon's final assessment of the creative phase is that it is a deadly period; because of the intense struggle involved, the creative period is inevitably a period 'where death is experienced' (Fanon: 222). The 'death' of the narrator is intertwined with the death of Stubby. After a few days of being harassed by Stubby, the narrator becomes convinced that Stubby will inevitably murder him, and so the narrator decides that rather than remain passive, he will launch a pre-emptive attack against his tormentor. As he observes a knife in his kitchen drawer the narrator remarks: 'For the first time in ages, I felt strength and purpose pervade my being' (Ibrahim: 107). As the narrator's shift in temperament occurs even before he grabs the knife, the narrator's decision to kill Stubby appears to constitute a kind of psychological death. In deciding to terminate Stubby, the narrator annihilates his vulnerable and passive side, so that he can assume power.

The third step towards creating national culture is the fighting period: Fanon asserts: 'The native, after having tried to lose himself in the people and with the people will on the contrary shake the people. Instead of according the people's lethargy an honoured place in his esteem, he turns himself into an awakener of the people' (Fanon: 222-3). In this period, the intellectual comes to declare and inaugurate a new way of living. He realizes that rather than simply recalling one's culture, one must 'substantiate its existence' by fighting against the colonial powers (223). This is the phase into which the narrator steps, after he is sentenced by the Committee.

After he kills Stubby, the Committee sentences the narrator with 'the harshest punishment on the books', and the narrator relinquishes his attempts at 'protecting my dignity' and he exits the Committee's hall (Ibrahim: 134, 116). He boards a bus called the 'Carter' bus, named after

American president Jimmy Carter (139). As he stands on the crowded bus, the narrator notices the dilapidated state of its interior, and remarks that it is a prime manifestation of the corruption of Western powers who export counterfeit products to Egypt under the guise of global partnership. The narrator also observes that the morose passengers around him greatly suffer from such treatment: 'I decided that all of them were oppressed and humiliated, but had remarkable powers of endurance' (143). The passengers on the bus are symbolic of the Egyptian populace, and the bus represents the colonial system of degradation in which they are forced to live.

In the spirit of Fanon's native in the midst of the fighting phase, the narrator decides to 'brush the cobwebs off national consciousness, to question oppression, and to open up the struggle for freedom' (237). A large and imposing man, who the narrator calls 'the giant', repeatedly taunts a female passenger on the bus by brushing against her backside. The narrator intervenes and reprimands the offender. But this yields violent results: 'My adversary … threw a knockout punch and hit me in the face, throwing me onto some seated passengers'; such assault 'made me see stars and made the world spin before my eyes' (Ibrahim: 147). The narrator's quixotic gesture is not just a means to its own end. It is aimed at inciting in his fellow passengers a spirit of defiance; he confronted the giant 'imagining that all the passengers would leap to my aid' (146). To his dismay, the passengers do not respond to his prompting.

The narrator's failed insurgence on the bus is not for naught. The fact that he addresses his own people is a victory in itself. Fanon says that the native's goal during the fighting phase is to turn his gaze inward: 'While at the beginning, the native intellectual used to produce his work to be read exclusively by the oppressor, whether with the intention of charming him or of denouncing him through ethnic or subjectivist means, now the native … progressively takes on the habit of addressing his own people' (Fanon: 240). Though none of the passengers rally behind him, by attempting to catch their attention, the narrator adopts the rhythm of the native intellectual at the core of the fighting phase.

The narrator continues to substantiate the makings of the native in fighting phase when he is at the (medical) doctor's office. He visits the doctor about his arm, which had been injured by the giant on the bus. He insists that his consultation be offered at no cost, as he had already paid an examination fee, but the doctor refuses to oblige. The doctor is yet another agent of colonialism; he is a self-professed humanitarian who in reality exploits the masses. When the narrator protests the doctor's unfair treatment, he is expelled from the office. Here, as in the bus, and in the Committee's hall, the narrator feels unheard. He finds himself without powers to protect his dignity and humanity.

The narrator returns to his apartment and nurses the emotional and psychological wounds inflicted by the Committee, Stubby, the giant and the doctor. He peruses through old pictures, letters, and other items that remind him of the events of his life thus far. In a bizarre ceremony, he sits at his desk and listens to the music of César Franck, Carl Orff, Beethoven and Shostakovich until the dawn breaks, and then he puts his wounded arm into his mouth and begins to devour himself.

This harrowing finale finds its meaning in the porter's prognosis earlier in the story. The porter of the Committee's hall had explained to the narrator that his sentencing is that he will consume his own self. When the narrator eats himself at the end of the narrative, the narrator demonstrates the powerlessness of himself and the Egyptian populace to liberate themselves from the powers of colonialism that intend to relegate them to consumerism at all costs.

The narrator's failure to deliver himself and his countrymen from colonial consumerism does not disqualify him from achieving the state of Fanon's native intellectual who creates a national culture. Fanon states that such an intellectual does not need to achieve liberation in order to produce culture; the intellectual makes the struggle itself a culture: 'It is not alone the success of the struggle which afterward gives validity and vigor to culture; culture is not put into cold storage during the conflict. The struggle itself in its development and in its internal progression sends culture along different paths and traces out entirely new ones for it' (Fanon: 245).

The particular culture that the narrator creates in the end is a culture of unmitigated hope in the face of defeat. Before he eats himself, the narrator performs a speech to kindle hope for his country's future. He decrees there would be a 'great day' when the Committee will 'gradually lose what authority it has while the power of those like me to confront and resist it will grow' (Ibrahim: 156). The narrator explains that his recent failure to overthrow the Committee's system is merely the natural upshot of his rash decision to challenge the Committee 'at an unsuitable time and place', and that his present sojourn in the depths of defeat is only transitory (157). The narrator's forward-looking approach to his plight is encapsulated in Fanon's statement that the native who creates culture 'work[s] and fight[s] with the same rhythm as the people to construct the future and to prepare the ground where vigorous shoots are already springing up' (Fanon: 233).

What Sonallah Ibrahim illustrates by the end of *The Committee* is the plight of the native intellectual who, after having done all he can to liberate the masses from colonialism, finds that he has effected no substantial change. Through the narrator's self-cannibalistic act, Ibrahim illustrates the gruesomeness of such moments of realization. Yet, Ibrahim also counsels, through the narrator's hopeful speech, that decolonization is an evolutionary process rather than an instantaneous act that precipitates liberation once and for all. Ibrahim's missive is thus a clarion call for the colonized to set their eyes on the promising future, as they contend with the despair of the oppressive present. In penning

The Committee, Ibrahim follows Fanon's injunction that: 'The colonized man who writes for his people ought to use the past with the intention of opening the future, as an invitation to action and a basis for hope' (Fanon: 232).

WORKS CITED

Brownlee, Jason. 'Peace Before Freedom: Diplomacy and Repression in Sadat's Egypt'. *Political Science Quarterly*, Vol. 126, No. 4, 2011: 641-68.

Fanon, Frantz, trans. Constance Farrington. *The Wretched of the Earth*, New York: Grove Press, 1963 [1961].

Ibrahim, Sonallah. *The Committee*, Syracuse: Syracuse University Press, 2001.

Labelle, Maurice. 'De-Coca-Colonizing Egypt: Globalization, Decolonization, and the Egyptian Boycott of Coca-Cola, 1966-68', *Journal of Global History*, Vol. 9, No. 1, 2014: 122-42.

Romance as Epistemological Aesthetic in the Fiction of Ahdaf Soueif

F. FIONA MOOLLA

> In this globe-scattered [Sri Lankan] family, we speak only of
> two kinds of marriage. The first is the Arranged Marriage.
> The second is the Love Marriage. In reality, there is a whole
> spectrum in between, but most of us spend years running away
> from the first toward the second. ...
>
> The rule is that all families begin with a marriage. And the
> other way around. (From the novel Love Marriage by V.V.
> Ganeshananthan)

Ahdaf Soueif (b. 1950) is one of the few Egyptian authors
writing in English, and probably the most well known.
Born in Cairo and educated in both Cairo and England,
Soueif combines activism and art in a range of genres that
encompasses short stories, the novel, autobiography and
essays. Translation, both of her own work into Arabic
and Arabic publications into English, is not only part
of her professional repertoire, but broader questions
of linguistic and cultural translation are key themes of
her fiction. Soueif has won a number of literary awards,
and was shortlisted for the Booker Prize in 1999 for her
second novel, *The Map of Love* (1999). Although her
literary reputation is not in need of 'favourable mention'
by intellectual and scholarly luminaries, it seems remiss
to neglect the importance accorded her first novel, *In the
Eye of the Sun* (1992), by Edward Said. 'The Anglo-Arab
Encounter: On Ahdaf Soueif' in the collection, *Reflections
on Exile* (2002), suggests that Arab-Anglophone cross-
cultural, translational exchange is inherent in Ahdaf's

72

project through the mere fact of the representation of Arab culture through the English language, refracted through English literature and culture. Ahdaf's fiction is striking for its acknowledged intertextual engagements with English literature, especially nineteenth-century literature. Furthermore, the novel's inherent structural 'worldliness', using the term in its Saidian sense, signifies the emergence of Arabic literature from the constraints of narrow nationalism into a liberatory internationalism. What Said observes about Soueif's first novel may as aptly be applied to her second novel, *The Map of Love*. Both novels are the focus of this essay, but through the lens of questions of human relations, which are a noticeably neglected dimension of cultural and literary studies generally.

While Said's remarks about Soueif's first novel act as a convenient index to the gist of most Soueif scholarship on questions of translation and cross-cultural exchange, it is to a different dimension of her fiction that I would like now to turn. One is struck in reading Soueif's fiction by her preoccupation with the theme of romantic love. Heterosexual intimate relations, sometimes offset by the unexpected homosexual encounter, are an enduring focus of Soueif's creative attention across her career in her short stories and her two novels. In fact, the short stories in the two collections, *Aisha* (1983) and *Sandpiper* (1996), introduce characters, events and motifs that are inset, reworked and expanded in the two novels. (The 2007 collection, *I Think of You*, is a selection from the previous short story publications.) One could say that, as an author, Soueif is entirely love-struck. Indeed, it is through romantic relationships that questions of translation and cross-cultural dialogue identified by most other scholars achieve social embodiment. The allure of love in Soueif's oeuvre is so pronounced that she was a featured author in *The Guardian's* 2009 series of articles on love fiction, titled '1000 novels everyone must read'. Soueif's piece, 'Great Arabic Love Stories', starts with a reflection on the significance of romantic love in Middle Eastern culture beginning with the ur-romance of Isis and Osiris in ancient Egyptian mythology. Isis, archetypal sister, wife, mother and, most significantly, lover, reassembles the dismembered body of her beloved husband, Osiris, when he is murdered by his brother, Seth. She further uses 'her great power as both healer and magician' to impregnate 'herself with his seed, so bringing forth life from death'. But love more generally seems to have been a consuming passion in ancient Egyptian culture, given the prominence of love as a theme in ancient Egyptian poetry. Soueif cites ancient verse and alludes to the myth of Isis and Osiris repeatedly in her fiction, most notably in the tapestry woven by Anna Winterbourne, the heroine of *Map of Love*, that depicts Isis, Osiris, and also the son, Horus.

Soueif's novels are epic novels that attempt through their expansiveness to capture a panorama of the history and the politics of the times they represent. One manifestation of the consciousness of socio-historical and political context in Soueif's novels is their foregrounding of time in various ways. *In the Eye of the Sun* sets the *zeitgeist* in the Arab world of the mid- to late-twentieth century in the context of global geopolitics. But its close attention to time is signalled through the organization of chapters by detailed but not teleological periodization, moving from July to August 1979 in Chapter I, to December 1975 in Chapter IX, and back to July 1976 to February 1978 in Chapter X. The earliest period represented in the novel is the Six Day War with Israel in 1967, where terse war-time reports are collaged with individual and family experiences. The non-teleological approach to time reflects the coeval approach in the novel to the sociology of human relationships embedded in contemporaneous contexts. The links between the individual life and wider networks in *In the Eye of the Sun* consciously remodel George Eliot's similar project in the nineteenth-century novel *Middlemarch* which shows the intimate connections between personal relationships and great cultural and social shifts. In *The Map of Love*, the second novel, the network of the personal and the political straddles two historical periods, namely the late nineteenth- to early twentieth-century period of British colonial intervention in Egypt, and the pre-millennial period of globalization and American imperial ambitions in the Middle East. Even in this novel that parallels two broad periods, the closeness of time to the intimate relations represented is signalled by the diary-like dating of the letters and fragments that constitute the narrative. The link between history, politics and the family is indexed in the preliminary pages of each novel by the family trees that extend across multiple generations. Thus the novels produce a striking sense of intimate and family relations inserted into and in dynamic exchange with politics and history.

The focus on intimate relations is suggested also through the numerous and often complex extended literary allusions in Soueif's fiction. The example of George Eliot has already been mentioned, but she is just one nineteenth-century novelist on whom Soueif draws. The others include Emily Brontë and the Russian Leo Tolstoy, whose novels in part pick up on similar European Enlightenment themes as do the English nineteenth-century novels, in the context of Russia's complex peripheral relationship with modernity. Common to all these novelist precursors is their focus on the romantic relationship and the ways in which class, traditional prejudice and, most importantly, social and political upheavals affect even the most intimate and apparently apolitical associations. Given Soueif's fascination with eros, it seems surprising that she does not allude to the eighteenth/nineteenth-century novelist whose name more than any other has been linked with romantic love, namely, Jane Austen. Unlike the novelists mentioned above, whose works form part of the cultural backdrop of the privileged, formally educated characters in Soueif's fiction, the novels of Jane Austen are never mentioned, even though that author is the acknowledged model for much popular romance fiction, and also recently romance film, with the success of the *Bridget Jones* movies as a case in point. I would like to suggest the reason for the elision of Austen from Soueif's exploration of romantic love occurs since Austen has been, arguably, presented as an apolitical writer of narrowly regional novels, an impression created by the author's own oft-quoted claim that her novels are cameos – a 'little bit, two inches wide, of ivory on which I work'. By contrast, the nineteenth-century writers who form part of the textual universe of Soueif's novels are all writers who show in texts like *Wuthering Heights*, *Anna Karenina* and *War and Peace* the wide and complex networking of personal relationships with social and political contexts.

Soueif's novels, in contrast to those of Austen, explicitly chart the intersections of romantic love and politics in a postcolonial age. In this respect, her approach is quite similar to that of the Indian writer, Amitav Ghosh, whose novels similarly track family histories, in particular the relationships that lead to marriage, across time and space in the postcolonial context. Soueif, in fact, has favourably reviewed *The Glass Palace*, the Ghosh novel in which the boundary-breaking and utopian potential of romantic love is most explicitly presented. While in Ghosh romantic attachments occur across race, class, caste and religion, in Soueif, affections often cross sharp political borders, in particular, the borders between empire and subject nations. This comes across most clearly in *The Map of Love*, where both of the parallel relationships cross fraught political divides. The marriage at the turn of the twentieth century of Anna Winterbourne, widow of a colonial officer in the Sudan and symbolic representative of British Empire in Egypt, to Sharif al-Baroudi, Egyptian nationalist, holds out the possibility of the reconciliation of colonial animosities. So too does the relationship in the 1990s between the American Isabel Parkman and the Palestinian-

Egyptian, Omar al-Ghamrawi, a character modelled on the biography of Edward Said, promise a defusing of American imperialist tensions as a consequence of its geopolitical ambitions in the oil-rich areas of the world. The distinctiveness of this element in Soueif's project has led postcolonial critic Bruce King cynically to conclude a partially favourable review with the assertion that: '*The Map of Love* seems a Harlequin Romance for the anti-Western intelligentsia' (453). Emily Davis in 'Romance as Political Aesthetic in Ahdaf Soueif's *The Map of Love*', the title of which is riffed in this essay, suggests furthermore that it is precisely the generic tension between the romance and political dimensions of the narrative that lost Soueif the Booker Prize in 1999, most specifically the novel's critique of Zionism and Israeli aggression in the Middle East that was deemed too politically radical. In her survey of reviews of the novel, Davis sums up the tension in reviews as either 'valoriz[ing] the novel's political content and criticiz[ing] its formulaic romance' or 'celebrat[ing] the romance as an escape from the realities of the book's political commentary and an indulgence in the guilty pleasures of mass-market fiction' (para. 30). Soueif defuses this tension through her frankness about the influence of popular romance fiction in her writing in the context of the multifarious potentialities of the intimate relation implied by its nuanced and complex exploration in her fiction. Mills and Boon is referred to in the fiction itself and Soueif has commented in an interview with Joseph Massad that: 'I am influenced by all the Mills and Boone [*sic*] books that I read as a teenager, which are a kind of subliterary rendition of **Wuthering Heights** and *Jane Eyre*' (The Politics of Desire in the Writings of Ahdaf Soueif': 88). Thus the popular romance tradition holds social justice possibilities for Soueif, as it does in many feminist analyses of the genre, resisting the highbrow dismissal of romance.

To sum it up in a slogan, for Soueif, drawing on second-wave feminism of the 1960s, the personal is political where politics *sensu stricto* is shown to be the matrix within which personal relations are forged. Davis, referred to above, interprets Soueif's employment of 'romance as political aesthetic' in the context of the work that romance has been called upon to do in various geographical and historical spaces. Davis situates Soueif's project within the context of colonial and national romance narratives. Drawing on the work of Anne McClintock and Laura Chrisman, Davis notes the ways in which the medieval romance tradition of male questers supported colonial narratives of 'grand adventure' and conquest that relied upon the constitution of subordinate and excluded groups. Davis then moves on to Doris Sommer's analysis of nineteenth-century Latin-American romance narratives, where, in contrast to colonial narratives, postcolonial romance across borders of race, class and religion effected 'gestures of conciliation between groups that had been positioned antagonistically within colonial hierarchies' (para. 2). Davis underlines Sommer's conclusion that romance in this context was ultimately a 'pacifying project' where the 'bourgeois ideal of the nuclear family, married to the national ideal of the unified populace, produces a revisionist historical narrative that contains dissent in the service of national unity' (para 2). The question Davis explores in the context of *The Map of Love* is whether Soueif's novel is able to harness the affective power of romance to explore 'transnational political coalitions for which neither masculinist nationalist rhetoric nor colonialist fantasy has provided a space' (para 4). The idea of the personal is political will be considered in this frame but also, calling on both novels, will be considered in connection with second-wave feminist insistence on the impact of the 'male' world of politics on the 'female' world of domesticity and personal relationships, and the more radical upending of the bourgeois nuclear family, dependent for its existence on gender stereotyping. More significantly, this essay will extend the debate to consider the possibility that Soueif's fiction more fundamentally presents the ways in which the personal is not only political, but also more profoundly epistemological, in its staging of culturally different approaches to personal relations, marriage and family.

The political is shown in the novels significantly to impact on the personal. In the first novel, the reader is presented with a plethora of relationships, sometimes leading to marriage, the course of which is determined by the politics of the day. The prime example of this, although there are many others, is the experience of Noora, a girlhood friend of Asya, the protagonist of *In the Eye of the Sun*. Noora marries a Palestinian, Bassam, against her family's wishes, since 'he'll bring with him a lot of problems' (252). The family's assumption is verified when, among other obstacles encountered as a consequence of her husband's statelessness, Noora has to turn down a PhD scholarship in England since her husband is denied a visa, and she does not want to separate him from their child. In *The Map of Love*, the relationships themselves are inherently political since they bring together partners from opposing camps, so to speak. By contrast to the scenario where politics impact on love, in the case of the relationship between empire and subject, embodied in the historical love affair of Anna Winterbourne and Sharif al-Baroudi, and the late-twentieth-century relationship of Isabel Parkman and Omar al-Ghamrawi, love is tantalizingly held out as a force that could, reversing the usual scenario, impact on politics. This is a possibility that is not realized since in the historical romance, mutual love in the idealized marriage of the colonizer and colonized is not sufficient to allow the 'other' to be accepted by the 'enemy'. In fact, the marriage estranges Sharif al-Baroudi even from his nationalist compatriots who begin to doubt his loyalty. Closure in *The Map of Love* is open-ended since we do not know who assassinates Sharif al-Baroudi, the nationalist leader. For complex reasons explained towards the end of the novel we are told it is rumoured that it could be the

Copts, or Muslim fanatics, or the British or the Turkish Khedive: '[t]hey say – they say' (506). In many of the possible explanations the marriage to Anna Winterbourne adds a possible motive to the murder that paradoxically undercuts the settlement of conflicts ideally envisaged in the marital union. With the twentieth-century relationship also, the possibility of the reconciliation of America and the Middle East is foreclosed by the ominous suggestion of the violent, politically motivated death of Omar, the Edward Said figure in the novel. Thus twentieth-century American-Middle Eastern hostilities, linked with what Walter Mignolo (in *The Darker Side of Western Modernity*) terms coloniality rather than colonialism, can also not be resolved through love.

A variation on the theme of the personal is political is presented also in the flashback when Asya recollects an experience that occurs before the time of Gamal Abdel Nasser's resignation after Egypt's loss in the 1967 war. The period she recalls was one where he was at the height of his power. A concert is held where the legendary Egyptian singer of love songs, Umm Kulthum, performs in his honour. Umm Kulthum uses a 32-line love lyric suggestively and subtly to critique the excesses in quelling dissent by the father of Arab nationalism:

> O my heart do not ask where is love,
> It was a fort of my imagination and it fell …
> My yearning for you burns into my side
> And the seconds are live coals in my blood.
> Give me my freedom! Let loose my hands! …
> I ache with your bonds drawing blood from my wrists …
> Why do I hold on to vows you have broken
> And this pain of imprisonment when the world is mine? (63)

The song of betrayal in love ambiguously alludes to the paradoxical admiration for Nasser and the betrayal of national trust represented by the nefarious activities of his intelligence service. The intimate connection of the personal and the political here is symbolized by the leader as lover of the nation. Indeed, Amal, the contemporary narrator/protagonist of *The Map of Love*, cites the maxim of second-wave feminism when a former lover, Tareq, expresses regret that they did not marry in their younger days. Amal cynically retorts that if they had married, he would be having a casual romantic flirtation with a third party, rather than with herself. Teased about her cynicism, Amal reminds Tareq of his cold, self-interested willingness to enter into business agreements with Israel. When Tareq responds asserting that he is talking about personal affairs, Amal interjects that '[t]he personal is the political' (338).

In the same way that second-wave feminism deployed the idea that the personal is political to challenge the hierarchy and gender division of labour in the nuclear family, throughout her fiction, Soueif challenges Arab expressions of patriarchy in the extended family. Mainly through pursuing their own love interests rather than submitting to family-approved marriages, the young, formally educated, middle-class female characters, especially in the first novel, challenge various expressions of Arab honour-and-shame culture.

The resemblance between Soueif's creative project which foregrounds romantic love and that of Amitav Ghosh, and Soueif's familiarity with Ghosh's work, has been identified above. Another comparable point relates to the significance of love in relation to marriage and the family. In this respect one begins to see an approach to romantic love that effects a seismic shift away from the personal as political to the personal also as epistemological. As noted in the epigraph, '[t]he rule is that all families begin with a marriage. And the other way around.' In the context of Soueif and Ghosh's work that challenges European Enlightenment certainties dispersed through colonization, the family is a crucial alternative matrix to the autonomous individual for the constitution of the postcolonial subject. Relationships and marriage noticeably predominate as a concern in

Soueif's novels, suggesting both the love of marriage in Arab culture generally, and the transition to marriage for love among the modernizing younger generation. It is the absolute inevitability of marriage leading to the creation of families in most non-modern cultures that underscores the role of the family in alternative models of subject formation. Ironically, Asya and Amal, the heroines of both novels end up isolated and alone outside of functional families. Asya of *In the Eye of the Sun* is in love with her husband but is geographically separated from him and emotionally estranged. Her own happily married parents teach at universities in different countries to weather tough economic times. Amal in *The Map of Love* is divorced and living in Egypt without her ex-husband and two sons, and appears to lose her brother to a violent political death at the end of the novel. Families created through marriage thus are presented as crucial to the constitution of the postcolonial self, but the transition to the love marriage in its paradoxical approach to self-fulfilment seems to undermine the very institution it would foster. Love as the main foundation of and rationale for marriage is an aspect of self-realization, rather than a social obligation with ethical and structural functions leading to love. But love on the personal self-realization model also allows the marriage bond to be easily broken when the love dyad is strained and collapses. If love leading to marriage is an element of individual self-fulfilment achieved through each other, when the horizon of personal realization changes, as indeed it must given the dynamism of this model, the marriage itself breaks down.

A fascinating aspect of the relationship of family and marriage that is encountered in Soueif and not in Ghosh, or any other postcolonial novelist to the best of my knowledge, is the entanglement of incest that makes the conception that marriage creates family break down since one is marrying family. Drawing on ancient Egyptian customs among royalty of sibling marriage and less frequently father-daughter marriage, Soueif takes the chicken-and-egg scenario of family as the foundation of marriage and marriage as the foundation of family into an abyss. Ancient Egyptian mores are overlaid by the Arab, and more generally Asian practice of cousin-marriage. In *The Map of Love* the Isis-Osiris-Horus triptych is a potent symbol of the sister who is also the lover-wife, mother and father. The incest motif emerges in the contemporary love story where the young American, Isabel Parkman, falls in love with Omar al-Ghamrawi, whose affections are ambivalently reciprocated since he is troubled by the fact that he is old enough to be her father. It is later revealed that he could, in fact, be her biological father since he had a physical relationship with her mother in the early days of his relocation to New York. When Omar suggests that she takes manuscripts in Arabic to his sister, Amal, in Cairo to be translated, it is discovered that Isabel is a descendant of a branch of the family with whom contact was lost in the grandparent's generation. Isabel and Omar are thus cousins and could potentially have been father and daughter, but this is a possibility the novel later excludes. Fascinated by her family history and superimposed by quite orientalist fantasies of sensuousness and sensuality, Amal, the narrator/focalizer of the greater part of the novel, dreams of being seduced by her forebear, Sharif al-Baroudi, again introducing the father-daughter incest motif.

Romance as epistemological aesthetic in Soueif's fiction is explored through the practices of arranged marriage, familiar in an Asian context, polygyny, a question often addressed in Arab and African fiction, and the seclusion of women, that is, the harem tradition that formed a frustratingly alluring dimension of colonial perceptions of oriental societies.

The two novels present a range of heterosexual marriages moving from the 'Arranged Marriage' to the 'Love Marriage', to use the convenient terms from the epigraph, with the expedient marriage lying somewhere in between. *In the*

Eye of the Sun presents more clearly than *The Map of Love* the apparent transition from the functional marriage that supports social structures where love is assumed to play no part, to the marriage whose foundation is located in romantic love. Of the three generations presented in the novel, the marriages of the third generation are, without exception, love marriages, with spouses unilaterally chosen often without parental approval. By contrast, the marriages of the older generations conform to the practices of the arranged marriage in Arab societies. Operating on a civilizational progress model, the distinction that emerges is between the non-modern arranged marriage and the modern love marriage, with an ineluctable transition from the former to the latter. What is striking about these marriages in Soueif's rendering of them is that the clear line between the non-modern and the modern is so deliberately blurred. For example, the parents of Asya's friend Karima, given the nickname Chrissie in her childhood in England, are cousins whose marriage was arranged by the family. Yet their marriage represents a case of *grande passion* against which the amours of the younger generation casts only a dim light. Among the cast of young friends and siblings, each chooses her/his own life partner, where the choices are motivated solely by love. In the case of the protagonist, Asya, her liberal parents turn down a good proposal of marriage in order to allow her the free choice to marry for love. Yet the ironies are multiple in every one of these cases. Most striking is the example of the protagonist, in whose marriage love is riven from sex. Asya has an enduring love for her husband Saif, but their sexual relation is marred by Asya's anxiety and Saif's bifurcated attitude to his wife vacillating between the paternal and the sadistic. Their marriage is only actually consummated when Saif rapes Asya after her adultery with the vulgar Englishman, Gerald Stone, whose attraction for Asya is only sexual. In Asya's marriage, thus, love and sex are divorced, motivating her yearning after the marriage fails – 'if only 'Sex' and 'Romance' were one' (564). This marriage from among the class of the privileged elite is contrasted with the materially and socially expedient marriages of the servant class where the novel intimates that love may not have been the foundation of the relationship, but affection in marriage and a vigorous sex life appear to overcome multiple obstacles, including severe disability. In both Asya's relationships, the love relationship with her husband and the sexual relationship with her adulterous partner, a level of violence towards the female is displayed that frequently is stereotypically linked with non-modern patriarchal abuse. After he discovers her adultery, the violence that had been suppressed in Saif's attitude to his wife is unleashed in extreme physical abuse. Psychological terror marks the deteriorating relationship between Asya and Gerald Stone, where at its worst, Asya creeps around in the dark in the house the freeloading Gerald has moved into with her, hoping that he has left after a vicious argument. Asya's fear and the depiction of her discovery that Gerald is still in the house with her has the suspense and intensity of the climax of a horror movie. She turns on a switch and 'as the bright light floods the hall she hears Gerald say, "You didn't even try to stop me –" and she hears her own scream, impossibly shrill and long but stopping suddenly as she feels the wetness between her legs and between her thighs' (612). Asya's love marriage to Saif paradoxically ends up in separation with occasional meetings shaped by the non-modern marriage model of fulfilment of relationship roles and companionship. In *The Map of Love*, again challenging expectations, Anna Winterbourne's marriage to the English colonial officer is subtly presented as a marriage of expedience, emotionally and sexually unfulfilling, while the 'oriental' marriage to Sharif al-Baroudi is a relationship forged, sustained and sealed by love.

The question of polygyny is a vexed one and often is a marker of the oppression of women mainly in Arab-Islamic and African cultures. In oriental society polygyny is, furthermore, overlaid by the practice of the seclusion of women within the domestic sphere. Soueif's fiction variously unsettles assumptions of the inherent elevation of women's rights in heterosexual monogamy. Going against her parents' wishes, Chrissie, one of the younger generation of characters from In the Eye of the Sun, mentioned above, marries an engineer, Fuad, for love. On his trips for work he forms a liaison and ends up marrying an unsophisticated lower class woman in Alexandria. Baulking against polygyny, Chrissie demands that he divorces the woman, but finally ends up living with a plural marriage. This relationship ironically reflects the relationship Asya's grandfather has with a maid in the household where his adultery is never legitimized by marriage, and where the woman is kept more on the French model of the mistress for life, despite his non-modern context. Mischievously playing with orientalist stereotypes, Saif, Asya's completely non-traditional husband, is presented as a harem husband. Saif's polyamory involving two women, Mandy and Clara, after their marriage break-up has Asya sardonically commenting when she sees them both in Saif's apartment: 'A scene from a modern harem, Asya thinks, except that here the women ignore each other; there's none of that mutual grooming and gazing you find in the classical stuff' (725-6). In The Map of Love, Anna Winterbourne finds it unnecessary to enforce a contract her husband prepares before their marriage in which he renounces his religious and cultural right to polygyny. Similarly, she chooses and finds comforting a life in the 'harem' with her husband's extended family.

Soueif's fiction in careful detail draws maps of love that demarcate different cultural approaches to intimate relations, but the focus falls on the boundaries between territories, paradoxically drawn to highlight their permeability. The personal, furthermore, is shown not only to be political, but conceptions of romantic love are also shown to be epistemological, where the significance of love is an index of the various ways in which the world has been culturally apprehended across time and space. Soueif's is a project both of epistemic resistance and potential epistemic justice, notwithstanding the fact that in both novels the central female characters end up alone outside of both family and marriage. Soueif uses a quote from Ama Ata Aidoo's play, *Anowa*, as an epigraph to a chapter in *The Map of Love*. Soueif alludes to Aidoo strategically, since like Soueif, Aidoo has had a concern with intimacies across her career, most obviously signalled by the title of an anthology she has edited, namely, *African Love Stories*. But it is to Aidoo's novel *Changes – A Love Story* to which I would like to turn in closing, where the protagonist, Esi, chooses a modern polygynous marriage since it promises her self-fulfilment – that ultimately proves illusory. Both Aidoo and Soueif are authors who explore border epistemes of intimate relations and who ask the question about their heroines, '[s]o what fashion of loving was she ever going to consider adequate?' This is the rhetorical question explicitly asked about the female protagonist, Esi, in Aidoo's novel *Changes* that also sums up the dilemmas of Soueif's women characters.

WORKS CITED

Aidoo, Ama Ata, ed. *African Love Stories: An Anthology*, Banbury, UK Ayebia Clarke, 2006.

——*Changes – A Love Story*, London: The Women's Press, 1991.

——*Two Plays: The Dilemma of a Ghost* and *Anowa*, Harlow: Longman, 1995 [1965].

Ganeshananthan, V. V. *Love Marriage*, London: Phoenix, 2009 [2008].

Davis, Emily S. 'Romance as Political Aesthetic in Ahdaf Soueif's *The Map of Love*', *Genders*, Issue 45, 2007: 32 paragraphs, www.questia.com/library/journal/1G1-179660944/romance-as-political-aesthetic-in-ahdaf-soueif-s-the

King, Bruce. 'Review: *The Map of Love* by Ahdaf Soueif', *World Literature Today*, Vol. 74, No. 2, 2000: 453.

Massad, Joseph. 'The Politics of Desire in the Writings of Ahdaf Soueif', *Journal of Palestine Studies*, Vol. 28, No. 4, 1999: 74-90.

Mignolo, Walter D. *The Darker Side of Western Modernity: Global Futures, Decolonial Options*, Durham, NC: Duke University Press, 2011.

Soueif, Ahdaf. *Aisha*, London: Bloomsbury, 1995 [1983].

——'Great Arabic Love Stories', *The Guardian*, 17 January 2009, www.theguardian.com/books/2009/jan/17/1000-novels-arabic-love-stories

——*In the Eye of the Sun*, London: Bloomsbury, 1994 [1992].

——*Sandpiper*. London: Bloomsbury, 1996

——*The Map of Love*, London: Bloomsbury, 2000 [1999].

——*I Think of You: Stories*. New York: Anchor, 2007.

——*The Glass Palace*. Review, 2011. www.amitavghosh.com/glass palace_r.html#gpm1_4

Said, Edward. 'The Anglo-Arab Encounter: On Ahdaf Soueif'. In *Reflections on Exile and Other Essays*, Cambridge, MA: Harvard UP, 2002: 405-10.

Literature as Prophecy

Re-reading Yusuf Idris's *The Cheapest Nights*

EUNICE NGONGKUM

In the early days of the 2011 Egyptian revolution, western media outlets like *The Baltimore Sun* newspaper and *The New Yorker*, proposed 'Best Books on Egypt' lists to their readerships, ostensibly to help them to better understand the country and its revolution. Interestingly, many of those proposals were fictional texts, some written more than fifty years before the revolution, chief among which were Yusuf Idris's *The Cheapest Nights*, Naguib Mahfouz's *The Cairo Trilogy* and Alaa Al Aswany's *The Yacoubian Building: A Novel*. Such indications bring to mind the interrelationship between literature and history which is a hallmark of African art. The functional premise often accorded African art forms by both writers and critics alike indicates that, in most if not all cases, readers expect the continent's literature to speak about its historical evolution. For instance, Chinua Achebe says that African literature, like all other literature, 'speaks of a particular place, evolves out of the necessities of its history, past and current and the destiny of its people' ('The Role of the Writer in a New Nation': 7). For Ngugi wa Thiong'o in *Writers in Politics*, the African 'writer's work is often an attempt to come to terms with the thing that has been, a struggle, as it were, to sensitively register his encounter with history, his people's history' (39). The books listed above might have been selected because they help the reader to understand the collective reality of the Egyptian peoples, their perceptions of the world and their place in it. At the same time, they underline the artist's role in 'bringing the incomplete picture that the historical perspective offers into sharper relief' (Fox 'Egypt: The Search for Identity'). This resonates with the Aristotelian perspective of the superiority of art to history because of the former's capacity to discuss events 'as they were or are, or as they are said to be or seem to be, or as they ought to be' ('On the Art of Poetry': 69). Herein lies the prophetic dimension of literature that is the focus in this paper.

This visionary quality occurs when the writer's composite representation of the historical moment informs both the present and the future. This is a recurrent strand in African literature for, as Wole Soyinka says, 'part of the essential purpose of any African writer is to write with a very definite vision by exposing the future in a clear and truthful exposition of the present' (quoted in Goddard *A Common Tongue*: 18). Evidently, Chinua Achebe's *A Man of the People*, John Nkemngong Nkengasong's *Across the Mongolo* and Ayi Kwei Armah's *The Beautyful Ones Are Not Yet Born* are among the works that belong to the tradition of the prophetic in African literary discourse. Yusuf Idris, whose *The Cheapest Nights* I analyse in this paper, is part of this tradition. His artistic vitality and vision reside in his ability to speak to Egypt's future through a sensitive and realistic exploration of the present. The stories in the collection under study, though set in the 1950s, can be said to constitute an archive of lived actualities informing the Egyptian past, present and future. How this record comes through to the reader, constitutes the main issue here.

I employ Ato Quayson's close reading practice known as calibrations, to explore how characters, plots, themes and styles in *The Cheapest Nights* (1957) illuminate the specific historical practices that enlighten contemporary Egyptian society and that might have informed the 2011 revolution. I argue that Idris's realistic depictions of Egyptian society betray his preoccupation with the subject of liberty, namely, 'the concrete liberties that men try to win and preserve at each stage of their historical development'

(Adereth 'What is Littérature Engagée?' 468). When such liberties are challenged, the writer intervenes to move the people to action. This constitutes his or her commitment; a commitment that can be said to be inspirational at every stage of a people's historical struggle.

Calibrations, otherwise known as reading for the social, is 'a situated procedure' that employs 'the aesthetic for the analysis and better understanding of the social; the social being coded as an articulated encapsulation of transformation, processes and contradiction' (Quayson *Calibrations: Reading for the Social*: xv). As an inter-disciplinary paradigm, it extends and complements other reading practices such as psychoanalysis, general sociology and Marxism. In this context, the concrete social situations identified or described in the literary text, transcend the 'disclosure of an authentic cultural or historical life to embed a thematic for change, process and contradiction' (xxxi). I find this reading perspective meaningful in my analysis of the prophetic dimension in *The Cheapest Nights* largely because its dialectical nature enables one to view how the text in question 'analyzes, synthesizes, has a view, and reaches out beyond the space and time of its location', as Ngugi wa Thiong'o notes in *Globalectics: Theory and the Politics of Knowing* (19). However, before analysing the text along these lines, it is expedient to contextualize Yusuf Idris, given that the writer's life as a committed artist is intimately bound up with his oeuvre.

CONTEXTUALIZING YUSUF IDRIS:
THE WRITER AS SOCIAL CRITIC

Yusuf Idris was contemporary Egypt's and the Arab world's outstanding short story writer, novelist, travel writer, editor, essayist and critic, whose work drew largely from his own life as a revolutionary figure. Born in 1927, the young Idris decided quite early on a medical career while also embracing leftist politics. Militating in anti-monarchical demonstrations in his student days, he displayed a marked sensitivity to questions of justice and equality which would become hallmarks of his life and writings. He eventually became the Executive Secretary of the Committee for the Defence of Students, a post that conferred on him responsibility for revolutionary publications. Imprisonment and temporary suspension from college were the outcome of this engagement which, however, was rewarded with the eventual overthrow of the then forces of oppression in Egypt. Appointed to Kasr el Eini, Cairo's largest government hospital, upon graduation from medical school, Idris continued his political trajectory by joining an underground anti-British organization. That organization supported Gamal Abdel Nasser's rise to power but Idris openly challenged the military leadership, when the promises of the revolution failed to deliver. He was arrested and imprisoned, and he had a brief stint with the Communist Party while in prison. His resignation shortly afterwards was hinged on his inability to embrace communism's totalitarian ethic.

The 1960s saw the artist's resignation from medical practice to embrace a literary career, as editor of the Cairo newspaper, *Al Goumhoureya*. Journalism was a boon as he travelled extensively throughout the Arab world observing the changes that were sweeping through several countries at that time. He fought with Algerian rebels against the French, convinced of the need of the Arab world's liberation from imperialist forces.

Until his death in 1991, Yusuf Idris was known to be deeply patriotic, and as one who conceived of the nation as an ontological category. He believed that a strong and independent nation was capable of delivering the people from the throes of poverty and the inadequacy felt by the majority of his compatriots. Roger Allen has observed that literary intellectuals, to which category Idris belongs, 'are shaped by their political and social environment [with] their reflections on social reality ... distilled in their fiction' (*Critical Perspectives on Yusuf Idris*: 53). In his entire oeuvre, Idris's 'political views and his determination to revolt against injustice remained strong, and his views often found expression in the stories he wrote' (Allen: 56). How he is able to marry matter and manner as to speak to the future in the stories I read here is worth investigating.

The short story was the genre in which he excelled most, bringing to it innovations at the thematic and aesthetic levels. For instance, critics find innovation and authenticity in his rejection of prevalent romantic tendencies of Arabic literature in favour of a realistic portrayal of Egyptian society specially focusing on the destitute and disadvantaged classes. This is a pointer to the need to inform the present and the future. The colloquial idiom in his dialogue is equally viewed as an authentic reflection of the changing Egyptian culture, even though some Arab authors and critics derided this formal perspective. Idris's engagement with politics and culture strongly situate his narratives as perceptive expressions of the Egyptian state in its march to nationhood. Such politico-cultural engagement is indicative of artistic commitment; a commitment to an evolving entity, namely, the nation of Egypt, which is the focus of this paper.

INTERROGATING SOCIO-POLITICAL SPACES: NARRATIVE AS PROPHECY

Idris's *The Cheapest Nights* is a collection of fifteen stories dealing, generally, with the changing values of twentieth-century Egyptian society. The stories realistically address issues of poverty, the relationship between the haves and have-nots, homosexuality, sexual impotence, politics, religious fundamentalism, urbanization and socio-cultural mores. In a variety of styles, the artist demonstrates a deep engagement with the battle for social justice; a battle that is as timeless as humanity.

The Egyptian landscape in all its ramifications constitutes the artistic canvass for the stories, providing characters, metaphors and spaces through which to lay bare all that is inimical to man's welfare. The opening paragraph of 'The Freak' is eloquent in this regard. 'Every town in this vast country that God gave us has got its own worries. It's got its own people, young and old, male and female, families big and small, Copts and Moslems. A vast universe regulated by laws and also troubled by them' (188). In this paragraph, the writer delineates the concerns that invite his critical eye, namely, religious, familial, communal and political relation-ships. As a committed writer, he raises them in the hope of initiating change, for, as Idris himself observes in another context, 'people are not born to accept the situations imposed upon them … for life is a constant process of change with which views and values must keep up' (x). When such views and values fail to meet with the people's expectations, there is bound to be revolt of the magnitude that swept across the Arab world in the recent past. Furthermore, underlining the country's socio-political landscape in a matter-of-fact manner here constitutes an indictment of the power politics at play at the national, traditional or familial levels; power politics which promote and sustain a class system that privileges a few at the expense of the majority. Interestingly, these are the foundation of popular revolutions for, as Nawal El Saadawi, Egyptian writer and activist, (commenting on the Egyptian Revolution of 2011) says, these 'burst out against the corruption of governments and the falsehood of absolute powers in all their forms, for absolute power only arises and continues in power, in both the nation and the family, on the basis of despotism, deceit, and arbitrary rule over millions of human beings through military, economic, political, cultural, intellectual, and religious force' ('The Egyptian Revolution Won't be Fooled': 1). That Yusuf Idris interrogated these issues more than fifty years ago points to his commitment as a revolutionary artist who is canny enough to speak to the future.

Wielders of power of any sort in society who misuse it for their own ends bear the brunt of the writer's satire. Satire is a weapon of commitment, being 'protest, a sublimation and refinement of anger and indignation' (Cuddon *The Penguin Dictionary of Literary Terms and Literary Theory*: 800). The satirist is 'a self-appointed guardian of standards, ideals and truth; of moral as well as aesthetic values. He is a man who takes it upon himself to correct, censure, and ridicule the follies and vices of society and thus bring contempt and derision upon aberrations from a desirable and civilized norm' (800). In the collection under study, Idris's commitment is largely foregrounded through satire. For instance, characters like Judge Abdalla in 'The Dregs of the City' and the aristocratic landlord in 'The Queue' are lampooned as representatives of the powerful who use their positions of authority to oppress or exploit the weak and vulnerable.

'The Dregs of the City' is an eight-part story of varying but connected episodes in the life of Judge Abdalla, a rich bachelor 'born and raised in easy circumstances' from the upper echelons of society who exercises enormous power as a judge in the city of Cairo. Abdalla's obsession with power is evident in the way he treats his subalterns. The focus of the narrative is the episode of him losing a wristwatch 'worth nothing in itself, and only the fact that he had lost it enhanced its value … neither platinum nor gold. Just a plain fifteen stone Ancre bought before the war that gave him a good deal of trouble as it frequently broke down and the cost of repairing it had come to exceed by far its original price' (Idris: 78-9). This episode becomes the writer's weapon of criticizing the abuse of all forms of power. In effect, words and phrases like 'worth nothing in itself', 'neither platinum nor gold', 'plain' and 'frequently broke down' reveal the fact that the lost watch is rather a bane to the judge's existence. The irony becomes evident when we discover that the entire story is woven around how Judge Abdalla seeks to bring the suspect to book simply to underscore the magnitude of his power. That the loss of such a trivial object should cause the judge to interrupt an important court session to the puzzlement of the attorneys, summon his servant Ga'afari and friend Sharaf and set out for the city slums to rope in the suspect, highlights the misuse of power by those in positions of authority.

The ironic posture of the writer further resonates in the forays he makes into the psyche of the main character via interior monologue. Through this technique, we are given explanations for the judge's attitude towards the weak and the vulnerable like the obsequious Farghali and the house-help-turned-mistress, Shohrat. Tormented by a severe feeling of inadequacy and inferiority, when he is among his peers, Abdalla perceives himself as 'a trivial being, a person of no consequence' whose 'appearance was not particularly impressive and [whose] conversation was uninteresting' (Idris: 82-3). Oppression of the poor then becomes an avenue to legitimize his power. Minimized then by women from his own circles, Abdalla hires the poor married woman Shohrat as domestic help and 'uses the sheer power he could exercise over her' to turn her into a whore, treating her 'a little more than a live mattress on which he sprawled and stretched and tossed and turned and relaxed without restraint' (94). His relationship with this woman is an exercise in subjugation as he slashes her salary for no reason eventually turning her into a thief and full time prostitute all in an effort 'to subjugate this woman ... to dominate her' (79).

Through Abdalla's relationship with the poor, Yusuf Idris lays bare the complex nature of power politics at play in society which is often the basis of the kind of revolution that Saadawi refers to above. Abdalla's fixation on power shows how such fixations often emanate from 'the complexity of individual experience in its interaction with an external world ... making visible the individual's encounter with reality, including the ideological representations of life that circulate within that reality and falsely define it' (Barnaby 'The Realist Novel as Meta-Spectacle': 44). The defining ideology in Abdalla's world is that of an oppressive and corrosive class consciousness that is destructive at best. It is only logical that the story should end with the judge wondering whether he is responsible for Shohrat's fate but, as people who are obsessed with power do, 'he wasn't bothered by qualms of conscience ... he had no punishment to fear' (Idris: 101) because 'being her master he had the upper hand' (95). At another level, when Abdalla narrates to his peers his exploits of capturing a common thief like Shohrat, he never gets into the details of his relationship with her, thus showing how the underprivileged are nothing more than a passing fancy to those in positions of power.

While in the preceding story the writer merely describes and presents a situation in which the underprivileged are the endless receivers of the brunt of power, in 'The Quest', we find them challenging power, corroborating Michel Foucault's thesis that 'where there is power, there is resistance' (*The History of Sexuality*: 98). The resistance here may not be in the magnitude of the recent uprisings in the Arab world but they, nevertheless, point to the visionary perspective of the committed writer capable of perceiving the active resistance of the downtrodden in situations of oppression. Indeed as James C. Scott observes, in another context, 'every subordinate group creates, out of its ordeal, a 'hidden transcript' that represents a critique of power ... behind the back of the dominant' (*Domination and the Arts of Resistance*: xii). This is what we find the peasants doing in this narrative.

In the story, the conflict is between the powerful 'rich aristocratic landowner from those parts descended from a long line of Turks or Mamluks' (Idris: 38) and the poor peasants from the surrounding villages of the countryside. The narrative focus is a 'barren piece of land where nothing would grow', belonging to the aristocrat but which is appropriated by the villagers for their weekly market. In the story, language serves to underline attitude and tone. For instance, descriptive words and phrases like 'barren' and 'part of the vast possession of the landowner' demonstrate the dispensability of the land given its infertility but, the ensuing conflict indicates that for the powerful, nothing goes for nothing. Firstly, the landowner encourages the peasants to come because the presence of their cattle was 'profitable; an excellent means by which to fertilize [the land] and eventually make it fit for cultivation' (38). Secondly, when the peasants trample and flatten the furrows, he resorts to exacting a toll fee from them each market day. To ensure that all of them pay, a wooden fence is constructed with a gate at 'which one collector is stationed' (39). Some of the villagers, however, find it complicated getting to the gate and simply improvise a short-cut by knocking down one of the wooden boards and slipping through the gap. That constitutes an affront at power and the landowner perceives it as such; angry that he has 'been defied by the worthless peasants' he resolves not to be 'dictated to by a lot of bare-footed vulgar peasants' (40). He consequently employs more drastic measures to subdue them. These include blocking the gap with two acacia trees, digging a trench around the patch and filling it with water, stationing guards and erecting iron spikes. In each of these situations, the peasants break through into the property and carry on with their activities.

The methods employed by the landowner to suppress the peasants, as well as their acts of defiance are highly symbolic in the context of committed literature. The oppressor's actions can be read as the different ways used by the rich to hold in check the liberties of the downtrodden, while the peasants' acts of defiance indicate that no matter how absolute a system of domination can be, there are always areas of weakness that can be infiltrated by counter-hegemonic discourses. The fact that the story ends on the note that 'and so, everywhere, there will always be a broken spike' (Idris: 42), shows that, at any time and place, people can always defy authorities and succeed. The recent past uprisings in the Arab world bear testimony to this view.

Idris's sensitivity to the world of the oppressed, whether in the countryside or the city, constitutes the focus of a good number of stories in the collection under study. These include 'The Cheapest Nights', 'You Are Everything to Me', 'Hard Up', 'The Errand', 'The Funeral Ceremony', 'Death from Old Age' and 'The Shame'. Here, the realistic portrayal of Egypt's poor, through vivid descriptions of the spaces they inhabit, their poverty, frustrations and efforts to make a living in the heart of misery, become the weapons through which the writer identifies with the vulnerable and the function they serve in the society which has marginalized them. Social realism in this case becomes the tool with which to register disgust with the status quo. A socially realistic work 'seeks to render social experience visible by accounting for what was possible to express and to observe within a particular social reality' (Barnaby: 43). At another level, it 'exposes the false consciousness of ideology, laying bare opportunistic constructions of history and stripping them of their compelling internal coherence' (38). The socialist realist perspective resonates with Quayson's view that the social identified in the literary text is always object produced out of an interrogation (xxxi).

In the title story, 'The Cheapest Nights', Idris offers vivid descriptions of the poverty and exasperations experienced by the major character, Abdel Kerim, who is burdened with many children, and has nowhere to go and nothing to do even on unfavourable winter nights. The cheapest pastime for him is to return to his bed and his wife and father more children he can hardly maintain. In a bid to highlight the man's desperate conditions, the narrative voice, like a camera lens, focuses on a number of poignant details. For instance, Kerim's physical features bespeak excruciating suffering. His 'brass-yellow face' is 'taut and dry' while his 'long hooked nose' is 'blotched with many ugly black spots' (Idris: 1). Furthermore, his feet are large 'with cracks

in their soles so deep they could easily swallow up a nail'
(1). Such hyperbole coupled with images of dryness and
disease like 'taut', 'dry', and 'brass-yellow' and 'cracks'
continuously emphasize the blighted nature of Kerim's life.

At another level, the spaces that the main character
inhabits are oppressive. His world, we are told, is a 'dark'
one of 'low grey houses nestled close to one another, with
heaps of manure piled before them like long-neglected
graves' (Idris: 2). Here, even the light from 'the few shining
lamps owned by some of the poor' (2) fails to penetrate
the darkness, indicating that the efforts made by the
downtrodden to overcome their situation are generally
insufficient. The environment is stinking and swampy, with
the inhabitants described as 'creatures packed beneath the
roofs' of houses that are shacks for the most part. Images
of death, disease and squalor like 'heaps of manure' and
'long-neglected graves' vividly capture the plight of these
poor; a plight further exacerbated by overcrowding, a result
of overpopulation. The reader is informed that it was a
wretched world in which 'brats sprouted out of the ground
in greater numbers than the hair on one's head' and 'the lanes
teemed with youngsters scattered like breadcrumbs … half
of whom will die of starvation, while cholera would carry off
the rest' (1-2). Hyperbole, here, evident in figures of likeness
such as 'brats sprouted out of the ground' and 'youngsters
scattered like breadcrumbs', serves to emphasize the writer's
disgust with the phenomenon of overpopulation especially
in situations of poverty. Through images of death, disease
and decay, Idris highlights and protests the destitution of
the poor and marginalized. The outer décor, described
above, reflects the oppressive interior inhabited by Kerim
who lives in a one-room house in which his wife 'lay like a
bag of maize and her brood of six scattered around her like
a litter of puppies' (4). Here, the children are described in
synecdoche and animal terms 'as six bellies so voracious they
could gobble up bricks', underscoring the extent to which
extreme poverty and destitution dehumanize the individual.

One would think that it is only jobless people like Kerim in the countryside who suffer, but poorly paid city workers, like Ramadan in 'You Are Everything to Me', equally experience crushing poverty. It is interesting to note that the 2011 'Egyptian uprising' according to Lisa Anderson, drew from 'economic grievances and social dynamics ... legacies of [the country's] decades under unique regimes' ('Demystifying the Arab Spring': 1). Yusuf Idris's delineation of the plight of the poor here not only outlines his visionary perspective but equally reminds one that historical processes have to be constantly interrogated in committed literature.

Ramadan's family is cramped into a one-room house and husband and wife are constrained to make love in the presence of their only son. While this points to the poverty of the family, it also demonstrates that in poor environments, young children are exposed early to sex and may develop loose morals through no fault of theirs. The writer here is concerned with the question of morality in the public and private spheres. Elements of glaring poverty and eventual decay, barrenness and disease are apparent through diction and imagery. The paint shining on Ramadan's cap, for instance, 'fails to conceal the grime and the signs of long wear' (Idris: 8), while his wife bathes with 'cheap soap' and dresses in a 'faded' cotton nightdress. Furthermore, the 'persistent wailing of a sickly child', a 'laborious cough' and a 'dry throat' (6) characterize the environment. There is no wonder then that such a world emasculates the individual, as Ramadan inexplicably loses his manhood and seeks ways to overcome his condition. His predicament offers the writer the opportunity to lay bare the desperate situation of the downtrodden who suffer varying indignities as a result of a poorly structured social system that fails to take the condition of the masses into account.

The perennial problem of unemployment is the focus of 'Hard Up'. Abdou, the central character, is almost perpetually hard up because he cannot keep a permanent job. Through his dilemma, Yusuf Idris discloses the inhuman world of the city where Abdou's neighbour, a nurse in the city's hospital, is ironically appreciated as a benefactor because he has secured a job for the former; a job which entails selling his blood to the hospital for a pittance.

Through the technique of enumeration, the precariousness of Abdou's world is exposed. His different jobs are enumerated to accentuate his precarity. The reader learns that he 'started out as a cook, got employed in the workshop next door' (Idris: 31), took on the job of a door-man, a porter, a hawker of vegetables, became 'a middleman roaming the alleys night and day, in search of a vacant room' (31) before picking up and then losing the job of a waiter. The details of Abdou's life poignantly reveal his abject poverty. His wife berates him when he returns home empty handed while he resents the neighbours' pity and wishes for better luck because 'their wishes were no good to his empty stomach or to [his wife] Nefissa's almost naked body' (32).

Abdou eventually picks up a job at the hospital which, as we noted earlier, consists of selling his blood to the Blood Transfusion Department for a meagre sum of money that paradoxically does not even meet the food needs of the week before he gives another dose. As every other job he has had before, even this one is bound to come to an end because, the rate at which the blood is collected does not match the rate at which it is replenished. When the hospital finally refuses to take blood on grounds that he is anaemic, the dialogue between him and the hospital authorities effectively conveys the writer's critical stance. The exchange is brief, made up of brief terse sentences and phrases that delineate the inhumanity of the situation. Abdou, for once, challenges the authorities who reject his offer on the grounds that it would not be human. His retort, 'And is what you are doing human?' points to the writer's criticism of the situation in which the weak and vulnerable are the prey of those in power.

CONCLUSION

My analysis demonstrates that literature constitutes an important site for understanding the socio-political environment that informs it. The short stories here narrativize the same socio-political concerns that informed the 2011 Egyptian revolution, namely, high unemployment, extreme poverty, dictatorship and human rights violations (Anderson: 6). This intimates that Yusuf Idris is a revolutionary figure who does not merely absorb material from his age into his fiction but, 'deriving from his own imagination and inner resources, [he] contributes to transform and embed the reality he has encountered' (Amirthanayagam 'Commitment in Literature': para. 5) for the liberation of his people. His stories gain significance because they reflect, enrich and inspire his people's struggle for freedom and democracy – thus justifying why the media outlets mentioned earlier might have made reference to them. The characters in the stories transcend their individuality to assume allegorical proportions as representative figures of the Egyptian landscape that engage the critical writer. The analysis highlights literature's forth-telling capacity in contexts of oppression and blatant disregard for human rights. *The Cheapest Nights* might have been inspired by 1950 Egypt but Idris's comments on that society translate beyond its time to appeal to the present and the future.

WORKS CITED

Achebe, Chinua. 'The Role of the Writer in a New Nation' in *African Writers on African Writing*, ed. G.D. Killam. London: Heinemann, 1975: 7-13.

Adereth Max. 'What is Littérature Engagée?' in *Marxists on Literature: An Anthology*, ed. David Craig. Harmondsworth: Penguin, 1975: 445-489.

Amirthanayagam, Guy. 'Commitment in Literature'. Speech delivered to the International Writers Conference, Edinburgh, UK, August

1962. © Estate of Guy Amirthanayagam. 2008. http://indranamir thanayagam.blogspot.co.uk/2008/05/guy-amirthana yagam-commitment-in.html (accessed 2 December 2016).

Allen, Roger M.A., ed. *Critical Perspectives on Yusuf Idris.* New York: Lynne Rienner Publishers, 1994.

Anderson, Lisa. 'Demystifying the Arab Spring: Parsing the Differences Between Tunisia, Egypt, and Libya'. *Foreign Affairs.* New York: Council on Foreign Relations, May/June 2011.

Aristotle, trans. T.S. Dorsch. 'On the Art of Poetry'. *Classical Literary Criticism.* Harmondsworth: Penguin, 1965.

Barnaby, Edward. 'The Realist Novel as Meta-Spectacle'. *Journal of Narrative Theory* Vol. 38, No. 1 (Winter) 2008: 37-59.

Cuddon, J.A. *The Penguin Dictionary of Literary Terms and Literary Theory.* London: Penguin, 1998.

El Saadawi, Nawal. 'The Egyptian Revolution Won't be Fooled'. *Words without Borders,* July 2012. http://wordswithoutborders.org/article/the-egyptian-revolution-wont-be-fooled (accessed 22 November 2016).

Fox, Elizabeth J. 'Egypt: The Search for Identity' www.duke.edu/%7Eefox/Mals_Paper.html (accessed 11 November 2016).

Foucault, Michel, trans. R. Hurley. *The History of Sexuality Vol. 1: An Introduction.* New York: Vintage Books, 1980.

Goddard, Horace I., ed. *A Common Tongue.* Quebec: AFO Enterprises, 1986.

Gramsci, Antonio, eds and trans Quintin Hoare and Geoffrey Nowell Smith. *Selections from the Prison Notebooks of Antonio Gramsci.* New York: International Publishers, 1971.

Idris, Yusuf, trans Wadida Wassef. *The Cheapest Nights.* London: Heinemann, 1978.

Ngugi wa Thiong'o. *Writers in Politics: A Re-engagement with Issues of Literature and Society.* Oxford: James Currey, 1997.

——*Globalectics: Theory and the Politics of Knowing.* New York: Columbia University Press, 2014.

Quayson, Ato. *Calibrations: Reading for the Social.* Minneapolis: University of Minnesota Press, 2003.

Scott, James C. *Domination and the Arts of Resistance: Hidden Transcripts.* New Haven and London: Yale University Press, 1990.

The Baltimore Sun, 11 February 2011.

Travel & Discovery

Hopes for a New Egypt in Mohamed Salmawy's
Butterfly Wings

KELVIN NGONG TOH

Mohamed Salmawy's *Butterfly Wings* is set predominantly in Egypt and Italy. In these macro spaces, the characters create and recreate themselves as they evolve from innocence to awareness. The narrative is focused on the principle of self-discovery with all the characters searching for themselves. This becomes more intriguing as Salmawy careful crafts this individual search to be included in the search for the Egyptian nation. The purpose of this essay is to underscore the fact that travelling out of the 'home' context begins the transformation process of the principle characters whose quests are carefully linked to the search of the Egyptian *nationness*. The transformation process, as perceived in this essay, ties in with Bill Ashcroft's interpretation in which he discusses the postcolonial people and cultures in the process of 'adapting' and not being destroyed. He writes: 'Many critics have argued that colonialism destroyed indigenous cultures, but this assumes that culture is static, and underestimates the resilience and adaptability of colonial societies' (*Post-Colonial Transformation*: 2). This polemics is relevant as it highlights different positions and responses to the colonial process. However, though adaptation has come to be the best option for colonial societies today because even resiliency is highly contested, it does not undermine the fact that many of the cultural values of people from Africa and many more of the Africa diaspora were destroyed. And so, adaptability, defined from a different temporal/spatial context cannot go without the feeling of loss or some void that is hard to fill. Salmawy's characters undergo transformation as they begin to define themselves as time/space becomes the 'addresser' that gives them the opportunity to be 'addressees' of their quest. Working within the framework of the postcolonial theory, therefore, this essay dwells on George Lamming's essay 'The Occasion for Speaking' and other salient tenets to defend the fact that with the political dilemma that dominates the Egypt that one finds in the narrative, both nation and citizens, as seen in the narratives, are in the search for themselves. This becomes possible, as the narrative programme suggests, only when one leaves the 'home' context. This means that even *nationness* is better constructed in the 'elsewhere'.

THEORIZATION AND CONCEPTUALIZATION

In Lamming's essay, the main focus is to argue that the colonized person lives in exile and that exile is a condition that the colonial person cannot avoid. He opines: 'We are made to feel a sense of exile by our inadequacy and our irrelevance of function in a society whose past we can't alter and whose future is always beyond us' (12). What this means is that colonized persons, especially those of post-independence Egypt that we are discussing in this essay, are rife with political tyranny to this day and that has rendered many, especially the free thinkers (the kind of intellectuals that Edward Said discusses in *Representations of the Intellectual*), to live in exile. The situation becomes even more pitiable in that even the people's revolution was very short-lived with the present installation of despotic pseudo-democratic leadership that gives no room for freedom of speech, and the shocking arrest of people and journalists. Egypt remains a place where exile becomes the strategy to exist such that, as George Lamming further propounds, 'to be an exile is to be alive' (12). Such an existential outlook therefore, is the base of my theorization in this essay. It becomes clear that if exile foregrounds existence, then speaking can only come from 'elsewhere' and so, identity construction and visibility as Lamming suggests may never come if the native remains in the 'home' context. I find this theoretical positon relevant here in that I hope to discuss that the discovery of self as Salmawy projects in this narrative, has always been constructed 'elsewhere'.

Travel and/or travel writing is one sub-discipline that connects to many other disciplines and fields of study. As Peter Hulme and Russell McDougall put it, travel writing has gained much of its steam 'from the context of postcolonial studies, which over recent years has been rewriting the history of Western imperial and colonial contact with other cultures' ('In the Margins of Anthropology': 6). Two things are fundamental about travel writing. First, travel, like its writing, rewrites and also writes history. This means that through travel and/or travel writing, one is capable of *making* and *knowing* him/herself. The history that is discussed here shifts from the records of the past to a complex organization of facts that define an individual, culture, nation and civilization. Secondly, travel foregrounds contact with others and this is also revealing as it ushers in the transforming process which, in the case of the postcolonial person and territory, may either absorb the traveller into other forces and global temptations or push the traveller to emerge. Travel as I discuss it in this essay has to do with moving to the 'elsewhere' to understand 'self'. It is to this understanding that I refer to in this essay as discovery, which does not in any way allude to sightseeing or touristic relaxation.

CHARACTER PERCEPTION AND SPATIAL CONSTRUCTION

The spatial representation of **Butterfly Wings** is shared between Egypt and Italy. This representation, from all indications, is built on a binary oppositional concept of Europe being better than Africa. As the narrative develops, the different places that play a role in the characters' transformation are topologically mapped. Miek Bal argues that 'places can be mapped out, in the same way that the topological position of a city or river can be indicated on a map. The concept of place is further related to physical, mathematically measurable shapes of spatial dimension' (**Narratology: Introduction to the Theory of the Narrative**: 133). The place in this sense focuses on the environment in which action and events are acted or narrated. As to whether these typological constructions are real or fictive in narrative fiction, Bal resolves by arguing that place, in fiction, is the imagination that helps the reader to put it in the **fabula**. The **writerly** nature of the reader, who becomes active in the creation of story and text is again highlighted in this kind of discourse. In the process of place construction, it is therefore the imagination of the reader and the character that builds it, based on the principle of **perception**. However, as Bal argues, it is the perception of the characters that transform a place into space. In this section of the essay therefore, spatial focus is based on the perception of the different characters and voices that dominate in the narrative.

My analysis in this section concentrates on the different gaze on the European space and the African space in the narrative and how these spatial constructions have built on the identity projection of the characters. However, in the narrative, except for Dr Ashraf's Italian friend and family, no European plays a central role in the narrative, though Italy becomes the centre for individual and collective transformations of Egypt in the novel. As the narrative opens, Doha al-Kenani, the wife of Medhat Bey al-Safti, prepares to travel to Italy.

> Doha had to pass by the luxury hotel on the edge of the square to collect the jacket she was taking to Rome. She had called the hotel dry cleaners in the morning, and they told her the jacket was ready for collection. At that point there had still been time, but now she was stuck in her car and might as well have been in a prison. (Salmawy *Butterfly Wings*: 1)

Though still at the level of desire and the anxiety that goes with it, one finds that the character is taking measures to have her trip to Rome without any obstacle. In terms of temporality, Doha is in the last stages of her preparation to travel and this is seen in the quote when the idea of time shifts from past to present, indicating the transition in time, is stressed by the adverb 'now'. The actant object of the subject here is her desire to get to Rome. At this stage, she is supported by the hotel dry cleaners and the traffic at Tahrir Square is a major obstacle as the narrative voice focuses, in terms of time, on the present. These very early stages of the narrative tells the reader that the 'now' in Egypt is chaotic, cruel and inhuman. This explains why the image of the prison comes so early in the narrative. Italy (Rome) therefore becomes the 'elsewhere' to go and to find freedom and expression of the 'self.' In this state, Doha's husband now comes in as the addresser that enables her to leave her 'prison-like' car to go to the airport just in time.

Going to Italy in the narrative is the result of a long standing relationship between the two countries since the reign of Cleopatra, queen of Egypt. These two states have been so close that kings in Italy have found refuge in Egypt. In *Butterfly Wings* the narrator informs us,

> The Egyptian embassy, with its luxuriant gardens, occupied a beautiful palace known as the Villa Savoia. It had belonged to the last king of Italy, Victor Emmanuel III, a member of the house of Savoy, who had been exiled to Egypt during the reign of King Farouk. When he returned to Italy after the

Second World War, he decided to gift the palace to Egypt, and the government turned it into the embassy. (66)

The narrator's perception of the space in narration, here called the Egyptian embassy, delves into the history of the two states, and in so doing historicizes relations between them as cordial. The cordial diplomatic representation is further seen when the Egyptian prime minister visits Rome. Again, the present in terms of timing becomes vital in the narrative. While the quote above tells us of a past, the visit of the prime minister, as the narrative projects, being third in command after the president and the secretary general of the ruling party, shows that even in the 'now' of the narrative, Egypt and Italy have a cordial relationship.

Therefore, going to Italy by some Egyptians, as we see in the narrative, has a long history. Doha, as the narrative reveals, has spent a long time preparing for her show at the international designer's salon in Milan. The narrator says, 'she had spent the whole winter working on the designs she would show in Milan … she was too busy with her designs for Milan. To help her, she studied all the fashion magazines she could get hold of and familiarized herself with the styles popular in Italy' (Salmawy: 6). This tells us that her journey is supposed to be an event that she hopes will transform her life as a designer and so she prepares so hard that it costs 'her a great deal of time, effort and money' (6); all markers that lead to any successful venture. Milan in this context is highly contrasted with Cairo. While Milan is seen as the space that exposes and builds, Cairo has its prison and also silences. Salmawy at this stage continues to foster the Lammingian discourse of the idea of Europe that showcases Europe as the dream-land and place of opportunities; a place where speaking is possible as opposed to Africa where 'silence' is the order of the day. The narrator says: 'This would be the first time she had participated in the Fashion Week, and she had high hopes, because big fashion houses signed up the best new designers there' (6). If Cairo could have offered her such exposure, then Milan would not occupy such important space in the mind of the character as she dreams to make it big in her art. And so, to travel is to be great and visible.

Salmawy's travel orientation from Africa to Europe shifts the paradigm; while much of the literature by Africans has described travellers from the perspective of Africans going to survive, to study and to escape the continent, Salmawy's narrative presents Africans who go to Europe to showcase themselves and talk about themselves. Doha is in Milan to present her art and it is to the delight of all, including Egyptians, that the Egyptian voice is heard in this international event. Unfortunately therefore, the voice of Egypt can only be heard in Italy. This is because the Italy/Egypt binary continues to represent what Gramsci had termed the hegemony and subalternity divide. John Beverley defines the subaltern identity or will as 'negative' seen from hegemonic eyes (*Subalternity and Representation*: 26). The dominant ideology in the narrative of Salmawy is an unconscious construction of this idea of Europe (hegemony) being good and non-Europe and Africa (subalternity) being bad. But interestingly, the character perception makes us see Europe not from the perspective of remaining in Europe and not from the perspective of accepting Europe but from the perspective of using Europe to construct 'self', as in the case of Doha, and also to rethink the nation as in the case of Dr Ashraf. While focusing on Doha, the narrative informs the reader that Doha has had her designs presented in Cairo but that presentation of Milan will make her go international. What this reveals is that, while Cairo 'might well have been a prison' (Salmawy: 1) with regard to her desires to be known the world over as a designer, Milan liberates her from the Cairo prison and exposes her to the world.

Italy is also seen as a place of free intellectualism where, interestingly, Egypt and other African countries are being narrated. In Salmawy's narrative, he presents the intellectual from Africa and Egypt as one that is silenced and is looking for a place to express her or himself. In the novel, Dr Ashraf is seen as one who is critical of leadership abuse in Egypt. This earns him a very bad reputation around pro-government agents. Doha tells Dr Ashraf in the plane that she does not follow opposition newspapers (20). Apart from his vituperative language in the newspapers about the government, he cannot speak in Egypt. This is proved when he is arrested. Thus, Dr Ashraf finds his occasions to speak freely only outside the 'home' context and, typically in the narrative, this is done in Italy. So at the opening of the narrative, we find him travelling to Italy to attend and present a paper at an NGO conference.

In his paper, at the conference in Palermo, Dr Ashraf freely exposes the misdeeds of the Egyptian ruling class and that of most of the African continent and the Third World. The narrative voice gives us a clue on his paper thus: 'The following day, after a rousing welcome from the audience, Dr. Ashraf al-Zayni gave his speech. He spoke of ruling parties' monopolization of political life in the third world, and explained how civil society in Egypt was working hard to bring about change' (101). This discussion already shows that it does not only give the presenter a voice, it helps him to learn from others but, much more like the intellectual that George Lamming discusses, Dr Ashraf's speech does not only remain in Europe because it adds a new dimensions into reading Egypt, also putting him at the centre of the national struggle.

Dr Ashraf's travelling abroad to speak does not show that he is afraid to speak in the police state of Egypt, but it does free him from the police and the instruments of state, which Guy Debord describes thus: 'The spectacle subjects living human beings to its will to the extent that the economy has brought them under its sway' (*The Society of the Spectacle*: 16). This spectacle is the state machinery that subjects all production including intellectual productivity to its control; Dr Ashraf is seen as impudent because he refuses to sway to the prescriptions of the spectacle. This explains why his move to Italy and his return to lead the revolution presents a different picture of Italy to the Egyptian ruling class. During the revolution, the government issues a statement about him:

> The interior minister's statement made it clear that the security agencies had had Dr. Ashraf al-Zayni under observation for some time. It stated that they had proof that he had returned from abroad a few days before the High Court demonstration. He had been in a European country to meet intelligence agents from an *enemy state* who had given him money to cause disturbances in Egypt by implementing a wide-scale plan, the details of which would be revealed at a later stage. (172, emphasis added)

This statement represents sabotage first on the person of Dr Ashraf because truth holds, from the narrative, that he has not done any of the things indicated by the ruling class. Secondly, it is sabotage to the image of Italy to be falsely represented to be training Egyptian dissidents. This only shows that the love of power can push the Egyptian ruling class to go to any length to protect itself and to continue ruling. In all, my argument in this section is that travel to Europe reveals an occasion for the Egyptian to understand him/herself and to speak about him/herself and the nation.

AYMAN AND IDENTITY QUEST

While moving to Europe enables the Egyptian in *Butterfly Wings* to speak and, in speaking, to understand 'self'; travel for self-recognition and identity construction also constitute a crux in the narration. At this point the desire to understand 'self' pushes the individual to move out of home. Ayman happens to be the youngest child in a home that has caused him to live in deception of who he really is. When he tells his elder brother 'I'm free to say what I want' (17), it shows that home has not been a place for him to speak. Ayman has the project of knowing his mother, claiming that, without her, his life is in a void. Interestingly, those in his home – his father and brother – are opposing actant agents to his quest. The addresser that enables him to get to the dream of ever seeing his mother comes from outside of the home context. Hagga Hikmet, his friend's mother, is said to love him and treats him as her son. She is the one that looks for information about his mother and lets him know.

Interestingly, the oppositional agents in the 'home' context will not let him go. His brother refuses to listen to him because of an obsession to travel to Kuwait. His father fears to reveal his past and prefers to cover it. But when Ayman insists, his father concedes. His acceptance and sponsoring of Ayman to go and search for his mother, thus seeking and searching for himself, is fundamental to Salmawy's narrative ideology. His call is for the ruling class in Egypt to accept and be tolerant of all so that a new Egypt can be constructed.

FROM CHRYSALIS TO BUTTERFLY

A dominating reference in Salmawy's narrative is the butterfly. A closer look reveals that the butterfly becomes a metaphor or metonymy, which is a theory of binary opposition. According to Roman Jakobson, metaphor is thought of as a horizontal line; 'one word is associated with another through contiguity' while metonymy is the vertical line 'where meaning can be substituted one for another' (in Cuddon *The Penguin Dictionary of Literary Terms and Literary Theory*: 507). In Jakobson's study on aphasia, he

> extends this model to metaphor and metonymy. Thus, language disorder acts on the two axes of language in different ways so that those suffering from a 'continuity disorder' tend to use substitution (i.e. metaphor) and those suffering from

'similarity disorder' tend to use associations (i.e. metonymy). (Cuddon: 507)

A close listening to the narrative voices show that the voices, especially those of the narrator that swings to and fro from the zero focalizer to the external focalizer; Doha and Dr Ashraf neatly demonstrate this binary. Though none of these speakers clinically exposes any symptoms of disorder in the mind, their disordered space – Egypt – may just have taken a toll in the way they use language. We learn that the strong representation of the butterfly in the novel is metaphorical when it is discussed by Doha, and metonymic when discussed by Dr Ashraf and the narrator. But at one point all voices seem to represent the butterfly from one angle of the binary. This is because, as we read, we discover that the butterfly is a transforming image. While to Doha, the butterfly transforms her, to Dr Ashraf, the metaphor of the butterfly is a force for transformation. This leads us again to the discourse of transformation in that the butterfly that is presented in the narrative undergoes total transformation. *Butterfly Wings* presents characters who are all transformed by their environment, strongly captured in the life of the butterfly. The narrator says

> Nevertheless, Egypt's butterflies had adapted to the harsh conditions and were able to survive and maintain their beauty despite the hardships. Some species were able to survive inside their chrysalises in the hottest and driest desert condition for years at a time. But as soon as it rained and vegetation sprouted and bloomed, the butterflies would emerge from their chrysalises with colored wings. (93)

In this discourse, one sees the use of associations more and more, so it becomes metonymic as the style of living in Egypt is associated with the process of the survival of butterflies. More importantly, these butterflies are specifically Egyptian. The transformation that these insects therefore undergo is associated with the struggle of Egyptians to survive in the harsh geo-political space in which they find themselves.

As the butterflies come out with beautiful wings, this gives hope that Egypt and Egyptians can survive the odds with valour. Dr Ashraf in his very long speech during the revolt reminds the people that, from 1919 to the Suez Canal Crisis, the Egyptians have always stood and won against injustice, dictatorship and enemy aggression and so the odds always end with Egyptian glory and never shame.

Besides the enduring nature of the Egyptian that is associated with the enduring nature of the Egyptian butterfly, the insect is so much a source of inspiration as it understands the times and responds accordingly. All through the narrative, Doha substitutes herself for the butterfly and so, for her, the butterfly is very metaphorical. This is justified by the fact that her female status makes her suffer doubly in a space that is highly patriarchal with even some women like her mother being male-programmed; Doha borrows from bell hooks' *Feminism is for Everybody: Passionate Politics*. The substitution is so visible that Doha says 'sometimes I think I was created to be a butterfly' (49). The time and space of this declaration is important. She is in Italy, a place that is far from the troublesome 'home' context and is having some good times with a girlfriend, Gabriella, the like of which she could hardly get in Cairo. By saying so, she declares that she has been set free from the burdens of political tyranny that governs Egypt, marital bondage and now carries the beautiful wings that allow her to fly.

In this, Doha learns some of her practical lessons from the butterfly that stands as a 'symbol of rebirth' (49). In the process of this rebirth, the butterfly moves from one space or state to another. This further stresses my concern of moving to *know* or to gain recognition. The meeting between Doha and Dr Ashraf begins the process of this rebirth. Yet, everything about them is built on coincidence and irony. In their very first encounter, they are in the air on a plane and Dr Ashraf says: 'What a strange coincidence that I should be sitting on a plane next to my political rival' (19). What is interesting is that Doha just smiles. Such a response is strange in African politics where people become enemies because they do not share the same political ideology or belong to different parties. Her smiles, for an answer, begin her connectivity with Dr Ashraf and this is represented in nonverbal language and soliloquy. 'She said to herself, "And I'm fated to have to deal with you, it seems"' (20). Later in the narrative, she becomes clearer and resolute: 'Doha decided that she was entirely Ashraf al-Zayni' (147). The rebirth that we find in her is because for the first time, her decisions matter to her, which shifts her from a life of domination from mother and husband.

Doha's next practical lesson is that, though she is the wife of a top government official, she is still obsessed with the 'elsewhere', and so justifies Tzvetan Todorov's claim in *Nous et les Autres* that 'there' is often thought to be better than 'here'. In Doha's desire to be a world class designer, she rejects Egyptian designs and goes for the exotic. Doha fails to understand that 'globalism' can only be developed in 'localism'. She is surprised to learn that there are butterflies that are specific to Egypt, thanks to the book that she buys in Italy. Doha is so transformed by this and decides to change her designs and make them Egyptian. This decision makes her remember a discussion with Dr Ashraf where he encourages her to go for Egyptian designs. Doha's freedom for the first time is evident in that, with this reality, she refuses to go in for the fashion show and quickly decides on change. At the time of her arrest, the narrator informs us:

> She sat at the dining table sketching new lines with her colored pencils. This time, her designs were for working women who needed clothing that was simple and practical as well as beautiful. They were nothing like designs for her old friends, politicians' wives that she no longer wanted to have anything to do with. Her inspiration came from the Egyptian tiger butterfly. (Salmawy: 148)

From the above lines, it is evident that Doha has already undergone her rebirth and is now on the side of the people. Her shift in paradigm is justified by the fact she goes for a demonstration and, as an artist, she now designs for the people. It is Ngugi wa Thiong'o in *Writers in Politics* who argues that all writers (artists) are political but the problem is whose politics? Doha opts for the politics of the people – those that Gayatri Chakravorty Spivak, in 'Can the Subaltern Speak', calls the 'sub-proletariat' (78). Besides the butterfly, Doha is further influenced by Dr Ashraf, a man who has transformed her way of seeing and, together, they commit themselves to work hard and struggle in the construction of a happy union and a better Egypt.

CONCLUSION

In this essay, my contention has been to show how the private lives of its citizens are so connected to the national construction of the state of Egypt. Interestingly, the narrative indicates a nation where awareness and the ability to construct self are broad. Salmawy's discourse here shows that where there is no freedom nor a calm atmosphere, it is difficult for people to speak. George Lamming's discourse on this subject shows that the ex-colonized may, because of the colonial legacy, be only able to speak out of the 'home' context. *Butterfly Wings*, as we see and defend in this paper, strongly reveals national construction and individual identity abroad, and what is positive is how all come back to Egypt to build a better future. It is because of this fact that the novel ends with the sun shining and youth getting married.

WORKS CITED

Ashcroft, Bill. *Post-Colonial Transformation*. London and New York: Routledge, 2001.

Bal, Mieke. *Narratology: Introduction to the Theory of the Narrative.* 2nd edn. Toronto: University of Toronto Press, 1997.

Beverley, John. *Subalternity and Representation: Arguments in Cultural Theory.* Durham, NC: Duke University Press, 1999.

Cuddon, J.A. *The Penguin Dictionary of Literary Terms and Literary Theory.* London: Penguin Books, 1999.

Debord, Guy. *The Society of the Spectacle.* Trans. Donald Nicholson-Smith. New York: Zone Books, 1995.

hooks, bell. *Feminism is for Everybody: Passionate Politics.* Cambridge, MA: South End Press, 2000.

Hulme, Peter and Russell McDougall. 'Introduction: In the Margins of Anthropology'. In Peter Hulme and Russell McDougall eds. *Writing, Travel, and Empire: In the Margins of Anthropology.* New York: I.B Tauris, 2007: 1-18.

Lamming, George. 'The Occasion for Speaking'. In Bill Ashcroft, Gareth Griffiths and Helen Tiffin. *The Post-Colonial Studies Reader.* London and New York: Routledge, 1994: 12-17.

Ngugi wa Thiong'o. *Writers in Politics.* London: James Currey; Portsmouth, NH: Heinemann; Nairobi: EAEP, 1982.

Said, Edward W. *Representations of the Intellectual.* New York: Vintage Books, 1996.

Salmawy, Mohamed. *Butterfly Wings.* Trans. Raphael Cohen. Cairo and New York: The American University of Cairo Press, 2014.

Spivak, Gayatri Chakravorty. 'Can the Subaltern Speak?' Patrick Williams, and Laura Chrisman, eds. *Colonial Discourse and Post-Colonial Theory: A Reader.* New York: Columbia University Press, 1994: 66-111.

Todorov, Tzvetan. *Nous et les Autres: La Réflexion Française sur la Diversité Humaine.* Paris: Editions du Seuil, 1989.

The Symbolic Relevance of the Use of the Eye in Nawal El Saadawi's Two Women in One & God Dies by the Nile

RAZINAT T. MOHAMMED

Symbolism is to literature what a good wine is to a good dinner. In this regard therefore, writers have used concrete symbols to invest things with a representative meaning or have used artistic methods of revealing ideas or truth through the use of symbols. Visual and concrete terms can easily represent abstract terms and thus give form to the formless. Nawal El Saadawi is renowned for the use of deliberate powerful diction which often has underlying meanings. This enquiry examines her language use, especially the recurrent use of the word 'eye' and its varied colours as an indicator to the central meaning and understanding of two of her novels, *Two Women in One* and *God Dies by the Nile*. Consequently, it is through the symbolic presentation of the 'eye' that the reader sees the author's themes unravel themselves.

Literally, a symbol is said to be a thing that stands for something beyond itself. This is to say that a symbol must always be considered beyond its outward presentation. Symbolism has been defined in various ways. For example, Arthur Symons in *The Symbolist Movement in Literature* refers to it as 'visual or pictorial'. Robin Mayhead believes that, in writing, '[i]magery is something bodied forth by the writer's imagination' (*Understanding Literature*: 135). This means that, through imagination, contrasting symbols and images can be artistically brought to bear on our reality, thus giving 'us a completely new and refreshing sense of the world in which we live' (135).

In the same vein, Fowler sees symbols in literature as attributes of an object 'which serve the rational idea as a substitute for logical presentation, but with the proper function of animating the mind by opening out for it a prospect into a field of kindred representations stretching beyond its ken' (*Dictionary of Modern Critical Terms*: 188).

Additionally, William Butler Yeats in *The Symbolism of Poetry* (1900) maintains that a 'continuous indefinable symbolism' is 'the substance of all style', and that 'the excellence of symbol consists in the suggestiveness that derives from the suppression of a metaphor's directly apprehensible terms of reference: "as a sword blade may flicker with the light of burning towers", so the symbol evokes unseen worlds' (quoted in Fowler: 188). Therefore, the fact that reality is embedded in symbols in works of art cannot be over-emphasized here. In this regard, the artist through his literary creation assumes the position of a high priest who is able to veil his perception of reality in cloaks that require an equally presuming mind to unravel. To this end, Jo Ray McCuen and Anthony C. Winkler emphasize the implicitness of symbolism in literature, which, thankfully, shields the effects of symbols from ruin by what they refer to as the 'peachiness' of readers in unravelling hidden symbols (*Readings for Writers*: 501-2).

Nawal El Saadawi is a well-known female writer whose major preoccupation is to champion the cause of oppressed Arab women especially in her country, Egypt. Critics and researchers have commented on her works and most believe that they tend towards the autobiographical. In this regard, Georges Tarabishi's intensive critique of her works in his 1988 book, *Woman Against Her Sex: A Critique of Nawal el-Saadawi* contends: 'The biographer's overwhelming desire to identify with her subject is something which ... we may regard as a guise for the author' (13). To him, El Saadawi's novels *A Woman at Point Zero*, *Two Women in One* and *Memoirs of a Woman Doctor* all enumerate the author's experiences as a young, struggling, and later, professional female.

Similarly, Abena P.A. Busia (1991) in her chapter 'Rebellious Women: Fictional Biographies – Nawal El Saadawi's *Woman at Point Zero* and Mariama Bâ's *So Long a Letter*', believes that El Saadawi's works tend to depict the realities of the author who is 'aware that for women, the ability to inhabit their own stories, and to become the subject of their own histories can be of itself an act or gesture of rebellion' (88-9).

Zainab Alkali ('Feminism and the Novels of Nawal El Saadawi') views El Saadawi's *God Dies by the Nile* as a novel that presents women as schizophrenics who desire a world that is devoid of men. Additionally, Alkali opines that Bahiah in *Two Women in One* is purposely presented as a rebellious young woman who opposes every role that society ascribes to her gender in preference for the roles and liberties of the opposite gender. In Alkali's opinion, Bahiah frequently assumes postures that are 'uncouth for a young woman' (84).

In her review of Nawal El Saadawi's *Woman at Point Zero* and *Memoirs of a Woman Doctor* Regina Nkere-Uwem (1997), traces the sufferings of female characters to the activities of other females to whom they are subordinated, especially the mothers ('Oppression of Women by Women in the Selected Novels of Nwapa and Emecheta'). These critiques of El Saadawi's works have no doubt, brought to light qualities that have further enriched the material resource of African literary studies. However, it is not enough to study characterization and themes of any work of art without paying attention to the language. In this regard, it is important to investigate El Saadawi's choice of words, especially, the recurrent use of the word 'eye'/'eyes'', and the various colours of eyes as having direct relevance to the execution of her themes in the works under study.

Two Women in One tells the story of a girl, Bahiah Saheen, a rebellious young woman who hates her gender and all the roles of that sex that she is made to play. She believes that the life of the female child unlike that of the male is restricted to the home, and especially the kitchen with its smell of onions and garlic. She also realizes that the upbringing of the female child is centred primarily towards the satisfaction of the male. However, Bahiah discovers early in life the shortfalls of such an upbringing on the over-all personality of the female and kicks against every aspect of it in the most radical forms. This novel gives voice to the author's belief in the fact that the emancipation of the woman is possible only through the radical and socialist ideological approaches.

God Dies by the Nile is about an elderly woman, Zakeya and her brother, Kafrawi with his two daughters, Nafissa and Zeinab. The novel unravels the gruesome oppressive experiences under which peasant women in the Egyptian village of Kafr El Teen are forced to live. The Mayor of the province, a dreaded, huge mechanical man, exploits the labour of the poor farmers by taking for himself the larger portion of their annual harvests. This tyrannical Mayor lives in the best house in the village and demands that young girls be sent to his house to do the cleaning. As events unfold, Nafissa, Zakeya's niece is sent to work in the Mayor's house and when he gets her pregnant, he dismisses her and asks for her younger sister, Zeinab to be sent to him as replacement. While all these were going on, the villagers could not complain. However, Zakeya is not able to contend with the excesses of the Mayor and her reaction in the end brings relief to the people of the village.

To this end, therefore, it is obvious from the synopsis that there indeed exists oppression, firstly in the life of Bahiah, and secondly in the lives of the villagers of Kafr El Teen. El Saadawi's consistent reference to the eye in these novels, *Two Women in One* and *God Dies by the Nile* suggests that the human *eye(s)* has or have symbolic relevance and indeed, speak a language that expresses the emotions of the characters. It is towards the exposition of these claims that this paper is aimed.

Through the use of the eye, the writer is able to give expression to emotions and character traits that would otherwise remain hidden. The eye has been used in *Two Women in One* to convey such character traits as those of defiance, determination, rebelliousness, lust, deception, knowledge, poverty, hate and wickedness.

The symbolic use of the eye to portray defiance and rebelliousness is seen in Bahiah's refusal to accept age-long traditions of bringing up girls. Girls she contends walk, 'with a strange, mechanical gait, their feet shuffling along while legs and knees remained clamped, as if they were pressing their thighs together to protect something they were afraid might fall' (*Two Women in One*: 7). This sort of upbringing she says is peculiar to girls because boys walk freely throwing their legs out with abandon.

The heroine's rebelliousness and defiance is therefore seen through her action of wanting to surpass the male in his liberty to walk and behave, she stands with her 'right foot on the edge of the marble table, left foot on the floor' (8), a posture that is even difficult for most males to perform. The only man that is able to stand in this way is Dr Alawi, her Anatomy lecturer, who intimidates his students with this ability and for the fact that his blue gaze is always unflinching. The only other person who is capable of check-mating Dr Alawi's posture and gaze is Bahiah herself, for when he stops before her table,

> she would never take her foot down. When he fixed his blue eyes on her, she would stare back at him with her own black eyes. She knew full well that black is stronger than blue, particularly where eyes are concerned. Black is the origin, the root that reaches back into the depths of the earth. (*Two Women in One*: 9)

In other words, Bahiah uses her *black eyes* to fight Dr Alawi's intimidating *blue eyes*. And since black is stronger than blue, she feels superior to him, hence the overwhelming feeling of liberation from restrictive female behaviours that she detests.

In addition, by way of expressing her rebelliousness, Bahiah sees her female self as an image that is unreal. Within her, she feels she is a different person though society forces on her roles and physical characteristics that are not acceptable to her real self. For this reason, she feels an encompassing desire to change the physical 'her' to the real self that hides within.

Even in this desire to redefine her person, Bahiah sees the eyes as the first point to consider because of her unflinching belief that no two people's eyes can ever be the same:

> She would be in the grip of a new, wild, nameless desire: the desire to be her real self and to trample all other wills down with hers, to tear her birth certificate to pieces, to change her name, to change her father and mother, to gouge out the eyes of those who had cheated and deceived her … so that no one would be able to take her own eyes and replace them with eyes that were not hers'. (97)

Furthermore, it is also through the eyes that traits such as those of lust and deception are revealed. Consistently, Bahiah realizes an overwhelming connection between Dr Alawi and herself. A feeling she has never been able to describe except that through his eyes she reads his lust for her; 'There was something between herself and Dr Alawi – something unspecified and incomprehensible, but nevertheless real and palpable. She sensed it in his blue eyes when he looked at her' (*Two Women in One*: 55).

Also, the author uses the eye to symbolically explain to the reader what important happening is to occur between Bahiah and her lover, Saleem Ibraheem, before the actual happening itself: 'As she jumped up he turned and there was his face directly before her, his eyes on her' (64). And again, 'his blue eyes fastened on her' and 'she expected him to take his eyes off her and look at the view, but he did not. His eyes remained on hers' and also 'his eyes still on hers' until Bahiah herself realizes the overwhelming effects of his eyes on hers and when he asks her 'why do you look away?' her reply still centres around the symbolic relevance of the use of the eye, for she replies: 'I don't know ... but your eyes sometimes seem not to belong to you' (65-6). And when he asks whose eyes they are, Bahiah claims ignorance. Here, it is important to note that the eyes that Bahiah sees on Saleem's face like all other eyes she has seen on men are deceptive. When he eventually attains intimacy with her, his otherwise blue eyes assume a tint of black and they glitter while Bahiah's very dark or black eyes, turn pale 'her eyes less dark and her nose less upturned' (70).

Similarly, Bahiah learns deception as a child from her mother 'who had taught her deception by lying to her' (12). Now as a young adult, she has grown to know that 'her eyes lied and that they hid her sexual desires' (97). In other words, Bahiah associates deception with the human eyes. In her own body, when she stands before a mirror, it is through her own eyes that she realizes that her sexuality is suppressed, in spite of herself.

Knowledge is also expressed through the eyes in this work of art. Bahiah discovers that real human desires are often suppressed by laws while the unreal ones are 'weak and need no laws to keep them in check' (*Two Women in One*: 12). In this ultimate search for what is true about her femininity, Bahiah's route is again the eyes. The author states clearly that 'Bahiah's deep black eyes remained focused on that strange sensation which reminded her that everything permissible is unreal' (13).

Also the author's description of the first meeting between Bahiah and Saleem is made concrete through the functions of the eyes thus: 'then their eyes met and she realized that the secret behind this extraordinary face lay in the way his eyes moved. It was strange, different from the other male students. Their eyes seemed not to see' (35), that is to say, it is only through Saleem's eyes that Bahiah knows of his special qualities which other males do not have.

Furthermore, on their first outing together, they climb Jebel al-muqattam, a very high mountain and it is here, that Saleem's eyes x-ray her entire person as it were, and gain knowledge of the real Bahiah that is hidden within: 'she raised her eyes in astonishment and they met his. They were black, with a strange penetrating gaze that tore the mask from her face, stripped away the layers, making her visible' (44).

Having so discovered Bahiah, his black eyes continue to probe while she in turn closes her own eyes repeatedly to cut out realities but 'then she opened them and realized that she was not dreaming and that the black eyes were still on hers. The blackness was not completely black; it was tinged with blue, a deep blue that spoke of unknown depths like the blue of the sky when we gaze at it and see that it does not exist' (45).

It is important to note here that the author's emphasis on the eyes and their colour is very symbolic because it portrays that which is real as opposed to the unreal and that which is known as against the unknown. The author specifically uses *red eyes* to symbolize wicked behaviours. In particular, Bahiah's detestation is for her father who is always trying to make her do things she does not want to do. For example, he wants her to become a doctor while she wants to be an artist. Like the policeman who sits along the street, her father's image on her drawing board, is given 'two red eyes and a black handlebar moustache, huge hands and fingers coiled round a long stick' (27) to give expression to his frequent attacks on her.

Just as red eyes symbolize wickedness, *yellow eyes* symbolize poverty. In her description of the poor living conditions and indeed, status of the working class people, El Saadawi describes their physical features thus: 'Their huge skulls swing back and forth like pendulums. Their broad, padded shoulders were stuck to each other … They leapt from their seats, holding their heads and staring around them, their yellow eyes wide and fearful' (31). In this respect, the yellowness of the eyes suggests jaundice and in the author's opinion, only the poor suffer jaundice.

As in *Two Women in One*, *God Dies by the Nile* presents an extensive use of imagery centring on the use of the 'eye'. Through the eye, the author has been able to draw the reader's attention to such human attributes as those of innocence, defiance, lust and knowledge, which are made manifest in the characters.

The innocence of peasants like Zakeya, the principal character in this work, is revealed through her mind's eye as she dreams away back into her infancy. Firstly, at dusk when she gets back to her hut after a tiring labour on the farm, she habitually squats at the door and stares into the dark oblivious night. Eating, to her, is simply a counter reaction to a burning pain inside her head and in her stomach, at which instance, she 'put out her hand and fumbled in the dark for the flat, straw basket containing the week's store of food. She pulled it up to her side, parted her tightly closed lips and began to feed little pieces of dry bread, dry cheese and salted pickles into her mouth' (4). After which she allows herself to drift into the innocence of childhood where 'she crawls on her belly over the dust-covered yard of their house, panting breathlessly, with her tongue hanging out of her mouth' (5). When in this trance, Zakeya sees everything through the purity of a child's eyes. For instance, when Kafrawi, her younger brother, and father of Nafissa and Zainab, slips in to sit beside her, the author says, 'she is looking at him through her child's eyes' (5). The image of innocence and the simplicity of her life as a peasant is clearly depicted here.

The eye, as a symbolic image of anger and defiance, is consistently depicted in the characters of Zakeya and Zeinab. When Zakeya walks, 'her eyes did not look at the ground, were not fixed to her feet. They were the same. They had not changed. They were raised, fixed to some distant point with the same angry defiance which looked out of them before' (2).

These short symbolic sentences portray an image that is militant in the old woman, Zakeya. And this anger and defiance are shared by all the oppressed peasants of the village of Kafr El Teen, especially Zeinab, Zakeya's niece. For, like her aunt, Zeinab will walk with anger expressed on her forehead or sit beside her aunt and, together 'their eyes continued to watch the lane with an expression of angry defiance' (65).

Furthermore, El Saadawi uses the eye as a symbol to illustrate lust in *God Dies by the Nile*. When the tyrannical Mayor and his young son, Tariq begin to discuss the circumstance that led to the birth of Nafissa's bastard child, the author tells us that 'as he listened to her story his eyes shone with the glint which can be seen in the eyes of a youth barely nineteen when he thinks of a woman's body' (38). It is the eyes, therefore, that express Tariq's lust in the way they shine excitedly in the dark night. When Zeinab succumbs to the plot to work in the Mayor's house, as she busies herself scrubbing the floors, the Mayor's blue eyes are said to be fastened on the reflection of her wet long dress 'and he could no longer take his eyes off her young body' (99). In addition to this, the author states that Zeinab's attention 'caught the blue eyes of the Mayor fastened on her with a strange look' (99). To this end therefore, the repeated mention of the eyes in this section of the work tends to symbolically relate the eye to the lustful desires of the characters. In addition, the realization of the fact that she and her entire family have been victims of the Mayor's tyranny comes to Zakeya through moments of pensive reflection that are portrayed through the description of her eyes.

Through the entire work, Zakeya's eyes have always been described as distant and bleak but at the point of the awakening of awareness she acquires knowledge of their predicament and, somehow, sees the solution to the problems through the activities of her eyes. Thus, 'she never slept or even closed her eyes. They pierced the darkness to the other side of the lane where rose the iron gate of the Mayor's house' (137). Her eyes piercing the darkness symbolizes knowledge of what has hitherto been unknown and when she claims 'I was blind, but now my eyes have been opened' (135), it completes the author's symbolic use of the eye as a medium for the expression of knowledge.

In conclusion, therefore, Nawal El Saadawi's use of the 'eye' has symbolic relevance to the execution of her themes in the two works studied here. It is obvious that a meticulous study of the human eyes can relate to an entire story about the realities of the human life. El Saadawi has, therefore, artistically opened up a new range of possibilities whereby complex human phenomena can be deduced through the activities or colours of her characters' eyes.

WORKS CITED

Alkali, Zainab. 'Feminism and the Novels of Nawal El Saadawi'. Unpublished PhD thesis presented to the Department of English and Modern European Languages, Bayero University, Kano, 1995.

Arthur, Symons. *The Symbolist Movement in Literature*. London: W. Heinemann, 1899.

Busia, Abena P.A. 'Rebellious Women: Fictional Biographies – Nawal El Saadawi's *Woman at Point Zero* and Mariama Bâ's *So Long a Letter.* In *Motherlands: Black Women's Writing from Africa, the Caribbean and South Asia*', Susheila Nasta ed. London: Women's Press Limited, 1991: 88-98.

El Saadawi, Nawal. *Two Women in One*. London: Saqi Books, 1985.

——*God Dies by the Nile*. London: Zed Books, 1974.

Fowler, Roger, ed. *A Dictionary of Modern Critical Terms*. London: Routledge & Kegan Paul, 1973.

Mayhead, Robin. *Understanding Literature*. London Cambridge University Press, 1965.

Nkere-Uwem, R. 'Oppression of Women by Women in the Selected Novels of Nwapa and Emecheta' Unpublished MA Dissertation submitted to the Department of English University of Maiduguri, 1997.

McCuen, Jo Ray and Anthony C. Winkler. *Readings for Writers*. New York: Harcourt Brace Jovanovich, 1983.

Tarabishi, Georges. *Woman Against Her Sex: A Critique of Nawal el-Saadawi*. London: Saqi Books, 1988.

African Epics

A Comparative Study of
Sundiata & *Al-Sirah al-Hilaliyyah*

KHALID ABOUEL-LAIL

This article focuses on D.T. Niane's *Sundiata: An Epic of Old Mali* and different narrations of *Al-Sirah al-Hilaliyyah* in Egypt, to investigate the similarities and differences between them in relation to the structure of the epic, represented by the stages through which the folk cultural hero passes: the prophecy, the birth of the hero, the alienation of the hero, and the final recognition of the hero. The article depends on the comparative method and the oral-formulaic theory (Finnegan *Oral Poetry*; Ong *Orality and Literacy*).

It may be somewhat striking that the Arab folk conscience has so far kept on the oral narration of 'Sirat Bani Hilal'; though its narration began as early as the tenth century. The *sirah* is an Arabic folk art while the epic is a Western folk art. Although they differ in name, structure and content, they share a great deal of their artistic characteristics. In his study of the relationship between the Arabic *sirah* and the Western epic, al-Hagagi has proved a high degree of similarity. He even considers the structure of the epic a part or a section of the folk *sirah*. The *sirah* is the whole of which the epic is a part. The similarities even transcend the few existing differences of structure and text, blurring the difference of language and locale (al-Hagagi *Birth of a Hero in the Folk Sirahs*: 25-6). Among the important similarities are focus on the topics of war, chivalry and motivation for revenge. Linguistically speaking, the lexical item 'epic'[1] is translated into Arabic as '*malhama*' which gives the meaning of bodily engagement in the heat of battle, thus, denoting raging battle, but technically speaking it is a 'long narrative poem recounting great deeds and extraordinary heroism'. Similarly, the *'sirah'* is the biography of a hero or a tribe including encounters, wars and fighting. Arabic dictionaries consider *malhama* and *sirah* synonymous (*al-Wageez Arabic Dictionary*) in the tradition of the scholars[2] that use the two terms interchangeably. Scenes of battle are so numerous in both that they can be seen as series of scenes of continuous battles where these scenes and battles are greatly similar. The two genres are not set apart despite the radical difference between them. The epic tends to display conflict among gods or demigods, sometimes with heroines that are goddesses as well. The *sirah's* hero, on the other hand, is human and it is populated by heroes who are mere mortals with human conflicts and characters, although some of its heroes and events are sometimes of supernatural proportions with unrealistic deeds.

In his pioneering study, al-Hagagi argued, 'Sirah is a wide world more spacious than the epic ... the latter being a part of sirah' (*Birth of a Hero in the Folk Sirahs*: 25-6). Perusing Tawfiq's (2010) translation, *Sundiata: An Epic of Old Mali*, one will discover that it does not go beyond the initial episode of those that the Arabic folk *sirahs* cover. This episode is the phase of 'births' which starts all Arabic *sirahs*. This proves the argument of al-Hagagi as was revealed in the above-mentioned distinction between *sirah* and epic.

In his well-known *Prolegomena*, ibn Khaldun comments on the old Mali Kingdom giving special mention of its king Sundiata Keita, the hero of the *Sundiata* epic, quoting his accredited historians, one of whom was Sheikh Othman, the most famous learned and pious cleric and Islamic jurisprudent of the Guinean people, who arrived in Egypt in H. 699 (around 1300 CE) with his family. He was familiar with the history he was recounting since it was relatively recent at that time. Quoting him, ibn Khaldun said:

[He was] their great king who defeated Sosso conquered their land and became their king Mari Djata … He ruled them for twenty-five years as they said. When he died, he was followed by his son Mansa Uli [i.e. Sultan Ali] … son of Sultan Mari Djata, then his son Muhammad ibn Qu. The line of kings was shifted then from the line of Sultan Mari Djata to the line of his nephew Abu Bakr, so they were ruled by Mansa Musa son of Abu Bakr. (Ibn Khaldun *History*, vol. VI: 200)

This reference gives the epic under study a historical nature especially when ibn Khaldun also refers elsewhere to the migration of the Hilali tribe to North Africa. The *Sundiata* epic runs within the context of the social and political history of the Mandingo country. Its people, according to some interpretations of the epic, belong to oriental Islamic origins as the descendants of Bilal ibn Rabah; they are Bilali.

It was said the name *Mali*, with the variants *Mallel*, *Mel* and *Melit*, as appears on some Middle-Ages maps, was a Berber name. The country had many names; it was the Mandingo country, Mali and the Takrur Kingdom. The common names used by the Mandingo tribes are Manenka, Mandinka, Mandin, Maning, Manenga, Mandeng or Manenka – all of a similar nature (Tarkhan *The Islamic State of Mali*: 27-30).

> The epic is based on the real life of the African king who lived in the 13th Century and established an empire in west Africa that extended from the coast of the Atlantic Ocean along the coast towards the east where there are now the following countries: Gambia, Guinea, Senegal and Mali. (Paterno *The True Lion King of Africa: The Epic History of Sundiata*: 3)

The old Mandingo country was composed of twelve kingdoms, one of which was the Niani Kingdom, ruled by Maghan Kon Fatta. This kingdom was under the rule of Sou-maoro, the King of Ghana, but soon got independence and Ghana itself came under the rule of the Kingdom of Mali. Seers had predicted that the King Maghan would have a son from an ugly hunchbacked woman, and that son was destined to lead the Mandingo people to victory. The epic sees the prophecy coming true through a number of folk motifs which connect this hero with Alexander the Great, with the heroes of Arabic epics and with heroes of the Western tradition such as Oedipus and Odysseus. On the other hand, connections are made with other African epics as other scholars, such as Konaté, showed the links between the Sundiata epic and the story of Shaka Zulu, king of the Zulu city in south-eastern Africa. However, this last reference relates historical events of a later time since Shaka was born in 1787 and fought against the English occupation of his country. Konaté confines the comparison to the phases of birth where the two works are similar in the vague atmosphere of their moments of birth. Paterno states that 'While this epic contains universal elements that are common in this genre, it also contains unique African roots' (3).

The phase of the birth of the hero in the *Sundiata* epic shows particular affinity to Western epics and especially the Arabic Hilali folk epic. The prophecy carried by the hunter/seer to the father King Maghan Kon Fatta in *Sundiata* is its first springing point as the seer himself says:

> I see two hunters coming to your city; they have come from afar and a woman accompanies them. Oh, that woman! She is ugly, she is hideous, she bears on her back a disfiguring hump. Her monstrous eyes seem to have been merely laid on her face, but, mystery of mysteries, this is the woman you must marry, sire, for she will be the mother of him who will make the name of Mali immortal for ever. The child will be the seventh star, the seventh conqueror of the earth. He will be more mighty than Alexander. (Niane *Sundiata*: 5-6)

The prophecy unfolds and the two hunters arrive to rid the Daw kingdom of the buffalo calf, a looming menace as in the King Oedipus myth or in many folk tales, the most famous of which being the tale of Saint George. As the king of the Daw kingdom had promised the hero to select the most beautiful girl of his kingdom for marriage, the hunters chose the ugly hunchbacked woman Sogolon leaving behind all the beauties of the kingdom, causing much ridicule on the part of the king and the people. The hunters carried Sogolon to the King of the Mandingo, Maghan Kon Fatta, in compliance with the prophecy. The marriage resulted in the birth of the legendary hero Sundiata Keita.

Prophecy also played an important role in *Al-Hilaliyyah;* it urged Rizq ibn Nayl al-Hilali to go on a journey to Mecca to marry a noble woman who would later bear him a male child to fulfil his heart's dreams. The urge came through a divine inspiration. The hero recites:

> Old age creeping, I was bent,
> It's God who fulfils all intent.
> Plights make me cry and crave,
> One little child brave.

> Heard and a divine call found,
> Everyman by his lot bound.
> Listen, Rizq, to God's divination,
> Get married and Mecca is your destination.
> (al-Abnoudi *Al-Sirah Al-Hilaliyyah*: 67-8)

The knot of marriage is tied and, similar to what happens in the African counterpart in fulfilment of the prophecy of the hunter/soothsayer concerning the fate of the offspring of the marriage, the 'the pool of birds' plays the role of the prophecy. It predicts the future of the new-born boy of the noble Khadra:

> Eighty maids of the Hilali tribe caught her eye,
> Sweet creatures brought up by the Lord of the sky.
> A pool of birds hovering in heaven,
> By seeking the Lord's blessing they are driven.
> (al-Abnoudi: 98)

The expected son would accomplish great deeds. He would resemble the crow in colour and bravery. It is the bird that would fly up and hit all the other birds around, 'all in reach will bleed'. Thus, the noble Khadra wishes she could get a child like this crow which fears nobody and gains the respect of everybody (al-Abnoudi: 103-5).

Thus, the prophecy is the nucleus around which all the events take place in both works; it also serves this central role in other Arabic and Western narrative poems. Prophecy plays a major role in 'transferring the hero from the domain of ordinary people to the domain of the mythical characters, i.e., from the realistic to the mythical. The hero, thus, enters the circle of the great universe and establishes his place in it' (al-Hagagi *Prophecy: the Hero's Destiny*: 18). The role and place of prophecy in the *Sundiata* epic is by no means unique to it since the same role and place is present in other world folk traditions such as in *The Iliad*, *The Odyssey* and *The Aeneid*, in addition to the myth of Oedipus, etc. Even religious narrative included such folk traditions as in the Prophet Muhammad biographies by Ibn Hesham and Ibn Isahq as well as other life stories of Moses and Jesus. Confirming this view, al-Hagagi said:

> Folk Arabic epic hailed prophecies which determined the destiny of their heroes, which makes them share concepts of other folk epics around the world. Such prophecies played a major role in the structure of these oral narratives ... Prophecies added to the role they played in folk narratives another role in religious stories. (*Prophecy: the Hero's Destiny*: 18-19)

Prophecy in these folk narrative traditions took a number of forms, such as visions, dreams, observing the stars and reading their clues, and telling the future through deciphering signs in the sand or extrapolating from the prophecies of old books (al-Hagagi *Birth of a Hero in the Folk Sirahs*: 49).

The hero's birth is almost always laden with mystique and mystery. The mystical events that surround the hero's birth do not shield him from hard times and extreme suffering. Unlike the birth of 'ordinary and normal' humans, the condition of possibility of the hero's birth is the commitment of the helping hands of a god or a supernatural force that either anticipates or delays the process of coming to life (Konaté *Violence in Two African Epics*: 3). We can find the same characteristic in both the *Sundiata* epic and *Al-Hilaliyyah Sirah*. In the epic of *Sundiata*,

> the noble king Naré Maghan determined to solemnize his marriage with all the customary formalities so that nobody could dispute the rights of the son to be born to him … Sogolon walked in front held by two old women. The king's relatives followed and, behind, the choir of young girls of Mali sang the bride's departure song, keeping time to the songs by clapping their hands. (Niane *Sundiata*: 9-11)

Marriage to Sogolon was motivated by the desire to see the dream of the birth of a legendary hero come true – a hero that would inherit the fathers' kingdom and kingship. 'You have ruled over the kingdom which your ancestors bequeathed to you and you have no other ambition but to pass on this realm, intact if not increased, to your descendants; but, fine king, your successor is not yet born' (Niane *Sundiata*: 5).

King Maghan Kon Fatta was already a father of more than one son, his eldest being Dankaran Touman, but neither he nor any of the other sons, was good enough to achieve the father's ambition for a king to inherit the great heritage of the ancestors. It was this same ambition that drove Rizq ibn Nayl to marry the noble Khadra. He was a father of a girl (Sheha). It was further said that he was also the father of another disabled son. This created permanent angst in Rizq's heart, wondering who will be his heir (al-Abnoudi: 85).

Every time Rizq saw fathers at an age similar to his playing with their children, his longing for offspring becomes stronger. Then, an inspiration/prophecy visits him in his sleep and urges him to start his journey to the Holy City of Mecca to marry the daughter of its noble ruler as she would be the one to give him the son/hero who would bear the name of his father and have a great status in the future.

Studying the way the African counterpart, Naré Maghan, married the ugly Sogolon shows the points of similarity with the manner another Arab lord, Shaddad ibn Qerad married an Abyssinian slave girl, Zabiba, mother of the Arab poet Antara ibn Shaddad, with the folk narrators' attempts to add a touch of beauty on the whole affair. Shaddad captured this slave girl following one of his triumphant battles. She refused to succumb to his amorous attempts unless they got married first and he promised to recognize the offspring of this relation as his legitimate children (Antara ibn Shaddad *Folk Epic*: 72-3). Zabiba abstaining from surrendering to Shaddad reminds us of Sogolon's reaction to her husband Naré Maghan who could not have his way with her until he threatened to kill her in compliance with the orders of the genies (jinns) (Niane *Sundiata*: 12).

Sogolon, Sundiata's mother, did have better luck than that of the noble Khadra and her son, or Zabiba and her son Antara. Khadra was accused of adultery and had to depart from the land of her tribe for the land of the Zahlah tribe where she brought up her son, Abu Zayd al-Hilali. She raised him on the principles of chivalry and heroism in his exile, hence his return as a hero to his hometown. Antara was accused of being a slave because of his black skin, and Sogolon suffered the same injustice and fate for herself and her son. Sundiata was the son of the ugly Sogolon whose person and the king's good care of the child since his prenatal phase, keeping in mind the words of the soothsayer, instigated hatred in the heart of Sassouma Bereté, the king's first wife. Sassouma feared for the future of her son Dankaran Touman who was then eight years old. Numerous attempts were made to get rid of Sogolon and her son. One such attempt occurred when the mother was pregnant, using tricks of senior magicians who admitted failure to do Sogolon and her son any harm. Another attempt was excluding Sundiata for his young age and physical disability to pave the way after his father's death for Sassouma to declare Dankaran Touman, her own son, king. In so doing she totally ignored the king's will based on the prophecy of the soothsayer. Khadra bore great sufferings caused by the colour of her son's skin, where she was accused of adultery and begetting that child from an illicit relation, which hurled on her a great deal of insults and bad treatment. Similarly, Sogolon endured terrible ordeals after the death of her husband and the apparent disability of her son. The first wife Sassouma 'banished Sogolon and her son to a back yard of the palace. Mari Djata's mother now occupied an old hut which had served as a lumber-room of Sassouma's' (Niane, *Sundiata*: 18). When Sogolon felt there was danger looming she decided to depart with her son in the company of Sundiata's brother Manding Bory and their sister Kolonkan (half-siblings). She chose them as she felt they were kind-hearted and loyal to their half-brother. The trick of King Dankaran Touman and his mother to get rid of Sogolon was to separate Sogolon and Sundiata Keita's griot (storyteller), Balla Fasséké, whom his father had appointed for him (Niane *Sundiata*: 27).

The mother Sogolon's decision to save her son by departure in the company of his siblings was wise. While Khadra travels with her maid Saeeda and her son Abu Qomsan who becomes a faithful follower of Abu Zayd, Sundiata travels in the company of his mother and half-siblings. Exile, or the hero's alienation, is forced on the hero who comes back after this obligatory journey to liberate his country as a hero saviour. 'Let us leave here, my son ... You will return to reign when you are a man, for it is in Mali that your destiny must be fulfilled' (Niane *Sundiata*: 26-7). Okafor refers to this common characteristic between the epics: 'It is noteworthy, here, that the exile of an endangered saviour of his people is recurrent in many traditions the world over' (*Oral Tradition and Civic Education in Africa*: 413).

The act of overthrowing the child king done by the step-mother who managed to banish him from his people and land resembles the act of sending Abu Zayd al-Hilali and his mother into exile. However, it denotes another angle of similarity to the folk epic of Sayf ibn Dhi Yazan in the ordeal he endured with his mother Qamaraya. Queen Qamaraya, the spy, who was planted by Sayf Araad in his father's Royal Palace with the purpose of getting rid of him together with her own unborn son, Sayf. When she gave birth she was overwhelmed with his great beauty and was terribly jealous of his succeeding to the throne. The king died for unknown reasons; he could have died of natural causes or been poisoned by Qamaraya (*Sayf ibn Dhi Yazan Epic*: 42-3). Sayf was raised away from his kingdom because of his mother who played a role similar to that of Sundiata's step-mother. Qamaraya left him in a desert where he was raised by a deer, which suckled him. He grew up in exile but managed at the end to return to his country to rule over it. Banishment and growing up in exile are common features shared by epics and *sirah*s except in rare cases. 'The birth of the epic hero is usually followed by rejection and ostracism. The hero travels through a string of crises that he surmounts' (Konaté: 3).

Similarities between *Sundiata* and *Al-Hilaliyyah* go further to include the destinations chosen by the mothers of the two heroes as safe havens for bringing up their children on the principles of chivalry and heroism. Khadra made for the Zahlah tribe territory with her maid Saeeda and her son Abu Qomsan. King Bassem al-Zahlan, ruler of the territory, took good care of them, providing sustenance and education for the little child. In one account, the name 'Barakat' (blesses) was bestowed on the child by the prophet al-Khidr, who also protects the mother Khadra when thugs tried to rape her.

In a similar way, the hero Sundiata goes through several

adventures while on the road with his mother to the land of Mema to settle down there. They left Niani, making for the city of Djedeba under the rule of Mansa (king) Konkon, who was a great seer. The king received them with some caution at the beginning but Sundiata soon got along with the children of the city. Here the child showed signs of heroism; he even won a sword duel with Mansa Konkon.

This is again similar to the phase when Abu Zayd was schooled in the madrasa. When Sheikh Saleh, his madrasa tutor, hurls insults at Abu Zayd and his mother and tries to torture him, instigated by one jealous mother, Abu Zayd kills the sheikh, whose brother – a minster of the state – tries to take revenge. The king however protects the lad. Another similarity appears in Sundiata's duel with Mansa Konkon (playing the game of *wori* in which the king excels) compared to Abu Zayd's duel with Gouda ibn Selim, nephew of King Fadl. Abu Zayd kills his opponent and faces attempts on the part of the parents of his dead opponent to revenge and send him to exile. Similarly, King Fadl protects him; he even suffers the enmity of his brother and sister-in-law for the sake of Abu Zayd whom he treats as one of his children.

Just as the land of the Zahlan tribe was the settlement haven of Abu Zayd and his mother, Sundiata was destined to find such haven in Mema, but not yet. He was expelled together with his company from the city of Djedeba after a sojourn of two months. They pass by the city of Tabon where they were well received by its king who was too old to take the challenge of keeping them for long in the face of threats from the king of Niani. They move to the city of Wagadou where the chief merchant recommends giving them the best of welcomes. Before the king of Wagadou, Sogolon went on presenting her case, depending on the ties of friendship between the king and her late husband (Niane *Sundiata*: 33). The impressive and welcome response of the king was:

No stranger has ever found our hospitality wanting. My court is your court and my palace is yours. Make yourself at home. Consider that in coming from Niani to Wagadou you have done no more than change rooms. The friendship which unites Mali and Ghana goes back to a very distant age, as the elders and griots know. The people of Mali are our cousins. (34)

The king's generous and hospitable reception was even extended more by sending them to the court of his nephew Tonkara in Mema. This corresponds with the welcome reception enjoyed by Khadra and her son in the court of king Fadle ibn Bassem al-Zahlan.

The Mema court was the last destination of Sundiata and his mother. There he trains in the use of weapons and shares in the king's conquests where he greatly excels. He gains people's amazed admiration as they even described him as a 'successor to Dhu al-Qarnayn', the Quranic name for Alexander the Great. The king and the army appoint him the king's viceroy, a decision hailed by the people. Abu Zayd al-Hilali achieved the same status in his exile in the court of King Fadl in the Zahl territory where he was first schooled for literacy then for chivalry and martial arts. 'Five years hence, listen to the tale's intent, I sent to the Zahlan king, I want my boy taught. Most important for me... I want a teacher for my boy, I want my lad literate' (Abnoudi: 175).

Recognition of the status of the two heroes after their long journeys of exile goes through comparable processes in the two epics. The Zahlan tribe, which gave refuge to Abu Zayd, was subjugated by the Hilali tribe and paid the tribe annual war tax, but when Abu Zayd al-Hilali grew up he refused to pay the tax and even cut off an ear of one of the two Hilali messengers (Abouel.leil *Accounts of al-Sirah Al-Hilaliyyah in Qena*: 196). In another account, the Hilali tribe supports the Ben Aqeel, which used to pay poll tax to the Hilalis, but Abu Zayd defeated them, killing off forty of their warriors including Atwan, Dagher, Jassar and Jayl. So the Aqeelis sought refuge with the Hilalis (Abouel.

leil: 340). Abu Zayd's sister, Sheha, was the means of the connection through the motif of the three apples, which he splits with his sword instead of catching and eating them. In parallel vein, the baobab leaves, the counterpart of the three apples, help in the recognition the hero in the *Sundiata* epic. When Sundiata settled in Mema, he learned that Soumaoro had invaded the Mandingo land and that his brother Dankaran Touman took flight leaving his people subjugated by Soumaoro. In the Mema market, Sundiata's sister Kolonkan, who used to live with him, met a woman and a number of Mandingo merchants who sold baobab leaves, *nafiola* and *gnougou*, used as condiment and only known in the Mandingo land. The sister Kolonkan, in the *Sundiata* epic, plays the role of the medium that connects the hero with his people. After consulting with her mother, she accompanies the Mandingo merchants to the mother who welcomes them and restores some of her withering powers. It transpires that these merchants were actually the courtiers of old king, Sundiata's father. Under the disguise of merchants they were searching for the hero Sundiata (Niane *Sundiata*: 45).

They beg him to come back to lift the oppression suffered by his country, softening his heart with the pleadings of the oppressed and the tears of mothers who lost their sons. One of his visitors tried to convince him in lines analogous to those expressed by the courtiers of the Hilalis while trying to convince Abu Zayd to come back to his homeland to liberate it of its enemies, leaving behind all the glory he achieved in the land of the Zahla tribe. The two heroes cannot but answer the call of their homelands and go back.

However, before the homecoming, both had to honour their mothers. Sogolon died and her son wanted to honour her with the right burial in a land granted to him by the king. He sought to express this wish when he took leave from the king to return to his homeland in the Mandingo country.

King, you gave me hospitality at your court when I was without shelter. Under your orders I went on my first campaign. I shall never be able to thank you for so much kindness. However, my mother is dead; but I am now a man and I must return to Mali to claim the kingdom of my fathers. Oh king, I give you back the powers you conferred upon me, and I ask leave to depart. In any case, allow me to bury my mother before I go. (Niane *Sundiata*: 45)

The king was upset and did not at first grant Sundiata the needed lot of burial land, but he eventually took the advice of an Arab Sheikh, a counsellor of his, since refusal meant peril for him and his kingdom. The Arab Sheikh's counsel is comparable to the advice of Sultan Sarhan's daughter to the Hilalis in the relevant epic. This is when Abu Zayd asked the Hilalis to honour his mother and pay her moral amends by spreading out some of the best silk cloth from the land of Zahla tribe (where he dwelt) to the Hilali land in Najd:

> Until we cross our doorsteps,
> Her camel on silk spread steps.
> Girls and women singing en route,
> Of her honour and good repute.

Sogolon underwent actual death in the *Sundiata* epic, while Khadra only experienced existential death as she had no subsequent role in the *Al-Hilaliyyah* epic after her son went back to the care of his tribe. The two mothers were absented after their sons found recognition in their homelands. The role each played was to prepare the son away from the homeland so that he can go back and liberate his people, take revenge and expel the enemy. Thus, they could restore the past glory of their lands and put other powers under their dominance after times of weakness, subjugation and paying poll taxes to others.

The two heroes went back to their respective homelands: Sundiata to the Mandingo land and Abu Zayd to Najd.

They then started their battles of destiny against their enemies, the Sosso country and the Aqeeli tribes, to restore the lost pride of their peoples after periods of subjugation and humiliation in their absence. The two heroes manage to accomplish their goals. 'Sundiata was able after a series of long battles to defeat Soumaoro Kanté and in a few years became the chief of their fighters in Mandinka' (Vij *History of West Africa*: 52). In 1235, Sundiata killed king Soumaoro in the battle of Kirina. In 1240 he seized the capital of Ghana and destroyed all vestiges of Soumaoro's former power. By acquiring the gold mine fields at Wangara, and by establishing his capital at Niani, a trading crossroads, Sundiata was able to bring peace, sovereignty and prosperity to his West African kingdom of Kangaba. In a comparable way, Abu Zayd was able to wage a battle against the Aqeeli tribe who wanted to avenge themselves for his previous killing of forty of their warriors, and waged war as well against the Jews who attacked Mecca.

The parallels in the two works appear in similarities of a number of folk beliefs and habits and the artistic properties of both. *First*, there is the *black bird*. A black bird hovering in the sky appears to the women of the Hilalis near the pool of birds at the beginning of the phase of births. It is the source of the prophecy for the noble Khadra, mother of Abu Zayd, and a propitious sign for her. She prays God for a child as black as this bird, 'all in reach will bleed'. This is the *Al-Sirah al-Hilaliyyah*, and again we come across the black bird in the *Sundiata* epic. It hovers above the battle field in the decisive battle between Sundiata and his opponent Soumaoro. Its hovering there is a propitious sign for Sundiata, an indication that he will triumph over rival Soumaoro in their battle (Niane *Sundiata*: 65).

Second, there is the *water pool*. It is the pool of birds in the *Hilaliyyah*, a great place for fulfilling wishes. Around the pool all those who have unfulfilled wishes would gather. Women go to 'the pool of birds where the rite of wishing is practiced as a strong belief' (Abdel Hafiz *Al-*

Sirah Al-Hilaliyyah in Some Sohag Villages: 135). The noble Khadra is

> deprived of male offspring and thus suffers a great deal especially the mocking eyes of all Arab women since women beget males who inherit their fathers, but her husband is left with no heir. At the pool of birds, she prays that God may give her male offspring like that black bird that hovered above and frightened off all other birds. (136)

In the *Sundiata* epic, there is the magic pool of water:

> In the middle of the mountain was a little pool of magic water. Whoever got as far as this pool and drank its waters became powerful, but the jinn of the pool were very evil and only the king of Rita had access to the mysterious pool. (Niane *Sundiata*: 65, 70)

The person who controlled this genie through offering a sacrifice could also control the pool. Sundiata won the favour of the genie guarding the pool through his offering: 'He sacrificed a hundred cocks to the jinn of the mountain' (Niane *Sundiata*: 70-71).

Third, there is the *custom of naming the new-born*. The *Sundiata* epic reflects this custom practised by the old Mandingo people. The new-born is given a name on the eighth day after his birth. According to this social custom, Sundiata was given his name on that day which was a great feasting day in the Mandingo land (14).

It is clear that this ritual combined the folk rites where old women contributed to the nutritional needs of the mother with some foods and beverages that were thought as of good health value for both the mother and the infant on the one hand and of symbolic fertility value on the other. The celebration has as well its formal nature when the entourage of the king celebrate the new-born by offering presents to the king. It is the same scene with all its symbolic, formal and folk meanings in the *Hilaliyyah* epic where the celebration of *Seboa* (seventh day, and not eighth) of the birth of Abu Zayd al-Hilali: 'the custom is

the day of seboa, with the crowd gathering ... They give
the babe a name, amongst maternal and paternal uncles ...
In the midst of Hilali gatherings ... The dignitaries come,
and words go round' (Abnoudi: 116). On that day the
new-born was given a name and the princes and the king
offered his father Rizq ibn Nayl presents.

Fourth, there is the *custom of declaring the honourable
chastity* of the bride on the morning following the
wedding night. After many failed attempts on the part of
the King Naré Maghan and adamant refusal on the part
of his new wife Sogolon, after one week and through a
ruse of his contrivance, he finally succeeds and manages
to both deflower and impregnate her (Niane *Sundiata*:
11-12).

The *Sundiata* epic depicts at length the scene of the
encounter between Maghan and Sogolon and his success
after many troubled endeavours. In contrast, while the
scene where Rizq ibn Nayl meets his wife the noble Khadra
gets the same interest, there is no rejection on the part
of the wife who, on the contrary, made herself ready and
beautiful for the expected meeting. On the following
morning women come to apparently congratulate her and
actually to make sure that she was deflowered as a sign of
her premarital chastity.

Fifth, there is a similarity of *folk games*. The *wori* game
(a kind of draughts or checkers involving pebbles and
sorcery) in the *Sundiata* epic resembles the draughts game
in the *Hilaliyyah* epic. The *wori* in the Sundiata epic is 'a
popular game in Upper Guinea and western Sudan' (Niane
Sundiata, Arab translation, footnote: 119).

Wori is almost the same as the draughts of the
Hilaliyyah, but engravings are made on the ground,
not on a tree trunk. The game plays a symbolic role
in the two works as they are not mere games. They
rather communicate certain messages between the
two opponents, similar to the case of a game of chess
between two rivals. Meaningful phrases are exchanged

during the game with the purpose of achieving a moral victory of one rival. The hero is one of the rivals, which explains the emergence of the game in the two works in the decisive moments of the events.

Consequently, Sundiata and his family left Djedeba for the city of Tabon. In a like manner, the game of draughts plays a role in decisive moments in the *Hilaliyyah* epic, comparable to that of the *wori* game. It appeared before the migration of Bani Hilal from Najd to Tunisia. In another decisive event when the draughts game was used in the *Hilaliyyah* epic, Abu Zayd played a game with his Tunisian friend Al-Allam who made a pact with him against his cousin Al-Zanati Khalifa.

This paper attempted to prove the existence of a strong connection between the *Sundiata* epic and Arabic folk epics (*sirah*s), especially the *Al-Sirah Al-Hilaliyyah*, in a number of aspects, among which are the different phases of the hero's life, e.g. phases of prophecy, birth, exile and his homecoming to gain recognition as a folk hero. The paper reviewed as well the common cultural characteristics related to folk customs, traditions and beliefs. The comparison between *Al-Hilaliyyah* and *Sundiata* would benefit from more study and analysis in the future.

NOTES

1   A long poem narrating the deeds of heroic or legendary figures or the past history of a nation, from Gr. *epekos*, f. *epos* = word, narrative, song. *Concise Oxford English Dictionary.*

2   Examples from numerous others are Dr Abdel Hameed Younis in his two studies – *Zahir Beibars in Folk Storytelling*, 1946 and *Al-Hilaliyyah in History and Literature*, 1950; and Dr Muhammad Ragab al-Naggar in his study *The Hero in Folk Epics: Issues and Technical Aspects*, 1976.

ENGLISH WORKS CITED

Finnegan, Ruth. *Oral Poetry: Its Nature, Significance and Social Context*. Cambridge University Press, 1977.
Konaté, Siendou. *Violence in Two African Epics: A Comparative Study of Chaka and Sundiata*, Université de Cocody-Abidjan, 19 December, 2012.
Niane, D.T. *Sundiata: An Epic of Old Mali*. London: Longman, 1965.
Okafor, Clement A. 'Oral Tradition and Civic Education in Africa'. *International Education Journal* Vol. 5, No. 3, 2004.
Ong, Walter J. *Orality and Literacy: The Technologizing of the Word*. London and New York: Methuen, 1992.
Paterno, Domenica R. *The True Lion King of Africa: The Epic History of Sundiata, King of Old Mali*, National Council of Teachers of English, University of New York, November 1994.

ARABIC WORKS CITED

Abdel Hafiz, M. Hasan. *Al-Sirah Al-Hilaliyyah in Some Sohag Villages: A Semiotic Study of Performer, Narrator and audience*. Unpublished PhD Dissertation. Folklore Literature Dept, High Institute of Folklore Arts. Cairo: Academy of Arts, 2014.
Abouel.leil, Khalid. *Accounts of Al-Sirah Al-Hilaliyyah in Qena*, Part I. Cairo: Egyptian General Book Organization, 2012.
al-Abnoudi, Abdel Rahman, compiler. *Al-Sirah Al-Hilaliyyah, Folk Storytelling of Gaber Abu Hassan*. Family Series. Cairo: Egyptian General Book Organization, 2002.
al-Hagagi, A. Shams al-Deen. *Prophecy: the Hero's Destiny in Arabic Folk Storytelling*, 2nd edn. General Organization for Culture Palaces. Folk Studies Library 2001.
——*The Birth of a Hero in the Folk Sirahs*. Cairo: Dar al-Hilal Publishing, 1991.
al-Naggar, M. Ragab. *The Hero in Folk Arab Epic: Issues & Technical Aspects*. Doctoral thesis. Cairo University Library 1976.
al-Wageez Arabic Dictionary. Cairo: Arabic Language Academy 1993.
Ibn Khaldun. *History* vol. VI. Beirut, Lebanon: Foundation of Gamal, n.d.
ibn Shaddad, Antara. *Folk Epic (Sirah)* Part I. Beirut, Lebanon: Public Library Publishing, n.d.
Niane, D.T. *Sundiata: An Epic of Old Mali*, trans. Tawheeda Ali Tawfiq.

Issue 1402. Cairo: National Centre for Translation 2010.

Sayf ibn Dhi Yazan Epic (Sirah). General Organization of Culture Places. *Public Studies Library* Vol. I, Issue 39, June 1999.

Tarkhan, Ibrahim Ali, *The Islamic State of Mali; Studies in African National History.* Cairo: Egyptian General Book Organization 1973.

Vij, G.D. *History of West Africa,* trans. Youssef Nasr and Rev. Dr Riadh Bahgat Saleeb. Cairo: Dar al-Maarif, 1982.

Younis, A. el-Hamid. *The Hilali in the History and Folk Literature.* Folk Studies Press, 2003 [1950].

Conversations with
Nawal El Saadawi

ONLINE INTERVIEW, 6 June 2017, Cairo Egypt

1 Can we as African women use the word Feminism without distancing ourselves from Western Feminism?
In Arabic we say '*Tahrir El Maraa*' which means: Women's Liberation, which means Feminism. All of these words, in different languages, refer to liberating women and children from the historical patriarchal capitalist racist imperialist colonial religious system, dominating the West and the East, the North and the South. We live in One World, not Three Worlds, dominated by the same oppressive system, globally and locally. We use one word today which is: 'glocally'.

2 What are the kinds of changes we would like to see in north/ south relations and gender relations?
We need to build a new world system based on: freedom, dignity, justice and equality for all peoples, regardless of nationality, religion, gender, class, race, colour, language, sect, creed, or any other so-called 'identity' differences.

3 Are all traditional societies pitted against women?
What do you mean by 'traditional societies'? In Ancient Egyptian society, for example, women were goddesses of knowledge, justice and medicine. But I think that all patriarchal feudal capitalist religious traditional, modern and post-modern societies are pitted against women.

4 How are your books received in the Arab world, especially in your country Egypt? Are they taught in schools?
Men and women in Egypt and other Arab countries have

received my books very well since my first novel was published, in 1958 under the title: 'Memoir of a Woman Doctor'. The governments of Egypt did not allow my books to be taught in schools, but they were taught in schools in some Arab countries like Tunisia, Libya, Syria, Lebanon, Yemen, Sudan and others.

5 *Has the condition of women improved significantly (in terms of human rights) in your home land between the time you were a young woman and now you are much older?*
The condition of women in Egypt and Arab countries changed, and is changing to the better, every day, in spite of capitalist colonial global and local powers trying to exploit women and the poor.

6 *Do you still write fiction? What are the things that occupy your time these days?*
Yes I still write fiction. I am now writing my new novel. In fact I have been writing fiction and nonfiction since childhood. In my opinion, fiction and nonfiction (facts) are inseparable. Dreams, imagination, the subconscious, are all part of reality.

7 *How did Egypt, land of past powerful and liberated women – Queen Hatshepsut, Cleopatra, and numerous goddesses/ deities, including Isis – transform into a hostile space of gender inequality?*
If you read my play, *Isis*, you will see how the female goddesses of Egypt were conquered brutally by the new male patriarchal feudal gods. You know our great grandmother, Eve, the goddess of knowledge, she was transformed to the devil Satan.

8 *How do Egyptian feminists confront problems of unequal political representation, inequality in opportunities, protection under the law, and struggle for human rights in the global arena for all?*

Egyptian women are confronting all these problems by two weapons:
1 - Unveiling the mind of peoples by writing and speaking up.
2 - Organizing politically and fighting together glocally.

9 *In some societies in which there has been significant progress in women's education, health and social advancement, there is now a backlash against women, especially in the form of gender-based violence. What can we do to fight this backlash?*
To fight this backlash we need to fight together locally and globally, to liberate our minds and liberate countries from (local–global) oppressive regimes, and to expose the 'link' between these global and local governments; who have used, and are still using, political terrorist religious groups, to kill and oppress people, especially, women, youth and the poor.

10 *In* The Hidden Face of Eve *you write that the male authors you have read are unable to free themselves from the 'age-old image of women handed down to us from an ancient past, no matter how famous many of them have been for their passionate defence of human rights, human values and justice' (2015: 325). Is this still true today or do you think there are male authors who understand and write about women in a different way?*
There are progressive male writers in every country of course, and they are increasing in number, but the deep historical psychological heritage of slave–patriarchy, still exists, in the body–mind, of humans, men and women. There are capitalist racist religious women who are more patriarchal than men. You see them today climbing the political ladder in the West more than in the East.

11 *What is the role of African literary production in the global age?*

African literary production is invading the world, after the progress in translation, and spread of post-modern electronic communications.

12 Can you discuss the emergence of women as leading writers in the field of contemporary African literature?
African women writers are invading contemporary world literature and not only African literature.

13 On the occasion of the pronouncement of Fatwa on your person, how did you receive the news? Were you in Cairo? If yes, how did you get out of the country considering the fact that the Muslim Brotherhood would have made sure to act with immediacy. Also, when the case was ruled in your favour, you returned to Cairo, did you not fear for your life? Or were you under some kind of protection by the state?
I was never under the protection by the state in Egypt or any other state in the world. There were many Fatwas against me, since the era of Sadat–Mubarak till today. A few days ago, on TV channels in Egypt, some Islamic terrorists swore to kill me, to stone me to death in Tahrir Square. They have not been punished by the state.

Seven trials were raised against me and my daughter (Mona Helmy) in Egyptian courts in the last three decades. Her crime was a poem she wrote, defending the honour of Mother's name.

We attended all of the trials with courage. My daughter stood up in court and defended me and herself creatively. Many progressive lawyers supported us. I did not fear death, nor prison nor exile. In fact I was lucky to experience all these agonies. Pain helps creativity. My power came from confidence in myself, and also the support of people inside and outside Egypt helped me.

14 Your works have been banned by some Arab countries like your birth country, Egypt, and Saudi Arabia especially, as a result, you've got into trouble with the state on more than one occasion; do you feel that your messages have been misunderstood over the years by these countries?

These countries understood my message very well, that is why they banned my books, and helped fanatic Islamic political groups to attack me and my family. They knew that my ideas will unveil the mind of their people, and hence be aware of the corruption of their regimes, and be able to over throw them.

15 What are your motivations? And, do you feel that you have been able to effect changes in the way that things are done today as opposed to forty years back?

My main motivation is to write my mind regardless of consequences.

I have been able to effect changes in Egypt and in other countries reading my books in Arabic or other languages. I receive a lot of emails and messages from young women and men all over the world, I meet them wherever I go, hearing each one saying: your books changed my life.

This is my only real reward.

16 Did you ever marry for love?

Maybe once, the first one, when I was very young, I am not sure, but I am sure today that I never met my real love.

17 What role does religion play in politics in contemporary society?

Religion is politics. They are inseparable since the beginning of human history. They are never separated. They only change their mask or head cover, or their disguise.

18 What, if anything, has changed about your ideological out-look over the years you have been writing?

Nothing changed (of the essential), except, I am more sure that I wrote my own mind, since childhood till today.

19 Why do you sometimes portray weak solidarity amongst

Arab women, particularly in **Woman at Point Zero?**
I portray what I see in real life. Arab women, and women in the world in general, are learning how to work together, in spite of patriarchal interventions and obstructions.

20 Have you at any point felt that your feminist tendencies made you marry thrice?
I married three times just to make my children honourable and legal (in official papers) and secure their safety under a very oppressive patriarchal system.

The three husbands were relatively good progressive men, but they could not cope with me in challenging the corrupt regimes.

21 Apart from the female subjugation happening in your native Egyptian society, what else motivates you and inspires to write?
My love of writing, my pleasure in writing, is my inspiration and motivation to write, apart from the subjugation of women and the poor.

22 Your fiction has touched and changed lives of women across the globe not just in the Arab world. What do you consider your greatest legacy … what does Nawal El Saadawi want to ever be remembered for?
I want to be remembered for my love of creativity and truthfulness.

23 'Feminism' as a term and as a movement has different connotations within different cultures. And your works portray a very different picture of the predicament of women – women in the Arab world, where farming animals like 'buffaloes', as I can recall from my reading of **The Fall of the Imam,** *are in a better position than women and are valued more than a human; a community where a woman is asked to 'hide your shameful parts' (the face). How do you think Feminism as a theory should be introduced to students in India where women's plight is not as bad as the women in the Arab world but rape* *has become almost daily 'breaking news'; and women activists run around with placards carrying the message, 'Don't Teach Me What to Wear, Teach Your Son Not to Rape'?*

Feminism as a theory (or theories) should be introduced to students in India by creative thinkers and writers who live mainly in India and understand the Indian women's plight, which is not very different from the plight of women in Egypt or in USA or Europe or China or other, since we live in one world (not three) dominated by the same patriarchal capitalist imperialist colonial military racist system. Sexual rape is not separated from economic rape, and is a universal political problem, not just sexual.

24 The Oxford English Dictionary defines, 'rape' as 'the act of forcing a woman or girl to have sexual intercourse against her will'. So this act of forceful sexual intercourse in marriage should also be considered as 'rape'. But interestingly, many people seem to have a problem with the phrase 'marital rape'. Your comments on such an issue.

Marital rape is more serious than any other rape because it is veiled by love and divine law.

25 'Women's rights are human rights' indeed; but they are there only theoretically. How do you think this can be made a practical reality in future? Who do you think is responsible for this treatment of women where they are at times even denied the basic 'human rights' – culture, politicians, common mass or women themselves?

Human rights like many other modern slogans (such as peace, justice, freedom democracy … etc.) are only theoretical, under a very unjust global – local (glocal) political religious military capitalist imperialist system. Women's rights and all other people's rights cannot be a practical reality without changing the ruling system globally and locally. Women and men should unite and work together globally and locally, to change the political and educational system.

Featured Articles

Little Magazines & the Development of Modern African Poetry

MATHIAS IRORO ORHERO

INTRODUCTION

Only a few dedicated studies have been done on the roles played by little magazines in the development of modern African poetry. These studies often limit themselves to a particular phase or period. It is this lacuna in scholarship that this paper investigates by engaging with the roles played by little magazines in developing modern African poetry from its earliest inceptions until the contemporary period. The influences of these magazines are identified from their roles as propagandist mechanisms, as nursery beds for poets, as forums between poets and readers, as catalysts to poetic criticism and as manifestoes for literary traditions. Little magazines examined in this paper include *L'Etudiant Noir*, *Présence Africaine*, *Drum*, *Black Orpheus*, *Transition*, *Staffrider*, *Okike*, *Kwani?* and *New Contrast*. Findings show that little magazines are the nucleus with which African poetry gained consciousness and attained maturation. Modern African poets have developed their craft, expressed their ideologies and experimented with new forms on the pages of these little magazines. Some of these magazines also serve socio-political and propagandist functions. Recommendations are made for the continuance of the little magazine tradition in the invention of future African poetic traditions.

This paper engages the historical evolution of modern African poetry and the roles played by little magazines.

African literary historians, critics and scholars pay little attention to the roles of formative little magazines in the development of modern African poetry. This lacuna in scholarship has relegated the roles of little magazines in the creation of a literary canon and the development of poets. The historical evolution of modern African poetry is examined with the view to emphasizing the place and importance of little magazines. Questions that the paper attempts to answer include: what roles have little magazines played in the development of modern African poetry? How have little magazines influenced African poetic traditions? What are little magazines doing now to promote the development of modern African poetry? These questions are answered with deep historical readings of modern African poetic history. This paper focuses on the poets and the magazines rather than the individual poems, and it presents a diachronic overview of African poetic history and the influences of little magazines from the colonial, through the post-colonial to the contemporary period. Attempts are made to cover the various regions of Africa.

Various definitions of little magazines have been given by scholars over the years. These definitions usually examine one or more forms of the tabloid that falls under the concept of little magazines. Suzanne Churchill defines the little magazine as 'non-commercial enterprises founded by individuals or small groups intent upon publishing experimental works or radical opinions of untried, un-popular, or under-represented writers' (*The Little Magazine Others and the Renovation of Modern American Poetry*: 8). Churchill's emphasis is on the fact that little magazines are non-commercial. This foregrounds the idea that little magazines do not charge writers for publication since they are not concerned with making profit. Churchill further asserts that the word 'little' refers to the audience size, which is usually small, rather than the magazine's size, budget, lifespan or significance (9).

Louise Kane conceives of the little magazine as 'a small-scale sort of publication whose pre-occupation with presenting good materials puts it in opposition to the commercial presses and publishing houses which will not publish a writer until they have become established. They are places of experiment and high-minded ideals and aims' ('The Little Magazine as Interdisciplinary Space': 2). Kane's conception emphasizes experimentation as one of the features of the little magazine as ideal avenues where avant-garde writers test their craft. Little magazines are always 'on the edge of something, furthering a cause or a certain set of aims ... having some sort of social or political function' (3). Kane's view is supported by Adam Augustyn who believes that a little magazine usually publishes works that are 'unconventional or experimental in form; or ... violates one of several popular notions of moral, social, or aesthetic behaviour' (*American Literature from the 1850s to 1945*: 104).

On the content of little magazines, Rahad Abir asserts that little magazines publish 'reviews, essays, fiction or poetry or more usually some combination of them' ('A Tale of Little Magazines'). Abir's position holds water for most little magazines that are solely devoted to the publication of creative works, especially poetry and short stories.

It is important to note that not all little magazines are traditional 'magazines'. The concept of little magazines has come to cover a wide variety of publications such as journals, periodicals and newspapers. Any form of the tabloid that publishes creative works, reviews and essays can take the appellation 'little magazine' or 'literary magazine'. The latter is another phrase that means the same thing as the former. The reason why other non-magazine media take this name can be traced to the historical evolution of little magazines. In this vein, Sue Waterman asserts:

> Literary journals evolved quite literally from the pages of newspapers in the 17th century, themselves a relatively

new genre, where advertisements for new publications were printed. From this initial role of announcers of new books, journals quickly took on that of providing excerpts for a growing reading public. Literary journals, which proliferated in the 18th century and became ubiquitous in the 19th, then began to review new works, giving their growing readership a means to judge and choose from an ever increasing availability of printed books. ('Literary Journals': 1)

Waterman's position is that little magazines, also called literary journals, owe their existence to newspapers which served as avenues for new works to be announced and for reviews. This early usage of newspapers must have warranted the inclusion of the newspaper medium in the broad concept of little magazines. Waterman lists some of these early newspapers, and they include *Les Journal des Scavans* (1665), *Spectator* (1711-14) and *Tatler* (1709-11). Other early little magazines include *Nouvelles de la Republique des Lettres* (1684), *North American Review, The Granta* (1889), *The Sewanee Review* (1892), *Poetry* (1912), *The Dial, The Masses, The Little Review* (1967-1977) and *Blackwoods* (1817-1890).

From the preceding, it is obvious that little magazines have been around for quite some time. These early little magazines have influenced the literary traditions in their various nations and continents. Their growths have been phenomenal, and their successes are striking. Little magazines have evolved to cover traditional magazines, newspapers, journals, periodicals and other tabloid forms that publish new and experimental writers.

MODERN AFRICAN POETRY

Modern African poetry is not an easy concept to define due to the peculiar nature of African literature. Various scholars have attempted to define and unveil the canons of modern African poetry. One such attempt is taken by Oniyitan Johnson who avers:

> Poetry is by no means a recent import into Africa from Europe. It is an important and living part of African culture, going back into the distant past in nearly all African societies there has been (and still in many places) a thriving oral tradition of poetry. Poetry and song are basic human … expression to accompany the activities of daily life, to give utterance to their joy and sorrow, to comment on life or simply to entertain. ('Understanding African Poetry at a Glance')

Johnson's view is anchored on the idea that poetry is not new to Africa. He attempts to show that Africans have had a thriving oral tradition of poetry before the advent of colonialism and Western education. Examples of these oral poetic traditions in Africa abound: examples include the *Udje* song-poetry tradition of the Urhobo people which has been documented and studied by J.P. Clark, Gabriel Darah and Tanure Ojaide, and the *Ijala* hunters' song of the Yoruba people which has attracted ample scholarship, among numerous others.

Kenneth Goodwin attempts to mark the beginning of modern African poetry, as opposed to African oral poetry, when he asserts:

> The first significant stage in the formation of contemporary African poetry in English was … emancipation from nineteenth-century cultural imperialism and the voluntary adoption of a foreign, but international twentieth-century style. It was a style comparable in many ways with that of the African Francophone poets … The adoption of the Anglophone African poets of an international style was due to their tertiary education. (*Understanding African Poetry*: ix)

Goodwin believes that modern African poetry owes its origins to the general twentieth-century literary conventions to which the earliest African poets were exposed in their tertiary education. This marked the beginning of a written tradition of poetry in Africa.

Romanus Egudu underscores African poetry as 'intimately concerned with the African people in the African society with their life in its various ramifications cultural, social, economic, intellectual and political' (*Modern African Poetry and the African Predicament*: 5). This postulation is an attempt to show the distinctively African nature of modern African poetry. In response to Egudu, Oyeniyi Okunoye posits that 'ironically, Egudu underscores the variety of experiences articulated in African poetry without drawing attention to its implication for the continued validity of an African poetic tradition. This unproblematic reading of African poetry betrays the weakness of pioneering scholarship' ('Captives of Empire: Early Ibadan Poets and Poetry': 771). Okunoye stands upon polemical grounds with Egudu's position. He attempts at defining African poetry thus:

> Modern African poetry, very much like other postcolonial literary practices, is defined in relation to European literary traditions which provide the paradigms, conventions and critical principles that are either appropriated or negated in the process of defining the identity of the newer literatures. ('The Critical Reception of Modern African Poetry', para. 2)

Okunoye's view rests largely upon post-colonial discourse which interprets poetic tradition as an appendage to that of a colonial power, such as Britain. In this light, modern African poetry is an appendage of European literary tradition and must be judged using European standards. Tanure Ojaide differs from Okunoye's standpoint in his attempt to define modern African poetry:

> Modern African poetic aesthetics are unique in possessing a repertory of authentic African features. This authenticity manifests itself in the use of concrete images derived from the fauna and flora, proverbs, indigenous rhythms, verbal tropes and concepts of space and time to establish a poetic form ... In fact, an authentic African world forms the backdrop of

modern African poetry. (*Poetic Imagination in Black Africa: Essays on African Poetry*: 104)

Ojaide's position is anchored on African aesthetics. That is, those peculiar stylistic and thematic features that mark off modern African poetry from European traditions. These aesthetics are mainly drawn from African oral lore.

On the periodization of modern African poetry, Sule Egya believes that modern African poetry can be divided into 'the pre-independence nationalist era', 'the roaring 1960s' and 'protest poetry' which he also dubs 'the Osundare generation' ('Power, Artistic Agency, and Poetic Discourse': 61-63). Charles Bodunde divides modern African poetry into 'the pioneer period' and 'the modern African period' ('Poetry in the Newspaper': 271-2). However, Egya and Bodunde's views have not addressed some salient issues in the canonization of modern African poetry. For example, their views have not been able to show the stylistic peculiarities of each phase. Friday Okon's attempt at the periodization of modern African poetry puts politics as the driving force. Okon divides modern African poetry into 'The Pioneers (Pre-Independence Echoes)' ('Politics and the Development of Modern African Poetry': 95), 'The Nationalist Struggle' (98), 'The Negritude Phase' (98) and 'The Post-Independence Period' (100) which he divides further into 'the older generation' (101) and 'the younger generation' (102). He also identifies the contemporary period as that of 'recent echoes' (107). Okon's categorization is peculiar because it covers a wide range of poetic traditions in Africa.

The preceding section has attempted a conceptualization of modern African poetry. The defining features of modern African poetry have been underscored, and the canons have also been outlined. In all, modern African poetry can simply be seen as a body of poetic works written by Africans, for the African audience and which handles the African experience using African aesthetics.

LITTLE MAGAZINES & THE DEVELOPMENT OF COLONIAL AFRICAN POETRY

African poetry, before the advent of colonialism, was essentially an oral form of art. It was not until the advent of tabloid poetry that African poetry got its modern manifestation, reception and widespread production. This was mainly due to the influence of little magazines. These magazines were published when the printing press was introduced into Africa. In the period before 1920, much poetry had not been written down, and little magazines were few. By the 1920s, modern African poetry had taken a new stand. The newspapers and new little magazines became a fertile ground for the publication of poetry. Southern African vernacular little magazines such as *Izwi, Labantu, Imvo Zabantsundu, The Xhosa Messenger* and *Isigdimi Sama-Xosa* became veritable mediums for poetic publication. These works thematized African culture and experience and were directed towards the African audience. Writers such as H.I.E. Dhlomo, R.R.R. Dhlomo, Josiah Mapumulo, Jordan Ngubane, Benedict Vilakazi and Emman H.A. Made, featured on the pages of these tabloids.

It was the proliferation of newspapers in the 1920s that led to a culture of literacy as well as literary awareness. With the construction of secondary/high schools and universities across the continent, a growing class of literates sprung up and the newspapers were used to instil nationalism in the people. Some of the newspapers include *The Anglo-African, The Lagos Observer, Lagos Standard* and *Lagos Weekly Record. The Nigerian Magazine,* asserts Gabriel Darah, was 'among the publishing institutions that nurtured and preserved Nigeria's creative literature, the greatest, perhaps' ('Literary Development in Nigeria': 1). This magazine was established in 1927, and it released 'Literary Supplement' which helped in the development of a truly Nigerian literary productivity in which poetry was much more favoured. Nationalist poets such as Dennis

Osadebey, R.E.G. Armattoe, Michael Dei-Anang and Casely Hayford used these early newspapers as vehicles for propagandist poetry.

Modern African poetry attained the peak of its genesis in the 1930s. This peak is reflected in the rebirth of black culture and ideals which is dubbed as Negritude. This term was coined by Aimé Césaire (Bruce King and Kolawole Ogungbesan *A Celebration of Black and African Writing*: xi). The birth of Negritude in modern African poetry was largely the work of Léopold Sédar Senghor, Aimé Césaire and Léon Damas. The concept of Negritude, its philosophy and ideals as well as its thematic thrusts, were all propagated through the medium of little magazines. The little magazine that influenced the birth of Negritude was *L'Etudiant Noir* (1935). According to Sunny Awhefeada, 'the magazine was influential in establishing the concept of Negritude which projected the dignity of the black man and his cultural values' ('Africa: Development of Modern African Poetry'). He further contends that the journal had a bias for political poetry and 'gave cultural and intellectual support to the independence movement of the fifties'. Although *L'Etudiant Noir* did not last for long, its influence cut across borders. The magazine's aim of propaganda was achieved, and it provided the foundation for Léopold Sédar Senghor, a poet whose name is almost synonymous with early Francophone African poetry. Speaking on the manifesto of *L'Etudiant Noir*, Lilyan Kesteloot, asserts that '*L'Etudiant Noir* is a little journal, without pretence, that propagated the problems which troubled them. It has permitted them to notice that these questions interest the entire black race' (*Anthologie Negro-Africaine*: 90).

The period between 1940 and 1960 is unique in modern African poetry. This period marks the rise of Anglophone African poetry as well as the maturation of Negritude in Francophone African countries. Many African literary historians date the beginning of modern African poetry to the 1940s. The attention that this period gets is largely due to the ample little magazines that were in vogue at the time. African poets, imitating the little magazine tradition of Modernist and African-American poets, set up their little magazines. Many of them were organized by student clubs and societies while others were published by individuals, groups or publishing houses.

In 1947, Alioune Diop founded a new little magazine titled *Présence Africaine*. This magazine was an offshoot of *L'Etudiant Noir,* and it was one of the strongest media for the Negritude propaganda. Awhefeada comments on this magazine that 'apart from its pre-occupation with socio-cultural and political didactics, [it] also took literary productions, especially poetry, and its criticism into fold. A large amount of the early poetry that came out of Africa first appeared in various editions of *Présence Africaine*'. The poets behind the workings of this little magazine include Paul Niger and Guy Tirolien of Guadeloupe, Bernard Dadié of Ivory Coast, Apithy and Behazin from Dahomey and Rabe Mananjera from Madagascar. The journal's manifesto, as captured in the first edition, was written by Alioune Diop thus:

> The idea was born in 1942–1943. In Paris, we were a number of students from overseas who – in the midst of the suffrage in Europe that was questioning its essence and authenticity of values – assembled to study the situation and the characters with respect to what defined ourselves. ('Opening Address': i)

The likes of Birago Diop, David Diop, Léopold Sédar Senghor, Bernard Dadié and almost all the Negritude poets, used this little magazine as a melting pot of their thoughts. The usefulness of *Présence Africaine* in establishing African poetry is made obvious through its publication of poems that deal with the African and black identity and experience both at the homeland and in the Diaspora. This little magazine also influenced the rise of other such Anglophone magazines at the time.

In Senegal, the little magazine *Bingo* was launched in 1953, and it echoed the Negritude tendencies of the emergent poetic tradition. Poets like David Diop, Birago Diop and Bernard Dadié have appeared within its pages. Awhefeada posits that 'the appearance of local sources of publications helped to create a more direct sense of community between the poets and their readers'. This position gives credence to the function of little magazines in fostering the poet-reader relationship by bringing the poets to the readers and the readers to the poets.

In South Africa, *Drum*, a little magazine, was making waves. Its influence on South African poetry was so much that literary historians do not hesitate to call the poets of the 1950s as 'the *Drum* generation'. It was first published in 1951 and continued uninterruptedly for 12 years. David Rabkin submits that 'in that time it gathered about it a group of writers and journalists who were largely responsible for black literature in South Africa' ('Drum Magazine (1951-1961)': 1). This submission shows the immensity of its influence in establishing South African poetry. Lewis Nkosi avers that the little magazine, *Drum*, 'seemed to be the place to be in for any young man trying to write' ('Apartheid: A Daily Exercise in the Absurd': 6). Such articles are concerned with the influence of this little magazine in fashioning the poetic output at the time. The magazine was a place of foundation for the young poets who wanted to air their voice. *Drum* was a magazine of protest: protest against white superiority and apartheid. It was a child of propaganda and history. It was also a cultural production of black South Africa. *Drum* had such imitators as *Zonk!* and *Bona* (1956) but none had the widespread literary acceptance of *Drum*. Some of the poets produced by this little magazine include Can Themba, Casey Motsisi, Bloke Modisane, Lewis Nkosi, Ezekiel Mphalele, Alex La Guma, James Matthew, Peter Clarke and Richard Rive. The greatest of them all was Lewis Nkosi.

In West Africa, this period marked the rise of the first generation of Anglophone poets. Many of these poets were college students and some even started writing from high school. The most veritable means of airing their voice was through the medium of little magazines. Many of them wrote at the time, but only a few did much in creating a unique modern African poetic tradition. Some of the high school students' little magazines include *The Umuahian*, a publication of the Umuahia Government College where Chinua Achebe studied and wrote his early poetry; *The Mermaid*, a little magazine by Kings College in Lagos; *The Interpreter* which was published by Aggrey Memorial College in Arochukwu; and *The Pathfinder*. Many of these high school little magazines doubled as almanacks and yearbooks, and short, witty poems were usually published in them.

The first students were admitted to University College, Ibadan, Nigeria, in 1948, and the development of Anglophone African poetry can be traced to this institution. Many of the well-known West African poets of the first generation attained literary maturation in the little magazines published at Ibadan. Starting with *The University Herald*, other little magazines started to rise in what culminated as an Anglophone little magazine renaissance. The titles include *The Beacon*, *The Horn*, *Aro*, *Catholic Undergraduate*, *The Bug*, *The Eagle*, *The Criterion*, *The Rag*, *The Scorpion*, *The Wasp*, *Tear Gas*, *Leepsteeck*, *Blow*, *The University Voice*, *Oke'Badan*, *The Abadina Unibadan*, *Horizon*, *The Sword* and *The Weekly*. The little magazine renaissance quickly spread to other schools such as the Nigerian College of Technology in Enugu where little magazines such as *Fresh Buds* produced a notable poet, Okogbule Nwanodi. This trend later spread to the University of Nigeria, Nsukka and to a host of others.

The greatest little magazines that influenced this period and its poetic output were *Black Orpheus* and *The Horn*. These little magazines published not only Nigerian poets but also the works of young poets from other African countries. *Black Orpheus* was first published in 1957 to a very professional standard and intended for a general readership. The title itself is based on an essay by Jean-Paul Sartre titled 'Orphée Noir'. *Black Orpheus* was created to cultivate Anglophone African poetry in the same way that *L'Etudiant Noir* and *Présence Africaine* had for Francophone African poetry. Ulli Beier, the founding editor, lamented the fact that African students of poetry had no indigenous works to look to and so *Black Orpheus* was created to foster and promote creativity from young writers. In the pages of this little magazine, criticisms were also published. Beier, formulating a manifesto for this tradition, asserts that the purpose of this little magazine was 'to make people feel they were not alone, even if they were writing in a part of Africa where there were no writers of their own calibre' ('The Conflict of Cultures in West African Poetry': 17). Beier further comments that the purpose of the magazine 'was to sell African literature abroad'. Most of the first-generation Anglophone African poets had their poems published within the pages of this magazine. Janheinz Jahn and Ulli Beier published criticisms on Negritude poetry and the new emergent poetry. The poems of Wole Soyinka, John Pepper Clark, Christopher Okigbo, Ezekiel Mphalele, Dennis Brutus, Léopold Sédar Senghor, Lenrie Peters, Vincent Kofi, Ibrahim Salahi and so many others, were featured in the pages of *Black Orpheus*. This little magazine can be regarded as a major catalyst for the development of early African poetry. The magazine bridged the gap between Francophone and Anglophone African poetry. Awhefeada argues that 'the various conferences on African arts ... and the introduction of African literature into the curriculum of African universities and schools, all owe much to *Black Orpheus*'. It did not just play the role of propaganda and experimentation but also of consolidation and formulation. It is the single most important phenomenon in early modern African poetry. The experimentation with Euromodernist tendencies as African poets fashioned their unique identities was also facilitated by *Black Orpheus*.

If *Black Orpheus* developed early Anglophone African poetry, it was *The Horn* that developed early Nigerian poetry. *The Horn* was established through the influence of Martin Banham, and it had J.P. Clark as its founding editor. Banham's idea was born out of the desire to replicate what obtained at Leeds University where he graduated. In 1957, the first issue appeared when J.P. Clark set up a committee of three which included Higo Aigboje and John Ekwere. Some of its earliest editors include Abiola Irele, Dapo Adelugba, Omolara Ogundipe and Onyema Ihema. *The Horn* published poets who would later turn out to be some of Africa's most well-known poets. On the pages of *The Horn* can be found the experimental tendencies of Africa's first-generation writers; the Hopkinsian syntax of Christopher Okigbo in his 'Idoto', the grandiloquism of Wole Soyinka, the allusiveness of Gabriel Okara, the imagism of J.P. Clark, the linguistic experimentations of M.J.C. Echeruo, and a host of others. This little magazine proved itself to be a fertile ground for new and experimental poets as they fashioned a unique literary identity. Some of the other poets that were nurtured in *The Horn* include Mabel Segun, Okugbole Nwanodi, Frank Aig-Imoukhuede, Mac Akpoyoware, Pius Oleghe, Bridget Akwada, Nelson Olawaiye, Glory Nwanodi, Gordon Umukoro, Yetunde Esan, Ralph Opara and Minji Karibo.

Without *Black Orpheus* and *The Horn*, African poetry may not have attained the heights it has today. The founders of these little magazines saw their utility and actively used them. The European expatriates in various African universities took cues from Modernist and African-American little magazines and invented a modern African poetic tradition through these little magazines. It is its diverse functions that earned *Black Orpheus* the title 'the doyen of African literary magazines' (Wollaeger and Eatough *Oxford Handbook of Global Modernisms*: 280). Meanwhile, in southern Africa, other magazines soon sprang up from the universities and beyond. Some of them include *The Purple Renoster* (1956) and *Contrast* (1960). There was also the *African Affairs Journal* which was devoted to African studies and oral literature. It was within the pages of this journal that Solomon Babalola published translations of 'Ijala' (Yoruba hunters' verse). This little magazine was used to propagate African oral poetry and incite the emergent poets to make recourse to orature.

One of the culminating effects of the little magazine phenomenon in West Africa was the publication of an anthology of Anglophone African poets with the title *Nigerian Student Verse* (1960). This anthology was published by Martin Banham with cues drawn from Olumbe Bassir's *An Anthology of West African Verse* (1957). Some of the poets, first published with little magazines, went on to publish their anthologies and poetry collections, such as Okigbo's *Heavensgate* (1962), *Limits* (1964), and Clark's *Poems* (1961).

The preceding section has examined the roles of little magazines in developing modern African poetry in the colonial period. Some of these little magazines and their contributors have been documented, and it has been ascertained that pre-independence African poetry owes much to such magazines as *L'Etudiant Noir*, *Présence Africaine*, *Black Orpheus*, *Drum* and *The Horn*. The poets that pioneered African poetry all experimented and attained maturation with these little magazines.

LITTLE MAGAZINES AND THE DEVELOPMENT OF POST-COLONIAL AFRICAN POETRY

The year 1960 was when many African countries attained political independence. Because of this, some African literary historians delineate the period after 1960 as the post-colonial or post-independence period. Post-colonial African poetry was informed by the historical consequences of independence and the creation of national identities. African poets had to distance themselves from Western tendencies and establish a unique voice. The poetry of this period was intimated by history; from the pessimism of the remaining years of the first decade after independence, to the bloody civil wars in some countries in Africa and then to the rise of Marxism, socialism and critical realism in the continent and finally to more ailing concerns such as corruption, environmental degradation, global affairs and other contemporary issues.

By 1960, several universities in Africa had already attained maturation, and indigenous poetry had been added to the curriculum. New universities such as the University of Nigeria at Nsukka, Ahmadu Bello University at Zaria, University of Lagos and Obafemi Awolowo University (then University of Ife) at Ile-Ife, were built and approved. Other universities were built in the 1970s and 1980s. These new universities adopted many of the student literary traditions from University College, Ibadan, Makerere University, Uganda and University of Witwatersrand in South Africa. The poets of this period took cues from the little magazines that proliferated in the last decade. At the University of Nigeria, *Pioneer* was first published in 1961 and was quickly followed by *The Muse* in 1963. *The Muse* was a publication of the English Students Association, and it acted as a catalyst for poetic production at Nsukka. It was on the pages of this tabloid that poets such as Pol Ndu, Okogbule Nwonodi, Bona Onyejeli, Uche Okeke, Sam Nwajioba and Romanus Egudu were produced. This magazine was a brainchild of Peter Thomas who took his cue from the Ibadan experiment by Banham and Beier. This little magazine was the foundation for a later class of writers who discovered and distanced themselves from Eurocentric tendencies and started to fashion a new and distinctively African poetry.

At the University of Ibadan, *The Horn*, now defunct, was soon replaced by *Idoto* and it continued to serve its function as a cultivation plot for the new writers at the University of Ibadan. At the University of Nigeria, *Fresh Buds,* now defunct, was replaced by *Omabe.* At the then newly created University of Ife, some little magazines were published to nurture creative talents. Some of them include *Ijala, Sokoti* and *Ife Writing* and tried to replicate the success of *The Horn* and *Black Orpheus.*

In South Africa, the influence of its quintessential literary magazine, *Drum*, was to lead to the proliferation of little magazines at the universities as well as outside the university walls. By the 1960s, the voices of the *Drum* generation had started to create a culture and tradition of protest poetry known as 'apartheid poetry'. The racial divide and prejudice of the South African white supremacists was known as apartheid. Both black and white poets expressed their anger against this system, and the little magazines were used as veritable means of propaganda. These magazines, which had widespread acceptance and readership in major cities and universities, heralded the finest of protest poetry ever to come from Africa. In 1965, *Unisa English Studies* was published at the University of South Africa.

Another South African little magazine, *The Classic,* was published in 1963 with Nat Nakasa as its founding editor. This little magazine, modelled after *Drum*, was created with the intention of seeking 'African writing of merit' (Nakasa 'Writing in South Africa': 4). This magazine published the early poems of Can Themba, Lewis Nkosi, Richard Rive, Leslie Sehume, Julian Beinhart, Ezekiel Mphalele, Andrew Motjuoadi, J.M. Brander and Casey Motsisi. As the little magazine evolved into a richer and more cultural production, the poems of Dugmore Boetie, Chris Macgregor, Finn Phetoe, Bill Ainslie, Wole Soyinka, David Rubadiri and Joseph Kariuki were published on its pages.

Most of these poems echo protest against apartheid while others were simply centred upon cultural consciousness. The earliest poems of Oswald Mtshali, Njabulo Ndebele, Mongane Serote and Mafika Gwala were published. This little magazine, thus, foreshadowed the new generation of poets in the South African literary space. Worthy of note also is the South African little magazine – *Contrast* – which was first published in 1960 by Jack Cope. This short-lived little magazine published both white and black South African poets. An anthology of South African poetry was published in 1967 with the title *South African Writing Today*, and the poems were drawn from little magazines.

In eastern Africa, the harsh and brutal colonial experience which was opposed by guerrilla forces paved the way for a protest tradition of poetry. At Makerere University, the little magazine, *Penpoint*, was already inventing a tradition. Poets such as Jonathan Kariara, John Nagenda, Pio Zirimu and David Rubadiri were incubated to poetic maturation in the 1960s as a result of the influence of this little magazine. *Makerere Beat* was another little magazine that was published in the Idi Amin era as a protest publication for students and new writers. At the University of Nairobi, there was *Mwangazawa Fasihi* and *Mzalendo* which published political and Marxist-oriented poems that attacked neo-colonialism. Jared Angira published his satirical poems in these little magazines. Other poets published in them include Peter Nazareth, Bahadur Tejani, Tilak Banerjee, Sadru Somji, Adolf Mascarenhas, Yusuf Kassam, Sadru Kassam and Mohamed Virjee.

The little magazine that influenced eastern African poetry of the 1960s most was *Transition*. This magazine was first published in Uganda in 1961 by Rajat Neogy. According to King and Ogungbesan, this magazine 'was more politically and intellectually oriented than the Nigerian *Black Orpheus*' (xviii). This assertion foregrounds the fact that this magazine was transcultural and pan-African. It was a formidable catalyst to African poetic output in the 1960s. *Transition* started off by publishing the works of local writers based upon Rajat Neogy's original vision to search for and encourage writers within eastern Africa. In the later part of the first decade after independence, *Transition* started to publish the works of other African poets, including Okot P'Bitek, Taban Lo Liyong, Grace Ogot, Wole Soyinka, Christopher Okigbo, Cameron Duodo, Ama Ata Aidoo, Dennis Brutus and David Rubadiri. This expansion of range took *Transition* from the eastern African poetic space to a pan-African poetic tradition. It was a magazine that actively sought, encouraged and published works that mirrored the African experience and culture. It was important in African writers' return to oral traditions as a means of creating a wholly African literary identity. Akin Adesokan posits that the little magazine, *Transition*, 'became the battlefield for such questions as African Socialism, Pan-Africanism, the status of ethnic and racial minorities, political partisanship as against free speech and literary "universalism"' (53). The influence of *Transition* in developing African poetry of the 1960s cannot be overstated. The coming-to-age of modern African poetry owes much to the influence of this little magazine. Other little magazines that played pivotal roles in developing eastern African poetry include *Nexus* (which was Mphalele's creation), *Busara Kenya Twendapi? Cheche Kenya, Coup Broadcast, Zuka, Darlite, Ghala, East African Journal* and *Juliso*. These little magazines were largely responsible for eastern African poetry in the 1960s.

By the 1970s, with new universities already established in Africa, the African poetry curriculum had been developed enough to include poets of the 1950s and 1960s. Most of these poets turned out to be the teachers of this new generation of poets. In West Africa, the Nigerian Civil War ended in 1970, and the end brought with it a new class of poetry that was different from the older generation. The poets of this period have been described as belonging to the 'Alter/Native tradition' (Aiyejina 'Recent Nigerian

Poetry in English': 112). Their poetry was marked by a return to orature as well as recourse to socialist and critical realism. Many little magazines proliferated at the time and these new poets vented their anger and pain on their pages. At the University of Nigeria, new little magazines such as *Nsukkascope*, the brainchild of Chinua Achebe, were founded in the 1970s. At the same time, *Okike* (1971) was also launched. On the influence of *Okike*, Lindfors asserts that it is 'Africa's finest extant literary journal' ('African Little Magazines': 87). This little magazine published poetry and its criticism and became a mouthpiece for several poets within and outside Nigeria. The influence of *Okike* can be seen by the sheer strength of poetic voices from eastern Nigeria – the likes of J.O.J. Nwachukwu Agbada, Catherine Acholonu, Obiora Udechukwu, Ossie Enekwe, Dubem Okafor and the others whom Aiyejina and Okunoye call 'the Nsukka poets'. As *Okike* expanded, its influences gradually spread to cover poetic output from other regions as well. The poetry of Niyi Osundare, Odia Ofeimun, Remi Raji, Femi Fatoba, and a host of other writers of the 1970s and 1980s, were all published in *Okike*.

With the establishment of Universities in Nigerian cities such as Maiduguri, Benin, Port Harcourt, Calabar, Sokoto, Jos and Ilorin, and in other places across the African continent, new student little magazines were inaugurated in other countries to cater for the poetic expressions of the new poets. This period also marked the beginning of modern newspaper poetry. At the University of Benin, *Oyiya* was launched by the creative writers' workshop alongside *Akpata*. The influence of Benin little magazines can be seen in the calibre of poets it has produced. Among these poets are the likes of Esiri Dafiewhare, Sonnie Adagboyin, Ogaga Ifowodo, Godwin Uyi Ojo, Ezenwa Ohaeto and Maik Nwosu. In Ghana, the little magazine *Okyeame* was already making waves.

Okyeame was first published in 1961, but it took on a radical shift in tendencies in the early 1970s. This little magazine was the nursery bed for poets like Kofi Awoonor, Kwesi Brew and Kofi Anyidoho. At the University of Sierra Leone, poetic output was encouraged by the publication of *African Literature Today* as a journal of criticism and review. Other journals that facilitated poetic output in Africa at the time include *Fourah Bay Studies in Language and Literature, Calabar Studies in Modern Languages, Lagos Review of English Studies, Cameroon Studies in English and French, NJALA, Ibadan Journal of Humanistic Studies, Nigerian Journal of the Humanities, Ife Studies in African Literature and the Arts, Ife Monographs on Literature and Criticism, Opon Ifa, Nsukka Studies in African Literature, Working Papers in African Literature, Work in Progress, Saiwa, Afa, Nka, Kiabara, Ganga, Gwani, Hekima, Marang, Pula, Ngoma, Ngam, Mould, New Horizons, Nigerian Theatre Journal* and many others. The importance of these journals is that they signified the mainstay of critical and meta-critical engagements in modern African poetry. This, in turn, raised the demand for more poetic outputs.

The eastern African poetic scene of the 1970s was not very different from what obtained in the 1960s. New little magazines such as *Umma* (1970) and *Dhana* (1971) were published. Others such as *Mawazo, Taamuli, East African Journal, Drum, Trust, True Love, Flamingo, Baraza, Afrika ya Kesho, Africa Nyota, Lengo, Target, Ukulima wa Kisasa, Uhuru* and *Musizi* published more populist poetry. The influence of *Transition* became even more pronounced as it changed its name to *Chindaba*. With this change, it became even more cultural than ever and served its purpose of pan-Africanism. At one time, in the 1970s, Wole Soyinka was its Chief Editor.

In southern Africa, some of the older little magazines of the 1960s forged on in the 1970s. Some of them, like *Contrast* (1960), continued with their original philosophy and produced new poets. Other little magazines by students and non-students were launched. At the University of Malawi, there was *The Muse* which was founded by Ken Lipenga and other undergraduate students. This little magazine produced some of the greatest Malawian poets such as Felix Mnthali, Jack Mapanje, Steve Chimombo, Frank Chipasula, Paul Zelaza and Ken Lipenga. Other Malawian little magazines that served similar functions include *Odi*, *Umodzi*, *Denga*, *Outlook* and *Kalulu* – which was devoted to translating oral poetry. In South Africa, *Snarl* and *Staffrider* were inaugurated in 1978 and both little magazines were largely responsible for English South African poetry as well revitalizing the spirit of racial co-operation. The works of both white and black poets were published, and focus was given to establishing literary conformity and a canon between white and black South African poets. *Staffrider* was a little magazine that was largely responsible for most of the contemporary South African poets. The first editorial had asserted that its primary objective was to provide a platform for the great surge of creative activity at the time. The same editorial goes forward to assert that the new writing of South Africa which it published has 'altered the scope and function of literature in South Africa in ways we are still to discover' (quoted in Oliphant and Vladislavić *Ten Years of Staffrider*: i). *Staffrider* provided a forum for the black and white South African audience to meet on equal grounds. Some of its poets include Michael Siluma, Joel Matlou, Bheki Maseko, J.M. Coetzee, Njabulo Ndebele, Peter Randall and a host of others. *Staffrider* marked the decline of protest poetry to a more liberal poetic content. One of the influences of the little magazines in South Africa in the 1970s is the relaxed tension between the whites and blacks. South African poetry started to gain a unification of traditions (white and black) as a result of these little magazines.

By the year 1980, modern African poetry had enlarged as a corpus with which scholars had already started to engage in the phases of African poetic evolution. The period between 1980 and 2000 marked the rise of new trends in African poetry. The poets became even more socially concerned with the conditions of the time, and they did this through Marxist lenses, but as the years went by, Marxist ideals met a decline. Many African countries had military heads of state while others had civilian dictators. The agitations for democracy were commonplace. By the early 1990s, all African countries had gained independence and apartheid was abolished in South Africa. The poetic space in Africa witnessed the rise of more socially and politically oriented works. The Marxist doctrines of the 1970s were gradually paving the way for a calmer and less revolutionary type of poetry. The poets were much less concerned with proletariat revolution. Their poems advocated against corruption which was commonplace in Africa. New trends such as ecological poetry, feminist poetry, Niger-Delta poetry, the free Mandela campaign, among others, came into vogue. The little magazines continued to play their roles as catalysts for poetic outbursts. They played roles that bordered on avant-gardism and it was due to their influence that the heralding of a more vibrant and younger generation of poets arose.

In West Africa, new little magazines were published in the universities. The poets that now occupy the contemporary space of African poetry were mostly students at the time in some of these universities. The little magazines became a medium to cultivate their skills. At the University of Lagos, the little magazine, *Iju Omi,* was launched in 1984. Assessing the functions of this little magazine, Awhefeada asserts that on *Iju Omi*'s pages, 'aspiring poets have also tested their powers'. This little magazine produced Hope Eghagha, one of the most formidable poets in the contemporary scene who, in 1984, was studying for his M.A. at the University of Lagos. At the then Bendel State University (now Ambrose Alli University), there was *Ivie* which was first published in 1991 by the Poetry Club. This little magazine was a starting point for Charles Omoife, a poet who is getting more critical attention. At the University of Port Harcourt, there was *Ofirima.* At

Ahmadu Bello University, there was *Kuka, Saiwa* and *Work in Progress*. At Delta State University, Abraka, there was *Abraka Voices*, which published poets such as Ebi Yeibo. These little magazines were the catalysts of Nigeria's status as the hotspot of African poetry in the 1980s and '90s.

Apart from the proliferation of these magazines, the newspapers also played pivotal roles in developing the African poetry of this period. *The Guardian* in Nigeria, in particular, was quite sympathetic to poetry. *The Guardian* gave a column to Niyi Osundare, one of Africa's most prolific poets. This column was titled 'Songs of the Season'. Osundare used this column to publish some of his earliest poems. Through the pioneer editorship of Femi Osofisan, 'The Guardian Literary Series' was floated, and it catered to the needs of the new poets for a place to air their voices. Some of the poets who published within the pages of the newspapers include Niyi Osundare, Femi Osofisan, Odia Ofeimun, George Asinaba, Ogaga Ifowodo, David Nwamadi, Afam Akeh, Tanure Ojaide, Esiaba Irobi, Balami Shaffa and Funso Aiyejina. In this vein, the *Daily Times* Newspaper also helped with its 'Poet's Corner'.

In Cameroon, the University of Yaoundé was creating its poets through such student little magazines as *Abbia, New Horizon, Ngam, Syllabus* and *Mould*. Some of the poets that these magazines produced were concerned more with the society than earlier Cameroonian poets. A new poetic tradition free from idealization was thus created.

In eastern and southern Africa, few new little magazines emerged. The older ones were still in vogue and were becoming stronger. The Ugandan *Transition* had an acclaimed international audience and was a continental symbol for African poetry. The South African *Contrast* was rebranded into a newer and more formidable *New Contrast* in 1989. *Staffrider* and *Snarl* played significant roles in the eventual end of the apartheid regime in South Africa in 1994. New little magazines such as *Stet* (1982), *Graffier* (1980) and *Taaldoos* (1980) were published in

South Africa as liberal white and black magazines to usher in a more tolerant society. Some of the poets that were produced include Breyten Breytenbach, Daniel Hugo, Rosa Keet, Antjie Krog, Peter Snyders, Wilma Stockenstrom, Barend Toerien and Marlene Van Niekerk. In eastern Africa, *Wajibu* was formed in 1985. These little magazines produced poets that still dominate contemporary poetry.

The preceding section presents the development of modern African poetry in the post-colonial period. African nations were attempting to find their unique identities, free from colonial identities. In this search, their poets acted as guides and priests. The little magazines provided the poets with means to express themselves and aid the new African nations in their search for identity and selfhood. The little magazines have stayed on course in their duties through one of Africa's most trying times and, with their aid, African poets have been able to create a unique tradition of African poetry.

LITTLE MAGAZINES & THE DEVELOPMENT OF CONTEMPORARY AFRICAN POETRY

The beginning of the twenty-first century marked a radical shift in African affairs. Most African countries were already witnessing steady democracies. The Marxist ideals of the later part of the twentieth century had already been given up as a lost cause. More contemporary issues were raised. Issues of corruption, violence, electoral malpractice, societal neglect, fraud and so many others, became the themes of social discourse. The maturation of technological advancement in Africa signified the birth of an internet era. The whole world transformed to a 'global village'. This period also marked the genesis of the security problems faced by many African countries. In Nigeria, Boko Haram engaged the nation in a religious war. In Nairobi, the Al-Shabab, allied to Al-Qaeda, orchestrated a bombing in 2013 that took the life of, among others, Kofi Awoonor. The genocide in Darfur, Sudan (2003-2009) also attracted international sympathy, and the culminating effect of these events is that the twenty-first century ushered in a new order of affairs in Africa. The problems that bothered new post-colonial states paved the way for issues that will determine the fortitude of these states. The poetic space of Africa in this period was as unique as the period itself. Most poets wrote in line with the conventions of African poetry in the twentieth century while others became more innovative and addressed new issues. These issues were so diversified that delineation becomes a tedious task. The little magazines also took new forms along with the winds of change. Publishers started to take advantage of the internet, and the result was that little magazines entered a digital stage where hard copies became rare and internet copies proliferated.

The little magazines, due to their sheer numbers, are not all known because the internet is a vast space where anything can be put by anyone. However, there are some prominent little magazines that have encouraged poetic output in the first decade of the twenty-first century. Most of these little magazines are a continuation of what obtained in the twentieth century, but changes have been made in the roles that they served. Among some of the little magazines that survived into the twenty-first century are South Africa's *New Contrast* and Uganda's *Transition*, which took its base to New York.

One of the most influential little magazines of the twenty-first century is *Kwani?* Launched in 2003 by Binyavanga Wainaina, it has been credited with starting an eastern African poetic renaissance. Many of the writers published by this little magazine have won awards both at the national and international level. Some of them include Yvonne Adhiambo Owuor, Parselelo Kantai, Andia Kisia, Uwem Akpan and Billy Kahora. *Kwani?* positions itself as the best of the new little magazines in eastern Africa because of its quality, milestones and avant-gardism. It has launched new and experienced writers into the poetic landscape, and it has utilized the internet perfectly. Other little magazines from eastern Africa include *Jahazi* and *Sanaa*. These magazines have engaged themselves with the projection of eastern African contemporary poetry. The *Nairobi Journal of Literature* was launched in 2002 and with its critique of poetry, showed the need for young poets to write becoming even more pronounced.

In West Africa, some little magazines have been used by poets such as Jumoke Verissimo, Chuma Nwokolo, Tade Ipadeola, Chika Unigwe, Oha Obododimma, Sefi Atta, Peter Omoko, Stephen Kekeghe, Mathias Orhero, Rome Aboh and Sade Adeniran, among other contemporary poets. These magazines include *Africa-Writing*, *Saraba*, *Maple Tree Literary Supplement*, *Sentinel Poetry*, *The New Gong* and *Farafina*. The magazines are usually accessible online, and some are packaged in a portable document format (PDF). These changes are as a result of the rise and acceptability of information and communication technology (ICT).

The list of little magazines that have emerged in the twenty-first century is not exhaustive. Frequently, new online/digital little magazines are published, and the diversity of themes and lack of adequate editing have reduced the nobility of this form. That said, the little magazine has a very bright future in constructing new African poetry, but the proliferation of many of them will greatly affect a uniform delineation of the poetry of this period.

CONCLUSION

This paper has shown that little magazines have aided in the development of modern African poetry by giving voice to new and experimental poets. Since their earliest inceptions, African poets have used these little magazines to develop their craft and attain maturation. It has also been seen that little magazines serve as 'editors' to poets whose poems first appear in magazines and are criticized before they are published in a poet's personal collection. This is true of Clark, Okigbo and Osundare. Little magazines also play huge socio-political roles. In this vein, *Transition*, *Snarl* and *Staffrider*, among others, served as tools of pan-Africanism and anti-apartheid.

This paper ends on a note of optimism for the future of little magazines in Africa. The tradition, which has always lacked the needed financial support, should be given more attention and monetary donations. New little magazines should be encouraged because they play huge roles in the creation of new African poetic traditions. This paper also recommends that further scholarship should be undertaken on the influences of little magazines in modern African poetry, especially with regard to individual poems and poets. The new internet poems have attracted little attention. This paper recommends that studies should be done on internet poetry, especially those contained in e-books, e-magazines, blogs and other social media. If adequate support and scholarship on little magazines are achieved, the qualitative and quantitative future of these magazines can be guaranteed.

WORKS CITED

Abir, Rahad. 'A Tale of Little Magazines'. *Asia Writes*, 2008. https://rahadabir.wordpress.com/2008/05/10/a-tale-of-little-magazines (accessed 11 September 2017).

Adesokan, Akin. 'Retelling a Forgettable Tale: *Black Orpheus* and *Transition* Revisited'. *African Quarterly on the* Arts Vol. 1, No. 3, 1996: 49-57.

Aiyejina, Funsho. 'Recent Nigerian Poetry in English: An Alter/Native Tradition'. In *Perspectives on Nigerian Literature 1700 to the Present* Vol. I, ed. Yemi Ogunbiyi. Lagos: Guardian Books, 1988.

Augustyn, Adam. *American Literature from the 1850s to 1945*. New York: Rosen Publishing, 2010.

Awhefeada, Sunny. 'Africa: Development of Modern African Poetry'. *AllAfrica* 21 October 2000. http://allafrica.com/stories/printable/ 200010210105.html (accessed 14 August 2016).

Beier, Ulli. 'The Conflict of Cultures in West African Poetry'. *Black Orpheus* Vol. 1, 1957: 17-21.

Bodunde, Charles. 'Poetry in the Newspaper: The Younger Poets in Nigeria and the Search for Artistic Medium'. *Okike* Vol. 34, 1996: 76-81.

Churchill, Suzanne. *The Little Magazine Others and the Renovation of Modern American Poetry*. London: Ashgate Publishing, 2006.

Darah, Gabriel. 'Literary Development in Nigeria'. In *Perspectives on Nigerian Literature: 1700 to the Present* vol. I, ed. Yemi Ogunbiyi. Lagos: Guardian Books, 1988.

Diop, Alioune. 'Opening Address'. *Présence Africaine* Vol. 1, 1947: 9-19.

Egudu, Romanus. *Modern African Poetry and the African Predicament*. London: Macmillan, 1978.

Egya, Sule E. 'Power, Artistic Agency and Poetic Discourse: Poetry as Cultural Critique in Africa'. In *African Literature and the Future*, ed. Gbemisola Adeoti. Dakar: CODESRIA, 2015.

Goodwin, Kenneth. *Understanding African Poetry: A Study of Ten Poets*. London: Heinemann, 1982.

Kane, Louise. 'The Little Magazine as Interdisciplinary Space: Literature and the Visual Arts in the Acorn (1905-6) and the Apple (1920-22)'. *Postgraduate English: A Journal and Forum for Postgraduates in English* No. 23, 2011.

Kesteloot, Lilyan. *Anthologie Negro-Africaine: La Littérature de 1918 à 1981*. Alleur: Marabout, 1987.

King, Bruce Alvin, and Kolawole Ogungbesan, eds. *A Celebration of Black and African Writing*. London: Oxford University Press, 1975.

Lindfors, Bernth. 'African Little Magazines'. *The African Book Publishing Record* Vol. 13, No. 2, 2009: 87-92.

Nakasa, Nat. 'Writing in South Africa'. *The Classic* Vol. 1, No. 1, 1963: 56-63.

Nkosi, Lewis. 'Apartheid: A Daily Exercise in the Absurd'. In *Home and Exile and Other Selections*, Lewis Nkosi. Boston: Longman, 1983.

Ojaide, Tanure. *Poetic Imagination in Black Africa: Essays on African Poetry*. Durham, NC: Carolina Academic Press, 1996.

Okon, Friday. 'Politics and the Development of Modern African Poetry'. *English Language & Literature Studies* Vol. 3, No. 1, 2013: 94-110. www.ccsenet.org/journal/index.php/ells/article/

download/25001/15583 (accessed 1 September 2016).

Okunoye, Oyeniyi. 'Captives of Empire: Early Ibadan Poets and Poetry'. *African Study Monographs* Vol. 19, No. 3, 1998: 161-70. www.africa.kyoto-u.ac.jp/kiroku/asm_normal/abstracts/pdf/19-3/161-170.pdf (accessed 14 August 2017).

——'The Critical Reception of Modern African Poetry'. *Cahiers d'Études Africaines* Vol. 4, 2004: 769-91. https://etudesafricaines.revues.org/4817 (accessed 14 August 2017).

Oliphant, Andries Walter and Ivan Vladislavić. *Ten Years of Staffrider, 1978-1988*. Johannesburg: Ravan Press, 1988.

Oniyitan, Johnson. 'Understanding African Poetry at a Glance'. *VoicesNet* 22 June 2011. www.voicesnet.com/displayonedoc.aspx?docid=206819 (accessed 6 September 2016).

Rabkin, David. *Drum Magazine (1951-1961) and the Works of Black South African Writers Associated with it*. Diss. University of Leeds, 1975. http://etheses.whiterose.ac.uk/2323/2/uk_bl_ethos_537912.pdf (accessed 14 August 2017).

Waterman, Sue. 'Literary Journals'. *Encyclopedia of Life Support Systems*. www.eolss.net/Sample-Chapters/C04/E6-87-04-03.pdf (accessed 12 September 2016).

Wollaeger, Mark and Matt Eatough. *The Oxford Handbook of Global Modernisms*. London: Oxford.

Locating African & Diasporic
Literatures in the Global Context

TOMI ADEAGA

African literature is written through the author's worldview
that is often firmly rooted in the socio-cultural settings
upon which the narration is based. The Nigerian author,
Chinua Achebe's assertion that African literature has never
been homogenous in nature is indeed valid. As is already
well documented in literary history, a number of the early
writers such as the francophone writers Léopold Sédar
Senghor, David Diop and Birago Diop, or Anglophone
writers like Wole Soyinka and Ayi Kwei Armah, had
the privilege of studying abroad. Senghor, along with
other students, Léon Damas (French Guiana) and Aimé
Césaire (Martinique) (see also Rabbitt 'In Search of the
Missing Mother': 36-54) were brought together in Paris to
produce *L'Etudiant Noir* journal between the 1930s and
1940s. Influenced by Edward Blyden's African Personality
Concept (Frenkel 'Edward Blyden and the Concept of
African Personality': 277-89), for which Léopold Sédar
Senghor called Blyden the 'foremost precursor both of
Négritude and of the African Personality' ('Foreword': xv-
xxii), Senghor, Césaire and Damas founded the *Négritude*
Movement in the 1930s. David Diop (Aitken and Rosenhaft
Black Germany: 191-92), who wrote avant-garde poems
such as the collection of poems called *Coups de pilon*
('*Pounding*',1956) that denounced European hegemony
over the African people and their cultures, and Birago Diop,
who is known for his lyrical poems and who also extolled
the African past through his collection of folk tales and

legends of his Wolof people, notably *Les Contes d'Amadou Koumba* (*Tales of Amadou Koumba*, 1947), were actively involved in the movement. The trajectories of Soyinka's and Armah's literary developments were also similar. While Soyinka studied at the University College, Ibadan, he also went on to study at the University of Leeds (1954-57), and Armah studied at the Groton University and Harvard University in Massachusetts in USA. Armah's book, *The Beautyful Ones Are Not Yet Born* (1968) that highlights the post-independent feelings of disillusionment in most of the newly independent African countries remains a classic to date. Helen Oyeyemi, like these authors, was born in Nigeria and studied in England where she wrote her first book *The Icarus Girl* about a young girl called Jessamy who is an *abiku*/twin. This *abiku*/twin story differs from the previous ones written by Okri and Emecheta because it begins in the diaspora, away from the African traditional rites performed for such special children.

This article will therefore focus on the works of some of the new crop of African writers (who are sometimes called the third-generation African writers) such as Oyeyemi's *The Icarus Girl*, and Okri's trilogy, *The Famished Road*, *Songs of Enchantment* and *Infinite Riches*. These writers' African diaspora narrative strands are closely aligned with the environments in which they thrive. This article seeks to highlight the significant developments in the works of these writers in the African diaspora. Attention will be paid to their positive contributions in driving the various shifts in this literature in the diaspora. In what ways are these third-generation writers building on the works of their predecessors? What sets them apart from those of the previous generations? These are some of the questions that will be explored in this article.

The works of famous writers like Ngugi wa Thiong'o, Wole Soyinka, Chinua Achebe, Nadine Gordimer, Assia Djebar, Senghor, Kourouma, for example, have dominated African literature for decades. However, this literary landscape has been changing because the works of younger authors like some of the third-generation authors explored in this article are among those works that are growing more visible both in the African diaspora and on the African continent. They are building on the strong literary foundations laid down by their predecessors. Thus, a younger writer like Chimamanda Ngozi Adichie, who has written books such as *Half of a Yellow Sun* (2006) and *Americanah* (2013), is treated like a celebrity in many parts of the world. Teju Cole, whose books include, *Every Day is for the Thief* (2007, 2014) and *Open City* (2012), frequently writes articles in major newspapers in the US, and Taiye Selasi, who is known more for her various speeches and articles such as 'Bye Bye Babar (or What is an Afropolitan?') (2005) and 'African Literature does not Exist' (Iduma 'No Selasi, African Literature Exists': 2013), than she is known for her book, *Ghana Must Go* (2013). The author, Binyavanga Wainaina, who published his first book, *One Day I Will Write About This Place* (2011), is also prominent in the social media where his satirical essays, such as 'How to Write About Africa' (2005), are featured. Oyeyemi's *The Icarus Girl* revisits an important aspect of Yoruba and African traditional beliefs surrounding *abiku*/twins by taking her readers on a journey through their spiritual world. The works mentioned above only reflect a small part of the activities that the writers engage in that have drawn attention to African diaspora literature in the different locations in which the writers have found themselves.

African creative works such as those of Amos Tutuola in his *The Palm-Wine Drinkard* (1952) or Ben Okri's trilogy have, along with South American literature written by authors like Gabriel García Márquez in his *One Hundred Years of Solitude* (1967) or Salman Rushdie's *Midnight Children* (1981), been concluded to be in the magical realism genre. But alluding to its origins, Kenneth S. Reeds says of magical realism:

In 1923 German art critic Franz Roh coined the term 'magical realism' and then repeated it in a 1925 book in reference to a new artistic tendency he saw appearing in European painting. It is unlikely he could have realized how far his notion would travel in terms of both geographic and inter-disciplinary debate. It has since formed part of Latin American literature, postcolonial studies, and can now be found in art and literary criticism related to India, Africa, Canada, Europe, and beyond. (Reeds *What is Magical Realism?*: 41)

So, the magical realism concept was coined in relation to art in the German art milieu in the early part of the 20th century. It has since been modified by those looking for a new word that expresses mythical realities either in their works or in their societies. The history behind this concept is such that:

Roh's 1925 book was published in Leipzig by Klinkhardt and Bierman and consisted of 134 pages of text followed by 87 reproductions of paintings. The first 14 were comparative paintings between Expressionism and magical realism ... The title of the book, *Nach-Expressionismus, Magischer Realismus: Probleme Der Neusten Europäischen Malerei*, put the term 'magical realism' as only a subtitle with the main title profiling the new art as a reaction to Expressionism ... Roh's work was centered on painting with little of the content wavering from this focus. (Reeds: 43-4)

Roh's disinterest in developing the concept beyond the works of the artists in his book further reiterates the looseness of the ideas surrounding it, which also enabled it to flow into new concepts as seen in the subsequent decades. This has led critics such as Irene Guenther and Anne C. Hegerfeldt to conclude that Roh's role in the development of literary magical realism is minimal. The lack of an actual definition born by a link to contemporary literary genre makes it flexible enough to be incorporated into North and Latin American literature as well as African literature and the *abiku* concept.

This concept was used to develop the narratives in the works of early Nigerian writers like Achebe who called it by its Igbo name, *ogbanje* in his classic, *Things Fall Apart* (1958). Okonkwo's daughter, called Ezinma, and for whom he had a 'soft spot', was an *ogbanje,* the child that kept on dying and being born again. Afterwards, John Pepper Clark-Bekederemo and Soyinka published poems called 'Abiku', in 1965 and 1967 respectively. In *Kehinde* (1994), Emecheta used the *abiku* concept to illustrate the bond between the main protagonist Kehinde and her dead twin, Taiwo, both in Nigeria and in London, to show that the dead *abiku*/twin can also have a positive effect on the twin who is alive, if given due honour in the form of an *èrè ìbejì* (statuette) and the traditional ceremony that goes with it. Emecheta has drawn attention to an African tradition that honours dead twins through appropriate ceremonies and rites. However, *Kehinde* differs from Oyeyemi's 21st century narration, *The Icarus Girl* in which she relocates to the diaspora this historical narrative of the relationship between the *abiku* and twins who are caught in the recurring process of life and death, and the family of the protagonist, Jessamy, fails to honour this age old tradition of carving the *èrè ìbejì* for the dead twin to appease her, until they are forced to do so when they get back to Nigeria.

Staying true to its origins, the *abiku* concept never dies, instead, it comes and it goes in the different generations of African literature. What is clearly important here is that Oyeyemi revisits the *abiku* concept through the *èrè ìbejì* (twin statuette) or 'twins' concept. Oyeyemi expands on the twinship concept that had been previously used by Emecheta in *Kehinde* (1994). Here, the twin sister Taiwo died at birth, along with the mother, but Kehinde lives on. Even before she became aware of her being a twin, she built a relationship with Taiwo when she started living in Lagos with her aunt Nnebogo whom she called mother until the age of eleven years:

When they gave me *akara* or *moyin-moyin* as a toddler, I would share it into two, a part for me, a part for my Taiwo – the one who came to taste life for me. I did this even though I did not know I was a twin, or that I deprived my Taiwo of her life. I even talked to her in my sleep, without knowing who I was talking to. (Emecheta: 19)

By this time, Kehinde was still called Jacobina, a name given to her at birth by her Igbo family in Ibusa, in the eastern part of Nigeria. When a woman came to the market where aunt Nnebogo had her fish stall, she performed a ceremony for her twins and then Kehinde finally realized that she was a twin after making eye contact with the twins held by the woman and she ran to her aunt and asked her for her Taiwo. She added 'when we got home from the market that day, I became ill. People made suggestions as to the cause of my fever' (Emecheta: 21). She became ill because she felt that she was incomplete, a part of her was missing. 'I was haunted by my past, so that Aunt Nnebogo put me on the hem of the skirt of her love. However, for me to get fully well, she asked a special *ibeji* carver to make me my Taiwo. They must have told her to start calling me my real name, Kehinde, and within a few years, I had forgotten that I had been called another name' (Emecheta: 21). Thus, Jacobina becomes Kehinde, the birth name of a twin, just as Lazaro, an allusion to the biblical Lazarus who had risen from the grave, becomes Azaro in Okri's trilogy, after he had been taken for dead and arose in the coffin where his parents were going to bury him. Titiola which means 'forever' replaces Fern and is shortened by Jessamy in Oyeyemi's *The Icarus Girl* into TillyTilly. Calling *abiku* and *twins* by their right names is quite important to the *abiku* concept because it underscores the special place they occupy in the Nigerian society in particular and African societies in general. Timothy Mobolade reiterates this point as he adds that *abiku* children are often given the following names:

Durojaiye (Wait and enjoy life); Pakuti (Shun death and stop dying); Rotimi (Stay and put up with me); Omolelebe (the child should be appeased); and Eloe (Appeal). Naming may also express the hope that the Abiku will be merciful and refrain from dying. Such names include: Igbekoyi (Bush [the popular cemetery for the Abikus] has rejected this [Abiku child]); Kokumo (It does [or will] not die again); Ajitoni (It wakes up [and is alive] today, and therefore we wish it many happy returns); Ajeigbe (Monetary expenses are never a waste [as our expenses on you shall be no waste]). In other cases, naming may take the form of complaints about the sorrows the child's several deaths have caused them and their neighbors. They believe that perhaps the child will be moved by this to relent and stay with them. Under this class of names are: Kosoko (No more hoe is available [to dig any grave]); Jolokoosimi (Let the owner of the hoe take a rest); Anwoko (We are yet to find a hoe [to dig a grave]). If at last the above types of naming fail to restrain the child from dying, on the reappearance of such an Abiku child the parents will identify it with contemptible names. Expressive of disgust, these are calculated to disgrace the child into a change of heart. Such are: Kilanko (Wherefore should the naming be ceremonious?); Oku (The dead, the deceased); Aja (A common dog); Omonife (It cannot be known by any better name than the mere one of a 'child'); and Tepontan (No longer feared, respected and cherished). (Mobolade 'The Concept of Abiku': 63)

So also are twins called by their birth names, Taiwo and Kehinde (Mobolade 'Ibeji Custom in Yorubaland': 14), during the ceremonies organized for them because it is an integral part of their cultural identity. Essentially, twins occupy a special space within most sub-Saharan African countries, and their lives are intrinsically linked with those of *abiku* in these cultures. This link is established when a woman gives birth to several twins and they die at birth. They are then *abiku*/twins.

Phillip M. Peek asserts that twins and twinning, along with dualities of many types, are fundamental for many

African societies; their importance is demonstrated by their continued veneration in the Americas among communities of African heritage (*Twins in African and Diaspora Cultures*: 6). The *twinship* concept gained more prominence through the pioneering research carried out by the English anthropologist, Edward Evan Evans-Pritchard on the Nuer people of the Sudan in the 1930s. 'They consider twins to be two physical beings but with one personality – a concept found widely throughout Africa. The Nuer also assert that "twins are birds" in that they share, symbolically, a similar relationship with "Spirit"' (Evans-Pritchard 'Customs and Beliefs Relating to Twins': 80-81). He also adds that 'twins form the closest possible human relationship' (234; see also Abrahams 'Spirit, Twins, and Ashes': 115-34; Beattie 'Twin Ceremonies in Bunyoro': 1-12; Beidelman 'Kaguru Omens': 43-59) which is the essence of Emecheta and Oyeyemi's narrative discourse on the subject that also resonates with most sub-Saharan African cultures. Victor Turner argues that 'twinship presents the paradoxes that what is physically double is structurally single and what is mystically one is empirically two' (*The Ritual Process*: 45). Turner concludes that 'when twins come into this world at the 'same' time and perhaps sharing the same soul, they disrupt carefully wrought social systems based on one entity in one position' (Peek: 7). Turner's argument is in alignment with most sub-Saharan African cultural beliefs.

In the Yoruba culture in Nigeria, twins are still perceived as special beings that need more attention than non-twins:

> Although twin births are relatively common among Yoruba people, with almost 5% of births resulting in twins, compared to just over 1% in Western Europe, a strong sense of anomaly still attaches to them. This is connected to the Yoruba belief that everyone on earth has a spiritual double. In the case of twins, that double has been born onto earth rather than remaining in the spirit realm, and as there is no telling which is which, both of the twins must be treated as sacred. (White 'The Trouble with Twins': 2010)

Babatunde Lawal adds: 'though they are physically two, twins are spiritually one' (Lawal 'Èjìwàpò: The Dialectics of Twoness in Yoruba Art and Culture': 35).

Thus, when these twins are born and they die or 'live' over and over again, as portrayed in Emecheta and Oyeyemi's narration, they are called *abiku* or *ogbanje* among the Yoruba and Igbo respectively. After the *ère ìbejì* had been carved for Kehinde's dead twin, Taiwo in Emecheta's narration, in Nigeria while she was still a child, Taiwo was pacified at an early stage and built a relationship with her twin that was not intrusive. She filled the vacuum in her life and she became more an invisible companion than a destructive rival. So, even while Kehinde was in London, she was only someone Kehinde turned to when she needed advice. So, she did not dominate the narration because family life played a central role in it. Oyeyemi's novel is different because its main focus is on the *abiku* child whose twin died at birth in the diaspora and the necessary rites were not carried out for her and the *ère ìbejì* was not immediately carved out for her, probably because Jessamy's Nigerian mother, Sarah did not believe that the dead twin would make contact with her sister while in London.

Oyeyemi taps into the Yoruba cosmology and double consciousness through diasporic *métissage* that is based on a split identity. Oyeyemi shows an adept understanding of this concept as she reaffirms the need for the reader to modernize the myth and see it through a different prism. By so doing, she stays within the traditions of African diaspora re-imaginings of African cultural traditions that have been displayed by people of African descent, especially in those areas with strong Yoruba ancestry. Christopher Ouma reaffirms the fluidity inherent in the *abiku* concept that enables the author to cross the temporal space and relocate to a new setting ('Reading the African Diasporic *Abiku*'). In countries like Cuba, Brazil, Haiti, etc., Yoruba traditions are re-adapted to their new environments where they reflect both their African ancestry as well as the cultures and traditions of their people:

> The Diasporic *abiku* lends itself to varied modes of storytelling, and of narrative practices occasioned by its new transplanted contexts, that allow Oyeyemi's novel to reframe the discourse on migration and race in relation to a continuously evolving cultural space of the African diaspora. Oyeyemi's *The Icarus Girl* does this without the aggregative and evolving logic of the "middle passage" that informed the syncretic nature of aesthetic practices in the cultural production and criticism of the historical diasporas, and of theoretical constructions of diaspora, such as Paul Gilroy's *The Black Atlantic* (1993). (Ouma: 189)

This dislocation and transplantation of the *abiku* concept basically sums up young African Diasporic literature and their place within world literature. Dislocation in the *abiku* concept centres round the move to the West and taking along one's cultural traditions to the new Western location. Transplantation here is associated with the *abiku* concept taking root in its new British environment, while still maintaining strong attachments to its Nigerian roots. Walter Benjamin said that 'translation is a mode. To comprehend it as a mode one must go back to the original, for that contains the law governing the translation: its translatability' ('The Task of the Translator': 76). These young writers have proved that this literature can be translated into new settings in the diaspora by following the footsteps of their predecessors such as Emecheta who left her country of origin, Nigeria to join her husband in London, England in 1962, and wrote more than twenty books there. Notable among them was her novel, *Kehinde* (1994) in which she introduced the *abiku*/twinship concept to the diaspora. Thus, this literature produced by the third-generation African diaspora writers shows similar translatability traits through the transfer of knowledge of their countries of origin and cultural traditions into the diaspora. By writing literature with roots in their countries of origin and the diaspora, as has been manifested in Adichie's *Americanah* (2013), and Oyeyemi's *The Icarus Girl*, they have displayed what Benjamin has called translatability. For, while Tutuola opened the doors of Yoruba magical realism to Africans, the African diaspora, and the rest of the world through his famous book, *The Palm-Wine Drinkard*, Achebe introduced the African past to the African diaspora and the rest of the world, most especially through *Things Fall Apart* (1958); these young writers carried on this tradition by transferring these shared cultural traditions in their literature into the diaspora where they have made their homes. Both Adichie's *Americanah* and Oyeyemi's *The Icarus Girl* illustrate the journey between two cultures, Nigerian and Western which meet and interact.

Oyeyemi's *The Icarus Girl* expertly showcases the fact that African cultural traditions are translatable into new ones and cohabit with them as Titiola, or TillyTilly, Jessamy's dead sibling relocates to London with her, and immediately adapts to life there by exchanging her Yoruba clothing for Western ones and her Yoruba accent to a British accent. Jessamy's mother, Sarah gave birth to two sets of twins and only one of them, Jessamy survives. When she goes back home to Nigeria on vacation with her parents, one of the dead twins from the first set, Titiola whom she starts calling TillyTilly makes contact with her and never let go of her. Sarah begins to feel uneasy after she reads the poem that had been written by Jessamy and TillyTilly which says:

All my thoughts have left, with her.
I thought I'd kept them in my head
But when I tried to find the thoughts
They all told me she was dead.
I asked if I could go to her
To find my thoughts, to think one day,
But they said 'No', 'cause she'd prefer
To keep me, too, and make me stay.
(Oyeyemi: 163)

After TillyTilly shows Jessamy a baby and tells her that she's dead, she add, 'I don't like to say it … but it's your mother's fault' (174). When Jessamy asks her for an explanation, she responds, 'ask her – there were two of you born, just like there were two of me. The other one of you is dead' (175). She reiterates that

> your twin sister's name was Fern. They didn't get to choose a proper name for her, a Yoruba name, because she was born already dead, just after you were born. You have been so empty Jessy, without your twin; you have had no one to walk your three worlds with you. I know – I am the same. I have been just like you for such a long time! But now I am Fern, I am your sister, and you are my twin. (176)

TillyTilly's allusion to 'three worlds' is expatiated upon by Sarah as she goes into a state of shock when Jessamy asks her if they were previously two babies. Sarah tells her British husband, Daniel Harrison, that 'Jess lives in three worlds. She lives in this world, and she lives in the spirit world, and she lives in the Bush. She's *abiku*, she always would know! The spirits tell her things. Fern tells her things' (Oyeyemi: 181).
Sarah's belief in this tradition indicates that

> African societies include the world of spirits, the dead, the living, and even the unborn … A legitimate part of the African view of life and the world involves the world of the spirits. The Africans, whether Christian or not, intellectual or illiterate in their great majority, still consult divinities and diviners when they have health problems or when their business is in a mess. Western ways are good, but you run back to your ancestral roots when things get out of hand. These things are deeper than foreigners may think. (Amouzou 'African Literature and Cultural Imperialism': 331)

Sarah cries 'we should've … we should've d-d-done *ibeji* carving for her' (Oyeyemi: 181). By admitting that the family made a mistake by not appeasing the *abiku/* twins and making an *ère ìbejì* for Fern, Sarah knows that this more than the British Dr Colin McKenzie's diagnosis is the solution to the crises, and calls her family in Nigeria. For, unlike the herbalist called to treat Azaro's illness in Okri's *The Famished Road*, who correctly diagnosed what was wrong with him by stating that he was a spirit-child, an *abiku* and gave the right suggestions as to how he could be healed; the British Dr McKenzie could not do so because he did not understand the culture that produced the *abiku*/twins. The diagnosis of the herbalist in *The Famished Road* underscores Lawal's submission on *abiku*/twins that:

> If one of them should die, a memorial, *èrè ìbejì*, would be commissioned ... to localize the soul of the deceased and maintain the spiritual bond between the living and the dead. If both twins should die, another memorial would be commissioned and the two statuettes treated like living children in the hope that they be born again to the same mother. Tradition requires that the carver give both memorials the same facial features to emphasize the *oneness* in their *twoness*, even if the deceased twins were not identical ... The memorial is normally carved from the wood of the West African rubber tree (*Funtumia elastica*). Apparently because its sticky latex binds two surfaces together, the wood of the rubber tree is believed to possess a high spiritual sensitivity. In fact, the local name of the tree, *ìré*, derives from the root verb *ré*, which means 'to unite, befriend, or reconcile'. Note that the same verb occurs in *èjìré*, the synonym for twins – the inseparable two – which explains why different parts of the *ìré* tree – leaves, bark, roots, etc. – are used in making charms or articles aimed at bonding friends, lovers, and social organizations. This notion is illustrated by the popular saying '*Ìré oko, lóní kí o wá bá mi ré*' ('The *ìré* of the forest has asked you to bond with me'...). The same root verb *ré* is implicated in words such as *òré* ('friend') and *ìrépò* ('social harmony'). Thus, to the Yoruba, twinship connotes a mutually beneficial relationship that infinitely doubles the dynamic that bonding generates in time and space, stabilizing families, societies and nations. (Lawal: 35)

Okri's *abiku* inhabited his African world in which the herbalist called to heal him correctly diagnosed the source of his illness by telling his parents that he was an *abiku* child. The remedy was that Azaro's connection with the spirit world had to be severed in which his secret special tokens brought from the spirit world were found and destroyed. But if this was not done, he was going to keep on falling ill and die. Azaro's friend Ade is also an *abiku* child who predicts his death because just like Azaro who's spirit friends are always trying to lure him back to the spirit world, Ade's spirit friends are also in contact with him. During a visit to Azaro:

> 'I am going to die soon,' he said. 'Why do you say that?' 'My time has come. My friends are calling me.' 'What friends?' 'In the other world,' he said ... 'Trouble is always coming. Maybe it's just as well,' he said. 'Your story has just begun. Mine is ending. I want to go to my other home ... 'My time is coming. I have worn out my mother's womb and now she can't have any more children. Coming and going, I have seen the world, I have seen the future. The Koran says nothing is ever finished.' (Okri *Famished Road*: 476-7)

Ade predicts the future of the world by juxtaposing it with the *abiku* concept as he claims: 'Our country is an abiku country. Like the spirit-child, it keeps coming and going. One day it will decide to remain. It will become strong' (478). Ade is comparing the recurring cycle of bad governance in most African countries to the *abiku* child and suggests that things will only change for the better when governments who have the interests of the common masses at heart come into power.

Sarah is also aware of this part of the Yoruba tradition. So, she takes Jessamy back home to Nigeria on a visit, before her ninth birthday. TillyTilly goes back with her and reverts back to her Yoruba mannerisms while the family is there. Sarah is however taken aback by her father, Gbenga's strong belief in the Yoruba tradition of appeasing a dead *abiku*/twin and his determination to take Jessamy to the traditional medicine woman, Iya Adahunse, after Jessamy speaks to him in Yoruba in a way only age-mates can speak to each other (Oyeyemi: 323). Sarah's husband, Daniel gets into a fight over it with his father-in-law and Sarah takes Jessamy away from them and decides to take her to Toyin in Lagos. On the way, they are involved in a car accident and Jessamy is seriously injured. Gbenga still arranges with Dr Adenuga, who is assigned to her to put Fern's *ère ìbejì* in a far corner of her room to watch over her (325-30). Oyeyemi erases the temporal divide between the Yoruba and British cultures as TillyTilly goes back and forth across the Atlantic with Jessamy. She affirms that, while the *abiku* concept upon which the twinship concept also thrives is firmly grounded in the Yoruba cultural traditions, it can also thrive in the diaspora. Thus, the only solution is to appease the dead twin or twins, otherwise the *abiku* cycle of birth will continue. This appeasement can also be done in the diaspora, where the *abiku* child resides.

This third generation of writers who mainly grew up in the diaspora and were predominantly born in the post-independence days, do not carry the burden of defining what African literature should look or sound like. Instead, they live and write in countries where their use of multiple Western languages is no longer widely questioned but accepted by both African and Western audiences alike. Their works are located in African literature because of their usage of historical backgrounds (Adichie's *Half of a Yellow Sun*), they use myths and African traditional cultures (Oyeyemi's *The Icarus Girl*) and like the first generation of writers – Wole Soyinka, Naguib Mafouz, Chinua Achebe, Léopold Senghor – they win international prizes for them. The first and the third generations of writers are like the *abiku*/twins that Lawal referred to earlier on in this article. Though they are two different generations, their core beliefs and world view are the same. This is visible in the continuity of the works started by the first generation of writers that is equally present in the works of this third generation of writers. The works written by these third-generation writers also come across as those written by local members of their societies with as much knowledge of their socio-political and cultural fabrics as well as those of their countries of origin.

This concept of magical realism was further concretized in Okri's trilogy in the figure of Azaro. 'Okri's reinvention of the motif is famously captured in Azaro's father's statement: "Our country is like an *abiku* country. Like a spirit-child it keeps coming and going..." The abiku motif resurfaces in Okri's work to engage with a fractious postcolonial national identity' (Ouma: 190). Okri's hybrid works, like Tutuola's *The Palm-Wine Drinkard* blur the boundaries between fiction and reality. The narrative voice, Azaro floats through nations, thoughts, past, present and future; through the born and the unborn, the living and the dead. By 'inventing a protagonist who mediates freely between the living and the dead, Okri resolves to feed an agonizing hunger, physical as well as metaphorical, by bringing in a mythic and magical dimension to the historical times he renders and relives in *The Famished Road*' (Zhu: 14), By so doing, 'Okri expands the spheres of reality and rejuvenates the mythos of African aestheticism.' (Zhu *Fiction and the Incompleteness of History*: 14). The melancholic Azaro who is more at home among spirits than human beings is driven by a loneliness that only this surreal world can satisfy. This existentialist alienation drives him into the other world where he lives a parallel life, similar to Hegelian assertion on alienation:

> We are not dealing with the Paradise which is ... lost due to some fatal intrusion – there is already in paradisiacal satisfaction ... something suffocating, a longing for fresh air, for an opening that would break the unbearable constraint; and this longing introduces into Paradise an unbearable Pain, a desire to break out – life in Paradise is always pervaded by an infinite melancholy. (Žižek *The Fragile Absolute*: 62)

But Mobolade concludes that 'the Yorubas believe that the Abikus form a species of spirits by themselves. As spirits, their places of abode are restricted to scheduled and obscure corners of towns and villages, to the inside of the jungles and to road-sides and foot paths in suburban areas' (Mobolade 'The Concept of Abiku': 62). Thus, this accounts for the melancholy that Azaro exudes because he is lonely without his spirit friends. Azaro's friends inhabit a communal world that is linked to the real world by a road which is in actual fact the mother's womb.

Okri affirms traditional African beliefs that these children are born with the intention to die at the time at which, in the spirit world, they already made the pact to do so. However, there are some of the children who are so well taken care of in the real world that they get carried away and break the pact. The consequences are that such children are 'assailed by hallucinations and haunted by their companions. They would only find consolation when they returned to the world of the Unborn, the place of fountains, where their loved ones would be waiting for them silently' (Okri *Famished Road*: 4). Thus, when the families realize that the children are *abiku,* they mark or mutilate their bodies before they are buried. For,

> we were often recognised and our flesh marked with razor incisions. When we were born again to the same parents the marks, lingering on our new flesh, branded our souls in advance. Then the world would spin a web of fate around our lives. Those of us who died while still children tried to erase these marks, by making beauty spots or interesting discolorations of them. If we didn't succeed, and were recognised, we were greeted with howls of dread, and the weeping of mothers. (4)

In the light of this, Azaro oscillated between the two worlds and was tormented by his spirit friends who wanted him to join them.

The *abiku* concept is therefore a recurrent process that has been used by the authors in different ways. In his trilogy, Okri has tapped into the cultural beliefs in which the concept is grounded. The repetitive style whereby Azaro travels in the spiritual realm both day and night, sees and takes part in the events going on there; the events taking place in Madam Koto's bar whereby Azaro and Madam Koto see the spirits that visit the bar and mingle with human beings that go there to eat, drink and have fun but are unaware of their presence, are some of the parts of the trilogy that have prompted Brenda Cooper to conclude that 'not much happens. What does transpire seems familiar and repetitive, as though one is living through many versions of the same dream or nightmare' (*Magical Realism in West African Fiction*: 68); or Kwame Anthony Appiah who claims, in reference to *The Famished Road*, that '500 pages with only the barest semblance of a plot' ('Spiritual Realism': 147). However, the repetitious events such as those mentioned above make up the *abiku* concept, a cyclic recurrent process that never ceases.

Emecheta's novel, *Kehinde* illustrates the essence of appeasing the *abiku/twin* at an early stage among the Yoruba people through the *èré ìbejì* carvings that are made in the image of the dead twin and given to the twin who is alive to appease the roving dead twin's spirit. Unlike Emecheta's *Kehinde* and Okri's Azaro, Oyeyemi's Jessamy is unaware of being an *abiku* or being a twin because she was born in London and was unaware of her being a twin because her parents did not perform the ceremony for her when she was a little girl. It was not until she went back to her roots in Ibadan, Nigeria that her *abiku/twin* contacted her. By this time, she was angry at the neglect and disrespect for tradition that she tormented Jessamy and those close to her. Thus, Oyeyemi explores the outcome of cultural alienation born of cultural dislocation within the *abiku/twin* cycle.

African literature is adapting to the realities of the 21st

century. African creative works written by African authors living in the diaspora are reaching out to a wider audience because they are not just read in hard copies but also read as mainstream stories that speak to both African and non-African immigrants in all parts of the world. These writers' contributions to the growth of African diaspora literature are reflected through their works that straddle themes from both their countries of origin and the West. The ever changing faces of this literature in terms of themes and locations portray their fluidity and multifaceted narrative composition.

They have also built upon the groundwork laid down by their predecessors in terms of contemporary magical realism to which the *abiku* concept also belongs. As stated earlier in this article, the magical realism concept is very much part of the postcolonial narrative today and it has featured prominently not only in the works of the Colombian author Gabriel García Márquez in his classic, *Hundred Years of Solitude* (1967); it has also featured in Salman Rushdie's *Midnight's Children* (1981). Thus, 'magical-realist novels were written in diverse parts of the world with the principal connection between them being their status as representations of the postcolonial experience. With this connection between magical realism and postcolonial writing, magical realism became an international literary phenomenon' (Reeds: 253). According to Reeds, Toni Morrison's storytelling also explores this concept because for her,

> fiction is not just a way to look back at history so a culture can improve its understanding of the present and hope for a better future. She sees storytelling as the key to cultural survival – especially in cultures like the African-American where prolonged violence has lasted for generations and the danger of cultural amnesia is pressing. Her novel *Song of Solomon* is both a manifestation of the storyteller passing on history as well as a didactic fiction which teaches about the importance of maintaining a living past or otherwise the

future may be lost. ... Morrison uses magical realism to both create and elucidate this message. (Reeds: 214)

In the same vein, the *abiku* concept that exists under different names in parts of Africa also shares these magical-realist traits as many African writers such as Tutuola, Soyinka, Clark-Bekederemo, Achebe, Emecheta, Okri and Oyeyemi among others have shown through their fictional works and poems. In the words of Ben Okri:

> The spirit-child is an unwilling adventurer into chaos and sunlight, into the dreams of the living and the dead. Things that are not ready, not willing to be born or to become, things for which adequate preparations have not been made to sustain their momentous births, things that are not resolved, things bound up with failure and with fear of being, they all keep recurring, keep coming back, and in themselves partake of the spirit-child's condition. They keep coming and going till their time is right. History itself fully demonstrates how things of the world partake of the condition of the spirit-child.' (*The Famished Road*: 487)

In Oyeyemi's *The Icarus Girl,* the *abiku*/twin, TillyTilly, tortures Jessamy because the necessary traditional rites have not been performed to appease her and, most importantly, an *èrè ìbejì* had not been carved for her after Fern's death. As a result of this, TillyTilly wants to take Jessamy's place in the family and grows stronger in London as time goes on until the family goes back to Nigeria and after the accident, the *èrè ìbejì* is placed in her hospital room by her grandfather. Thus, Oyeyemi joins her predecessors in highlighting the importance of *abiku* children as special children who must be treated differently through appeasements. Okri also reiterates this point in his trilogy, whereby Azaro, the *abiku* child only stays with his parents because he wants to do so. Anytime he falls ill, they show him love and implore him to stay with them. Since he does not shut the door to the spirit world because he enjoys wandering through it, he is able to inhabit both worlds without dying. He is what Tutuola has called the 'wonderful child' in *The Palm-Wine Drinkard*. Tutuola's translation of the word from the Yoruba ọmọ àràmòndà into 'wonderful child' to describe the palm-wine drinkard who travels from the land of the living into the land of the dead and back also puts the life of Azaro and his friend Ade into perspective because they, like Oyeyemi's TillyTilly are 'wonderful children' who are spirit-children and wanderers on the famished road.

The fact that the image of *abiku* has been successfully woven into the fabrics of these narratives and poems shows its fluidity because 'as the notion of the *abiku* travels from Clark to Soyinka to Okri, it evolves and adapts, effectively (re)constructing varied reading practices. As it travels in different contexts, the concept of the *abiku* morphs, shape-shifts, and complicates previously constructed frameworks of engagement, whether spatially or temporally contextualized' (Ouma: 190).

Have this new literature and their writers in the diaspora succeeded in creating a new direction for African literature both in Africa and the African diaspora? Yes, they have, because they affirm that African literature is part of the *abiku* concept. It keeps on developing in new environments. In Okri's *Songs of Enchantment*, Azaro's father who was an illiterate asked him to read to him. He then asked him how a child of his age could read that well. In his mind, Azaro thought

> that was probably the first time that I felt the doors to my other lives – my past lives – opening on me with frightening clarity. Sometimes my other lives would open and then shut, and what I glimpsed didn't make sense. Other times I could see far into an aquamarine past; I saw faces that were both entirely alien and familiar; and my mind would be invaded with the black winds of enigmatic comprehension. The lives in me increased their spaces, languages of distant lands bore my thoughts, and I found I knew things I had never learnt. I knew the charts and tides of the Atlantic, I understood complex principles of higher mathematics, the sign-interpretations of

the forgotten magis, the sculptural traditions of the ancient Benin guild, the lost philosophies of Pythagoras and the griots of Mali. (Okri *Songs of Enchantment*: 30-31)

Thus, African literature did not stop growing after most of the first generation of writers either died out or stopped writing. Instead, those third-generation writers, especially the ones in the diaspora have localized it and offered their audience narratives that reflect the writers' multifaceted worldviews that are grounded in their African origins and formed by their diasporic environments.

Alluding to the Somali born British poet, Warsan Shire's collaboration with Beyoncé on Lemonade: The Visual Album, Ainehi Edoro expertly drives home this point as she states that *Teaching My Mother How To Give Birth* and *For Women Who Are Difficult to Love* 'are some of the most iconic texts of contemporary African literature. By using these texts as the poetic scaffolding of Lemonade, Shire plants seeds of African literature deep within one of the most significant works of our time' (Edoro 'Beyoncé is Not Shining a Light on African Literature'). Shire's texts are iconic because they reflect the wandering spirits that populate Okri's famished road, who are in search of a place to belong. Thus, Shire and other third-generation African diaspora writers have planted seeds of African literature across the world and those seeds have germinated to produce narrations that promote the development of African diaspora literature.

For: 'Through Shire, Beyoncé is given access to the rich archive of texts and images we call African literature. But this also means that African literature now commands one of the points of access into the complex of meanings in a cultural object as globally situated as Lemonade' (Edoro). Indeed, African diaspora literature is giving the world access into Africa's rich archive of myths and legends, stories, images, art, traditions and cultures that have survived for centuries because 'everything is connected' (Okri *Songs of Enchantment*: 147).

WORKS CITED

Abrahams, R.G. 'Spirit, Twins, and Ashes in Labwor, Northern Uganda'. In *The Interpretation of Ritual*. J.S. La Fontaine (ed.) London: Tavistock Publications, 1972.

Aitken, Robbie and Eve Rosenhaft. *Black Germany: The Making and Unmaking of a Diaspora Community, 1884-1960*. Cambridge: Cambridge University Press, 2013.

Amouzou, Akoété. 'African Literature and Cultural Imperialism'. *Revue du CAMES – Nouvelle Série O* Vol. 008, N° 1, 2007.

Appiah, Kwame Anthony. 'Spiritual Realism'. *The Nation* 255/4, New York, 3 August 1992.

Beattie, J.H.M. 'Twin Ceremonies in Bunyoro'. *Journal of the Royal Anthropological Institute* Vol. 92, No. 1, 1962.

Beidelman, T.O. 'Kaguru Omens: An East African People's Concepts of the Unusual, Unnatural and Supernormal'. *Anthropological Quarterly* Vol. 36, No. 2, 1963: 43-59.

Benjamin, Walter. 'The Task of the Translator: An Introduction to the Translation of Baudelaire's *Tableaux Parisiens*'. Translated by Harry Zohn, 1923. In *The Translation Studies Reader* 2nd edn, Lawrence Venuti (ed.) New York and London: Routledge, 2004.

Cooper, Brenda. *Magical Realism in West African Fiction: Seeing with a Third Eye*. London: Routledge: 1998.

Edoro, Ainehi. 'Beyoncé is Not Shining a Light on African Literature – It's the Other Way Round'. 8 June 2016. www.theguardian.com/books/booksblog/2016/jun/08/beyonce-lemonade-african-literature-warsan-shire (accessed 27 July 2016).

Emecheta, Buchi. *Kehinde*. Oxford: Heinemann Educational Books, 1994.

Evans-Pritchard, E.E. 'Customs and Beliefs Relating to Twins among the Nilotic Nuer'. *Uganda Journal* Vol. 3, 1936: 230-8.

——*The Zande Trickster*. Oxford: Clarendon Press, 1967.

Frenkel, M. Yu. 'Edward Blyden and the Concept of African Personality'. *African Affairs* Vol. 73, No. 292, 1974. www.jstor.org/stable/720808 (accessed 25 July 2016).

Harris Joseph E. 'Introduction', in *Global Dimensions of the African Diaspora*. Joseph Harris (ed.) Washington, DC: Howard University Press, 1982.

Iduma, Emmanuel. 'No Selasi, African Literature Exists'. 10 December 2013. www.mriduma.com/no-selasi-african-literature-exists (accessed 1 July 2016).

Lawal, Babatunde. 'Èjìwàpò: The Dialectics of Twoness in Yoruba Art and Culture', *African Arts* Vol. 41, No. 1, 2008.

Mobolade, Timothy. 'The Concept of Abiku'. *African Arts* Vol. 7, No. 1, 1973: 62-64. www.jstor.org/stable/3334754 (accessed 4 October 2016).

——'Ibeji Custom in Yorubaland'. *African Arts* Vol. 4, No. 3, 1971: 14-15. www.jstor.org/stable/3334423 (accessed 5 October 2016).

Okri, Ben. *The Famished Road*. London: Jonathan Cape, 1991.

——*Songs of Enchantment*. London: Jonathan Cape, 1993.

Ouma, Christopher. 'Reading the African Diasporic *Abiku* in Helen Oyeyemi's *The Icarus Girl*'. *Research in African Literatures* Vol. 45, No. 3, 2014: 188-205.

Oyeyemi, Helen. *The Icarus Girl*. New York: Anchor Books, 2005.

Peek, Phillip M. *Twins in African and Diaspora Cultures: Double Trouble, Twice Blessed*. Bloomington: Indiana University Press, 2011.

Rabbitt, Kara. 'In Search of the Missing Mother: Suzanne Césaire, Martiniquaise' *Research in African Literatures* Vol. 44, No. 1, 2013.

Reeds, Kenneth S. *What is Magical Realism? An Explanation of a Literary Style*. New York: Edwin Mellen Press, 2012, www.kennethreeds.com/uploads/2/3/3/0/2330615/what_is_magical_realism_-_first_chapter_-_kenneth_reeds.pdf (chapter 1, accessed 14 August 2017).

Roscoe, A. *Mother is Gold: A Study in West African Literature*. Cambridge: Cambridge University Press, 1971.

Selasi, Taiye. 'Bye-Bye Babar'. *The LIP*, 3 March 2005. http://thelip.robertsharp.co.uk/?p=76 (accessed 16 June 2016).

——'Stop Pigeonholing African Writers'. www.theguardian.com/books/2015/jul/04/taiye-selasi-stop-pigeonholing-african-writers (accessed 1 July 2016).

Senghor, Léopold Sédar. 'Foreword'. In H.R. Lynch (ed.) *Selected Letters of Edward Wilmot Blyden*. New York: KTO Press, 1978.

Turner, Victor. *The Ritual Process: Structure and Anti-Structure*. Ithaca, NY: Cornell University Press, 1977 [1969].

White, Anthony. 'The Trouble with Twins: Image and Ritual of the Yoruba *ère ìbejì*'. *emaj* Issue 5, 2010 https://emajartjournal.files.wordpress.com/2012/04/white.pdf (accessed 14 August 2017).

Zhu, Ying. *Fiction and the Incompleteness of History: Toni Morrison, V.S. Naipaul, and Ben Okri*. Bern: Peter Lang, 2006.

Žižek, Slavoj. *The Fragile Absolute: Or, Why Is the Christian Legacy Worth Fighting For?* London: Verso, 2009.

The Postcolonial Writer
& the Existential Ordeal

Day and night my toils redouble,
Never nearer to their goals;
Night and day I feel the trouble
Of the wanderer in my soul.
(William Wordsworth, 'Song for the Wandering Jew': 146)

It was three days to my departure to Cambridge for a
much-anticipated professional development opportunity,
but offices, shops and airports were closed. The usually
bustling network of roads that run like the veins of a leaf
through the city of Lagos, Nigeria's commercial capital,
were desolate. And every tick of the clock increased my
apprehension over a career advancement opportunity that
was swinging on the pendulum of uncertainty. And so,
early on that first Monday of July 2003, I called Patricia,
the officer in charge of the arrangements at the British
Council, my sponsor. She was a soft-spoken, dimpled, and
amiable lady who walked so rhythmically one would think
she was waltzing to some ghost music in her head.

'Hey, Nduka', she responded on the other end, as if she
had been roused from a reverie. 'I've been trying to get hold
of the travel agents on the phone without luck. I hate to
believe that the proprietress has switched off her phone on
a day like this. Other workers of the travel agency I tried
are also unavailable.'

'So what do we do?' I asked.

'I'm not about giving up, Nduka', Patricia assured me. 'I'll keep trying until I get through. But then, even if I succeed, how would you handle transportation from the mainland where you live and pick up the ticket on the Island? I hear the roads are barricaded and, besides, I understand the airport is dead.'

'Just leave that to me. Let's get the travel documents first. You haven't forgotten that as a journalist I am permitted to cover the strike?'

Patricia's loud chuckle on the phone forced a smile out of me – a relieving act at a time when laughing seemed like a luxurious exercise unless, of course, you were a Nigerian, curiously described by a UK-based research group, as 'the happiest people on earth'. Indeed, Lagos could force one into believing that claim. Despite prevalent privations, the streets of Lagos were a theatre of tragicomedies and melodramas. In that instant, a scene I had witnessed flitted through my mind like a dreadful dream. A man was almost lynched for allegedly causing the disappearance of a young boy's genitalia by means of a handshake. But for the intervention of the police the Lagos mob would have sent that man to his ancestors. Obi Nwakanma, a friend, poet and fellow journalist had rightly written at the time:

> Poetry walks on the streets in Lagos. It is in the incredible dynamic of life which enacts, like some incandescent power, the moment of each living hour: it is in the sense by which, living in this city, a poet glimpses a whole new form of life, and an alternative way in which to experience it fully. This vast, tense and bristling city, its social tendon tautly held by imprecise impulses, reverberates in the poetic propensities which she inspires.[1]

As Patricia's trademark chuckle trailed off at the other end of the phone, she assured me that she would call back later in the evening to provide an update on any lucky break we may have with the arrangements. She informed me that she had contacted the High Commission earlier to possibly pick up my passport and was told that they were able to process a visa for me before the labour strike took effect that Monday morning. I thanked her and looked at my wristwatch. It was 12.45 p.m. Another sit-at-home labour strike and scorching petrol scarcity had paralysed the sprawling city of millions of inhabitants, some of whom lived in slums floating on the lagoon.[2] Even in high density ghettos such as Ajegunle and Mushin, the residents yielded to the stay-at-home orders of the labour union. There were no residents in the streets chasing one business or another. No residents loitering in clusters, sharing rumours. The Nigeria Labour Congress (NLC), perhaps the only viable opposition to the then ruling political party, Peoples' Democratic Party, had indeed succeeded in impelling the strike to cripple socio-economic activities. It had been called to protest unending devaluation of life via incessant hikes in the prices of petroleum products instigated by the deregulation policy of the Bretton Woods Institutions – the International Monetary Fund and the World Bank.

The NLC president, Adams Oshiomhole – a diminutive man with a heroic stature – had deployed his oratorical gifts to convince a reluctant populace already strike-weary and buffeted by adversity to abide by Labour's call for a total strike. Like other radical leftist ideologues, Oshiomhole was a major critic of the deregulation pill prescribed by global financial institutions and Nigeria's creditors. The rising levels of poverty, double-digit inflation, and spiralling graduate unemployment were hallmarks of corrupt political leadership. Oshiomhole faulted the religious implementation of hostile economic reforms imposed as *conditionalities* for loans by international financial institutions. And many were persuaded by this argument. So convinced were the masses that the strike action turned Lagos into a ghost city. Others who would have ventured out in search of their daily bread rather stayed indoors for fear of social miscreants. Known in city argot as Area Boys, these hoodlums took advantage of such strikes to rob people and unleash mayhem. Lagos had shut down.

So the opportunity offered me by the British Council was in jeopardy. I was travelling to participate in the British Council Cambridge Seminar as a writer and general secretary of the Association of Nigerian Authors. My interest in the seminar was heightened by the promotion of the 2003 programme as one that would 'feature an eclectic mix of famous and lesser-known writers, poets and critics and includes sessions on the work of emerging writers now influencing the UK literary scene, including those shortlisted in *Granta's Best of Young British Novelists*'. One of those novelists was Zadie Smith, whose wave-making novel, *White Teeth*, had been introduced to me by E.C. Osondu, a friend and co-editor of a 1998 controversial anthology of short stories, *We-men: An Anthology of Men Writing on Women*. Ms Smith's inclusion of a wiry Nigerian character in her novel, and her beautiful and youthful face, had aroused my curiosity about what she would be like in real life. Another writer on the programme who I really wanted to spend some time with again after his relocation to the UK upon winning the Caine Prize for African Writing was my compatriot Helon Habila. He had been the latest in the unending exit to the West of talented Nigerians as part of a painful brain drain. Other members of the literati that were listed in the programme and who I longed to meet included Ali Smith, Julian Barnes, author of the intriguing book, *A History of the World in 10½ Chapters*, and the famous Marxist critic, Terry Eagleton.

The sun had gone under on that Monday and, ironically, Lagos had just begun to stir to life rather late in the day when my phone rang. For a city that was responding to the terror of night marauders by cutting back on moonlighting and nocturnal life, dusk looked like dawn, with screeching and cursing commercial bus drivers and commuters anxious to take advantage of the remains of the day before the city was plunged yet again into darkness owing to regular power outages. I picked up the phone, full of expectation. Indeed, it was Patricia. She revealed that she had picked up my passport and extracted a promise from the travel agency handling my reservation that I would receive a return ticket by the next day, 'no matter'. Only trouble was, Patricia had been unable to get my basic travel allowance (BTA) because her office accountant was not on duty. Even if he was working, how was I to gain access to any bank when they were all closed?

'Can you arrange your BTA?' Patricia's voice sounded more like that of a woman thinking aloud than asking a question. I must have been dumb for an unusually long time for next I heard, 'Are you still there, Nduka?'

'Oh, yes, I am', I replied. 'Aha! You asked about getting BTA?' Without waiting for her confirmation, I added, 'I'll try. But, as you noted already, the time is too short and the banks are on strike too.'

Patricia asked me to call her the next day as soon as I had an update. It was more a command than a request. As the phone clicked off, I pondered how I was going to overcome the obstacles that threatened a much-cherished opportunity. Such obstacles were part of the existential struggles of a postcolonial writer operating in an environment where, to appropriate Marechera (*House of Hunger*: 1), 'every morsel of sanity is snatched away from you as some bird of prey snatch [sic] food from the very mouth of babes'.

As a journalist in Nigeria in the late twentieth century and the turn of the millennium, every opportunity offered by a professional travel grant – and I did get quite a few then – was ringed with a marvellous paradox of more sadness than joy. My first international trip abroad seemed to have set off a tough pattern that subsequent trips would follow. Facilitated by Isidore Okpewho, mentor and friend, and Edris Makward, with funding from The Ford Foundation, the trip was to Morocco as a guest writer at the African Literature Association conference in 1999. The poet and journalist, Odia Ofeimun, had also been invited. Due to extenuating socio-political circumstances, I obtained the travel visa late and arrived at the conference on the second day to a warm welcome by Professor Makward, convener of the Morocco conference. I suffered comparable late arrivals during similar intellectual trips abroad. The most memorable were trips respectively sponsored by the French Embassy (in Chambéry, France), Goethe Institut Lagos (in Frankfurt), and the US Department of State for the International Visitor Program on the theme 'The Role of Theatre in U.S. Society'. Reliving those experiences in my mind, sleep eluded me for the most part of that night.

* * *

Dawn arrived with Kika, my four-year-old daughter, arched over me, nudging me gently to wake up and informing me that I had a guest. In the living room Ifeanyi, a cousin who I had come to rely on for critical support in times of crisis, was ensconced on the sofa. He was watching cable news on our ageing television, to which I had a bit of sentimental attachment because it was a wedding present. A tall lad with big, smoky eyes, Ifeanyi spoke with a loud voice and was ever ready to help solve problems.

'Bros, how na?' he asked in Pidgin, rising from his chair as a mark of respect as I approached him. 'E be like say you no dey feel well, abi na the strike?'

I was hardly listening as I sank into the sofa. We made quick conversation and I told him about my preparations for the UK trip and the BTA challenge.

'I don tell Ndu make e no worry himself about this trip', interjected Onyi, my wife, strolling toward the kitchen. She had barely finished speaking when my cell phone rang upstairs.

'Kika, please fetch my phone quickly'.

As she ran up the stairs, the phone stopped ringing. I imagined it might be Patricia. Ifeanyi cast an understanding look at me, and said, 'Bros, e go be network problem. You know how this *kwashiokor* GSM dey do.' I had barely absorbed Ifeanyi's critique of the epileptic service provided by Nigeria's relatively new global system for mobile communications when the phone rang again. And Kika was well near me, bearing it.

'I just picked up your passport with the visa issued by the High Commission', said Patricia, her voice sonorous like a weaverbird's. I thought she was teasing and told her so. She said she was not, and doubled down by asking how soon I could pick up. I told her 'immediately'. But she would rather that I waited so that she could try to get the ticket from the agency later that afternoon as well.

That morning, Ifeanyi and I squandered hours discussing national politics, as was usual with most gatherings of two or more Nigerian citizens. We interrupted our discussion once or twice to eat at the invitation of Onyi. Outside, people sat in clusters discussing the third hike in prices of petroleum products since Olusegun Obasanjo, a retired soldier-turned-politician became president four years before. President Obasanjo had secured a dubious re-election early in the year, but the optimism with which he and his cohort in the ruling party had been welcomed after the most brutal dictatorship in the nation's history had begun to dissolve into mists of despair and hopelessness. It was not surprising, then, that the strike action proved hugely successful. It was an opportunity to protest the gradual slide into another season of anomy.

This was the background that inspired my Cambridge escape to recoup creative energies. And there it was, hanging in the balance like a crooked pendulum, the result of an otherwise salutary labour strike. I was momentarily lost in thoughts when my cell phone rang again, like the cock's third crow on the night that Apostle Peter denied Jesus Christ.

'Hi Tricia'.

'Hi Nduka. You must be the son of God!'

'What's new?'

'I have your ticket at last. Only snag is you have to pick up your BTA from my UK counterparts at Heathrow. That's the best I could get for you, and that shouldn't be much of a problem anyways.'

'Oh, Tricia! You've been marvellous. Yes, that shouldn't be a problem really. I'll manage to scrape up enough FOREX for airport rituals both in Lagos and in the UK. I doubt that I'll need more than the basics before meeting your colleagues at Heathrow.'

'Terminal Four, that's where. Details when you come to pick up the travel documents. How … when are you coming?'

'Right away.' I turned to Ifeanyi as if he had the magic wand to overcome the inevitable mobility difficulties that confronted us.

Out in the street Lagos was a tumultuous multitude chasing too few vehicles and *okadas* – commercial motorbikes. Everyone appeared to be rushing to make the most of eventide before darkness and dread enveloped the city. After all, it was on one such dark night that I was shot at by suspected car snatchers or assassins at the Apapa wharf area while I worked as a Literary Editor for *The Post Express*. That was three years earlier, and I had gradually surmounted the trauma that discouraged me from nights out. Lagos is an enigmatic city whose artistic haunts – or 'watering holes', as a friend fancifully calls them – I liked to explore. A city which has been the subject of several collections of poetry,[3] it was populated with joints where one could enjoy local delicacies and live West African highlife music or West Indian reggae laced with a peculiar Nigerian-ness. Ifeanyi and I hunted for bootleggers who might have fuel for sale at cut-throat prices under such strike conditions. I had a Honda Civic, fortunately a fuel-efficient car. Frustrated, I eventually returned home while Ifeanyi took the search to some dangerous dark alleys, or *lungus*. After about forty-five minutes searching several *lungus*, he returned with a ten-litre jerrican of petrol. We emptied this into the tank of the car, caring little that it might have been typically adulterated, and we set out for

Lagos Island to pick up the travel documents from Patricia. The drive to Ikoyi was surprisingly uneventful. At the gates of the British Council office the security men said we had narrowly missed Patricia, that she had been waiting. Anxiety got the better part of me. I called Patricia. She assured me that all was well. We arranged to meet at La Source, a mixed-culture restaurant and popular artists' hangout at the French Cultural Centre. At the meeting, Patricia was business-like in the manner she handed over the documents. 'Have a great trip, Nduka', she said.

I looked at the documents for a while, wondering about this wanderer in my soul forever yearning for new trips. I did not know when Ifeanyi ordered a bottle of my favourite lager, *Star*, for me. I looked up from the document and saw the sweaty, green bottle daring me not to engage it. It had been a long day and a sip could sooth frayed nerves. Or so I thought without sacramentalizing the drink, as my friend and self-styled god of poetry, Borojah, would do.

An hour and two bottles later, Ifeanyi was driving us back home. Inside the car, the wind whistled jazzy tunes as we drove on the long Third Mainland Bridge. I tracked several threads of possible twists and turns that my Cambridge trip could take.

* * *

Back home, the clock seemed to tick faster. The humid air, exacerbated by a power cut that denied me the luxury of using an electric fan, worsened my discomfiture. My alternate source of power, an overworked power generating set, had packed up from overuse. I had hoped that Ifeanyi would, in his characteristic resourcefulness, imagine a plot to save me from the BTA threat. But, like me, he was in one of those moods when the mind is bereft of ideas and too lazy to think creatively. The jarring sounds of late-night Pentecostal worshippers in neighbourhood churches competed with the chants of a muezzin from an adjoining mosque. I tried calling up a couple of acquaintances to ask for a short-term loan but met with hard luck. So, what was I to do? Even at the best of times the country had no facilities that could provide a creative artist with a modicum of financial support for his work, much less in a crisis situation like the labour strike. I was reflecting on hopes and impediments as an interesting existential dilemma when Onyi provided a *deus ex machina*. She had an emergency fund hidden in her trunk box, she revealed. It wasn't much but she was proud to prove, as she often argued, that women save the world through common sense.

I was in no mood for gender debates and was more inclined to be on my best behaviour, lest she changed her mind. It was 10.30 p.m. From the balcony where we sat for fresh air, I could see market women returning from the night market. The chants of believers in the churches and the mosque had stopped and a semblance of sanity was beginning to descend on the neighbourhood. Long after the household had gone to bed, I sat glued to my chair outside praying that 'almighty' National Electric Power Authority plc (NEPA) would restore power so I could finish packing. It seemed like the longest night. NEPA, which the Nigerian humour mill had aptly nicknamed 'Never Expect Power Always, Please Light Candle', had not returned power, and sporadic gunshots in the horizon announcing armed robbery operations in progress seemed to mark each hour, waking me intermittently.

It was 7 a.m. when I woke up. Onyi was already busy preparing breakfast of *moin-moin* and *akamu*. Though NEPA had restored power to our community and the heat had abated that morning, I was in a dour mood, still agitated about the impending trip later that day. It was the third day of the strike and it had begun to lose its momentum. Still, there had been reports that regular flights were yet to resume at Murtala Mohammed International Airport. I tried to shunt the negative thoughts aside but they persisted. It was as if, to appropriate Dambudzo, the acid of disappointment was eating the base metals of my will to succeed. As I summoned the determination to confront the challenges of the day, I was assailed by echoes of memorable lines from Chinua Achebe, saying in a documentary film that 'living in Lagos is like living in a war front'. I resolved to win the war that day.

As I packed my stuff for the trip, focused more on how to overcome any more challenges the day might offer, my phone rang. A friend that I had asked for a loan the previous day asked me if I still needed the money. I was excited because that would reduce the sense of insecurity I felt travelling without a reasonable BTA. The friend even offered to bring the money to me before I left for the airport at 5 p.m.

Soon it was five o'clock and my friend was yet to arrive. He called to say he was held up at the notorious Oshodi flyover where the usual go-slow had built up as a result of bonfires set up by youths who were still in the strike mood.

We waited.

It was almost 6 p.m. when Onyi suggested that we leave for the airport and notify my friend to redirect his journey to the international airport instead. As we drove around the small roundabout by the local airport, I sighted a burnt corpse on top of a heap of ashes and incompletely burnt tires. A casualty of the strike, I thought! At the airport there was bumper-to-bumper traffic, with vehicles snaking up about one-and-a-half kilometres to the departure terminal.

'This is now the worst part of the trip, after all the *wahala*', Onyi intoned, trying to suppress her agitation about my meeting the check-in deadline.

We had overlooked the fact that, being the first day of full flights since the strike began, the airport was going to be besieged by delayed travellers. By the time we got to the drop off point, it was thirty minutes past check-in time. Two customer service clerks told me that they had concluded check-ins for my flight. I looked back at my family as if in search of a clue as to what next to do. I saw my friend who had brought money for me with them. Their unsmiling faces seemed to be the catalyst I needed to unleash my most persuasive powers.

'Please may I see your station manager?' I asked the two clerks who were trying to calm many frustrated travellers.

'No, you can't. He is not around.'

'Where is your office here?'

'There.' One of the clerks pointed up to a section of the upper floor of the departure lounge. I hurried in that direction, Ifeanyi wheeling my luggage behind me. When we arrived at the office, I met an old senior from my department at the University of Ibadan. She introduced herself as the Public Relations Officer (P.R.O.) for the Airports Authority. I brought out my Press ID card. I also showed her the letter of invitation for the Cambridge Seminar which I was supposed to be attending and told her I was late to check-in and was unable to board, and that I had already missed a day of the seminar. When I noticed that there was quiet in the room, with a middle-aged man who looked like the station manager listening attentively, I emphasized that I was not a businessman but a writer and scholar out to promote Nigeria's literary arts and culture in Cambridge. The small crowd there gazed at me as sweat hugged my shirt to my skin.

The P.R.O. ushered me into a posh office. The man I had suspected of being the manager trailed behind us. As I sat in the revolving chair, my favourite lines from Sola Osofisan's poem 'One Afternoon at a Roadblock' twinkled in my mind:

> In my dear homeland,
> If you are not a cobweb hugging
> Some god's extended branch-work,
> You belong in an unmarked grave. (8)

The manager vetted my documents, processed a boarding pass for me, called an assistant and directed him to escort me to the boarding gate, while he worked the walkie-talkie, perhaps to notify the crew that one more passenger was on his way.

We got to the boarding gate after a twelve-minute walk that seemed like forever. Three or so passengers were boarding the aircraft when we arrived. Soon, the aircraft door was shut. Thoughts of the difficult circumstances surrounding the trip persisted as the aircraft taxied off.

* * *

When we arrived in Heathrow airport early Thursday morning, I was too tired to think about the next stage of my trip – a train ride to Cambridge. Good enough, my cousin, Charlie, had come to pick me up. He was an easy-going, fast-talking, fun-loving guy with a large heart. He had reserved a first-class ticket on a 3 p.m. Cambridge-bound train and had insisted that I had to rest in his house first, before embarking on the one-hour or so ride to Cambridge.

I really cannot account for how I spent the six or so hours before Charlie drove me to Kings Cross Station to take the train to Cambridge. But I remember eating a rather heavy breakfast and then drifting away while Charlie and I talked. When I regained consciousness, I swung into another rushed exit from the house, this time to catch the 3 p.m. train to Cambridge. Fortunately, the unpredictable London traffic was nowhere in sight as we drove to Victoria Station. I was feeling like a recovering drug addict as Charlie drove, managing to astonish me with his knowledge of the London road map in spite of my drowsiness. Although the air of the city was fresh compared to the heavily polluted atmosphere of Lagos, I was already beginning to miss my family and the madness of Lagos. Those who are amused by the irony of the city's slogan, 'Centre of Excellence', only need speak to the 'real Lagosians' of *Isale Eko* – downtown Lagos. Only Lagosians know why, in spite of their love-hate relationship with the place, they remain so addicted to the city by the lagoon. Indeed, as I had said in an interview by John Vidal (2005), Lagos is 'made up of people stranded in the city. They work [there] but cannot go home. Most people live in squalor and cannot imagine any other life' ('Voices of Lagos').

Images of Lagos and the near-overwhelming experiences of the trip kept playing in my mind as Charlie escorted me to the boarding point at the train station. We had some free time to shop there for basics before departure time. Inside the first-class compartment of the train at last, there was just one other passenger. How money filters people into classes, I thought. I reflected on how the British Empire had exploited indentured labourers to construct the amazing London underground railway tubes. As the light train travelled at a moderate speed to Cambridge, I stared out the window at London suburbs and the countryside, drifting in and out of consciousness as I slept and woke, slept and woke.

* * *

Cambridge seemed long getting to. The trail was punctuated by billboards which created the illusion that one had reached the 'big' destination several times before actually finally arriving at the historic home of one of the world's oldest and best-preserved bastions of knowledge. Several years since that visit, the magnificent sixteenth-century constellation of edifices at Cambridge University is still fresh in my mind. The burnt brick and limestone walls and the spring-fresh River Cam hooded from the sun by a canopy of trees combine to make the setting a perfect environment for reflections on the offerings of the mind.

I collected my apartment keys at the porter's lodge at Downing College, strolled along the sidewalks, past manicured green lawns toward L Block. It was summer holiday and without the students in session the college was quiet, like a cemetery, especially for a traveller from sizzling Lagos. Inside the small but well-appointed room,

I unpacked only a few of the items I needed, rushed to the bathroom to freshen up, and went in search of the seminar venue.

The seminar activities were held mostly in the garden as much as the summer weather permitted than inside the medium-sized hall at Howard Building. At the venue, I met David Steven, an averagely-built policy analyst, strategic consultant and researcher with a veiled British conservatism and a warm disposition typical of a technocrat accustomed to dealing with unconventional writers. He was a co-director of the event. He briefed me, trying in spite of the demand on his time by other participants to focus on giving me sufficient update on the activities I had missed. He sympathized with the difficulties that had forced me to arrive late enough to miss Helon Habila, my friend and compatriot, who had to leave because his wife was due to be delivered of their first child that weekend in East Anglia. I soon realized that I had joined the delegates at break time that day, and so participants were dispersed. While some participants milled around the garden, others could be seen snacking and bantering. I felt like an outsider struggling to fit into a social space that was out of joint with his consciousness.

When the seminar reconvened, Zadie Smith, the novelist and essayist who a year later was recognized as one of the top twenty most influential cultural figures in the UK, was on the panel. She radiated like the poster girl the seminar's promotional photographs had projected her to be. She had penetrating eyes that seemed to see beyond the surface of things. Yet she was so casual in manners you would wonder how the kind of maturity evident in her novel *White Teeth* melded with such girlish carefreeness. She was on a *Granta* panel on new writing with the *Granta* editor, Ian Jack. It was a lively session during which Ms Smith expressed her concerns about the tedium of becoming a marketing tool for publishers through promotional tours. As she spoke, I could not help thinking about the contrast between the trajectories of writers from the advanced world and that of those from the so-called Third World that Charles Larson had explored in his new book at the time, *The Ordeal of the African Writer*. For there was Ms Smith, about 28 years old then, unhappy about an opportunity that many writers her age in Nigeria would give an arm and a leg to get, as the cliché goes.

Unfortunately, my phlegmatic mood got the better of me throughout the seminar, prompting me to occasionally brood over how terribly expectations can be so far from reality. Here was an event I had so looked forward to, worked so hard to attend, only to become moody through it. The feeling was akin to one's experience with writing a book. The process can be thrillingly challenging but the end sometimes leaves one disillusioned and wondering: 'Is this all?' or 'Now, what next?'

I managed, however, to hit it off with a few participants at the seminar, especially Mark Stein, then Editor of *Wasafiri*. No sooner had we met than we discovered that we had common interests and so we spent a lot of time talking. Mark commissioned me to write a review essay on Habila's new novel at the time, *Waiting for an Angel*, for *Wasafiri*. He had inferred from our conversation that I was in a vantage position to offer insights into how the original collection of short stories, *Prison Stories,* morphed into the novel. There was also Rachel Holmes, an academic turned founding website manager for Amazon UK until she left in December 2002 to become a full-time writer. The author of *Scanty Particulars* and a recurrent name in the jury of literary prizes such as the Whitbread Prize and Orange Prize for Fiction, Rachel is the kind of writer who could best be described as a free spirit. She surprised me by her generosity when she offered me free accommodation in London whenever I needed it.

Without a doubt, I learnt a lot in the seminar sessions which had in attendance other great literary personalities such as Kate Mosse, who was decorated as Officer of the

Order of the British Empire (OBE) in 2013; Toby Litt, award-winning novelist and short story writer; Ali Smith, celebrated novelist and short story writer; Tariq Ali, historian and novelist; and Michael Schmidt, poet, publisher and director of the Literatures of the Commonwealth Festival, to mention but a few. Nonetheless, the trip to Cambridge lives in my imagination as a sad reminder of dragon-ridden days that have assumed new proportions in my homeland, climaxing with the gargantuan corruption that has bred an unprecedented recession and poverty. Survival is no longer just 'a cruel battle of wits' in the postcolony as I had written in *The Night Hides with a Knife* (1), survival is now literally everyday resurrection from death itself. It is even doubly so for the creative artist.

NOTES

1 Obi Nwakanma, 'Nigeria: Lagos and a Life of The Poets', *Vanguard*, 15 January 2006, http://allafrica.com/stories/200601170183.html (accessed 15 August 2017).

2 Tolu Ogunlesi offers a panoramic view of the slum in his essay, 'Inside Makoko: Danger and Ingenuity in the World's biggest Floating Slum' published in *The Guardian*, Tuesday 23 February 2016. Interestingly, one of my earliest assignments as a Staff Writer for *The Guardian* was a feature article on Lagos slums entitled 'Echoes from Lagos Ghettos'.

3 The best examples include Simbo Olorunfemi's *Eko Ree: The Many Faces of Lagos*. Ikeja-Lagos: HOOFBEATS.com. 2003, and *Lagos of the Poets* (2010), an anthology of several poems by 113 poets about Lagos edited by Odia Ofeimun.

WORKS CITED

Barnes, Julian. *History of the World in 10½ Chapters*. New York: Alfred A. Knopf, 1989.

Granta 81: Best of Young British Novelists. London: Granta Publications, Spring 2003.

Habila, Helon. *Waiting for an Angel*. New York: W.W. Norton, 2003.

——*Prison Stories*. Festac Town, Nigeria: Epik Books, 2000.

Larson, Charles. *The Ordeal of the African Writer.* London: Zed Books, 2001.

Marechera, Dambudzo. *House of Hunger*. Harare: Zimbabwe Publishing House, 1978.

Nwakanma, Obi. 'Lagos and a Life of the Poets', *Vanguard*, 16 January 2006. http://allafrica.com/stories/200601170183.html (accessed 10 March 2017).

Ofeimun, Odia ed. *Lagos of the Poets*. Lagos: Hornbill House, 2010.

Ogunlesi, Tolu. 'Inside Makoko: Danger and Ingenuity in the World's Biggest Floating Slum'. *The Guardian*, 23 February 2016. www.theguardian.com/cities/2016/feb/23/makoko-lagos-danger-ingenuity-floating-slum (accessed 10 March 2017).

Olorunfemi, Simbo. *Eko Ree: The Many Faces of Lagos*. Ikeja-Lagos: Hoofbeats.com, 2003.

Osofisan, Sola. *Dark Songs*. Ibadan: Heinemann Educational Books Nigeria, 1991.

Otiono, Nduka. *The Night Hides with a Knife*. Ibadan: New Horn and Critical Forum, 1995.

Otiono, Nduka and E.C. Osondu. *We-men: An Anthology of Men Writing on Women*. Lagos: Oracle Books, 1998.

Smith, Zadie. *White Teeth*, London: Hamish Hamilton, 2000.

Vidal, John. 'March 2005: Voices of Lagos', *The Guardian*, March 2005. www.theguardian.com/pictures/image/0,8543,-10605140635,00.html (accessed 13 March 2017).

Wordsworth, William. 'Song for the Wandering Jew'. In *The Complete Poetical Works of William Wordsworth, Poet laureate, Etc., Etc.* ed. Henry Reed. Philadelphia: Troutman & Hayes, 1851.

Literary Supplement

My Mother
(Nawal El Saadawi)

MONA HELMY

She
taught me
how to be proud of my head
not
how to go with men to bed
—

She
taught me
how my dissident creative writings
can be my honor, my pride, my sky
a sky where I can sing, dance, laugh and cry
where I can sleep undressed
without being in the least shy
—

She
told me that my destiny
was to swim under water
to go against the stream
to soar above the cloudy weather
of the 'Hareem'
—

She said to me:
'the pleasure of writing
is your only reward
not prizes not critics' reviews
never suppress your true self
it is a sin
that has no excuse'
—

She told me
that my freedom is priceless
not to be compromised
without any hesitation or regret
for it is my complexion my existence
my blood and my sweat
—

My mother Nawal al Saadawi
Always reminds me
that my free life
is the most creative poem
I can ever write

And the Stars Beckoned

Short Story

NADIA WASSEF

When you were a little girl, playing with your neighbour's discarded dolls, you looked up into the deaf sky, and wished that when you were all grown up, you would be a belly dancer. The stars teased your secret out of you. They could be trusted not to whisper pungent rumours. They weren't your neighbours. They would never tell.

Your thoughtful body couldn't help itself. It had the knowledge no-one gave it. Your knees knew that only they could instigate the most vibrant of hip shakes; the incline of your buttocks produced that perfectly undulating stomach roll; and the see-sawing of your shoulders tilted your breasts to mechanical perfection. And when the beat of the *tabla* came at you, you didn't think to fight it. You allowed it in because it was part of you in a way that your family wasn't.

When you got your period you thought you had injured your core. Your urban mother didn't share her womanly knowledge. Just like her rural mother. They only passed on recipes. They discounted the body that wouldn't listen to them anymore. But your body listened. It heard the *taqsim* of the *tabla*, the fanciful misdirection of the *'oud*, and it played along. Your eyes devoured the old black and white Egyptian movies of Samia Gamal and Taheya Karioka. Their beauty and their grace mesmerized you; and it brought all the ugliness in your life centre stage.

You locked yourself in your own room – the only privilege of being the eldest daughter – and replayed the beats in your head while dancing with abandon to decaying walls. When your parents asked you each passing year what you wanted for your birthday, you made something up that was well suited to their world. You never said a professional belly dancer's costume. Although you could feel its sequins on your curious breasts, the rough netting rubbing at your honest belly, and the faux gemstone crowning your navel. You imagined the sequined hip band directing your movements while the dagging on the generous tulle and muslin flirted with your thighs. Your bare feet, sometimes gliding, other times shouting to the world: you are alive.

Your parents insisted you go to school. You needed that degree. They needed the income from any job you could find. It would help with the growing wants of their growing family. Then they would second you to a man to start his family. Your five younger siblings were as different as the five fingers of your hand. You served them breakfast, braided their hair, stuffed their lunchboxes with white cheese and tomato sandwiches, made sure they got to school on time, and helped them with their homework. Your mother's health was unreliable. Your father blamed it and her for only supplying girls. You were the pillar of your family, yet they knew nothing about you. They were so surprised when you rejected the husband they got you, packed a suitcase of clothes that wouldn't be handed down to your sisters, left breakfast laid out on the table, and made your exit.

You thought to leave a note explaining the reasons behind your departure, like you had seen all the tragic heroines do. But why crowd them with information they would have no use for? You just called after the dusk prayers of the day you left. You suggested they tell the neighbours you had been selected for a special training course and you would be gone for a while. Rather than committing lies to paper, the phone call seemed nobler to you.

And finally, your life began. Haram Street's bright lights beckoned, their clubs pulsing through the night. You auditioned for a troupe run by a woman, thinking she would be kinder, like a mother. She was like your mother: she maximized on the use she got out of her girls. You finally danced to an audience, but you chose not to fall in love with the drummer, preferring to dispose of your virginity more efficiently. You managed the demands on your body. You practised every day from noon prayers till dusk, listened to advice from other dancers, paying closer attention to the stories of those who had fallen.

If you'd ever been on a stage, you would understand the addiction. The fantasies and fears of desperate men lying at your feet: kick up or stomp – your choice. You were different because you embraced this life; you weren't coerced into it out of desperation like the others. Even your style spoke of that difference: uncorrupted because you had only revealed your dancing to chipped walls all your life.

You didn't mind that money was thrown at you while you performed; finally you could step on the bills that had eluded your family and ruled their pitiful existence. Nor did the diminished drunks that approached the head of the troupe bother you, because you appreciated the extra income. You learnt how to get out of them more than they took away from you. At first it was a loan to fix the rip in your outfit, then it was gifts of new outfits, until you finally graduated to the higher calibre of man who would take you on short trips. You visited the Giza Pyramids, saw views of the city you never imagined, and travelled to other cities. You never knew how much pieces of paper could please you: your first driver's licence, your first passport, your first bank statement. You played your grateful part with dignity, and most of the time, you were content. You saved pennies, invested pounds, and discovered the delicious joy of spending on yourself. You now had a manicurist, a woman who waxed you and then scrubbed you with crushed lupine beans, another who massaged your aching body to invigorate it for the next performance, and yet another who applied red, then black, henna to your hair. Your dresser remained one of the two most important people in your life: she would arrange your outfits, clean them, mend any tears, and suggest new ones. The other permanent fixture was your driver/bodyguard who waited for you after each performance, who stood outside your changing room filtering people, and who steered you through the city, protecting your body with his own. This was your family.

Had you had more time to dwell on the past, your parents might have surfaced in your thoughts. You might have missed your sisters. You might have pitied them for the life they didn't choose, but would live out anyway. Every couple of months you would send clothes, meat, and imported foods that were out of the reach of their Egyptian pound-denominated life. Only after leaving had you found the common ground with your family. You understood that there was one thing more frustrating than being poor, and that was not being poor enough. Being able to almost afford, but not quite. Unfulfilled hopes chiselled away at their hearts more than no hope at all. Your packages of daughterly care probably dulled the ache. You assumed, but didn't care enough to find out.

When you changed your name to match your rising star status, you did it for yourself, and then for them. You didn't want your absent presence to thwart the chances of your sisters when they reached marriage age. You had to allow them to make the same mistakes your parents made. Nor did you have the inclination to absorb the confused expressions that your life would trigger on their faces. Above all, you enjoyed reinventing yourself and then un-leashing it onto this world.

You were so blessed. Every Ramadan you would spend the entire Holy month fasting, feeding the poor, resting your body, and praying. You needed to thank the God who had not stood in the way of you, who had let circumstances enable your choices. Nightclubs and cabarets closed throughout that month allowing piety to prevail. You performed your five prayers at their set times as though you were performing maintenance on your car. You confessed to God all your sins as you knelt on your silk prayer mat, your hands travelling down your toned thighs, your heels warmed by your buttocks. You didn't actually perceive them as sins, but from what God had said, you knew He would see things differently. You weren't going to try His patience by explaining or arguing with His viewpoint, you merely apologized for all that had passed, and paved the way for what was to come. You had both been through this, year after year, and you took comfort in the formulaic nature of your bond.

You toyed with the idea of marrying. But you had married an art form. The notion of falling in love appealed to you, then you remembered those ghastly heroines in your cherished films, and how love had led them astray. But you had fallen in love with your own independence. You had looked for the man. The man who would protect you. There was the one who stole from you while you slept; the one who admitted he would never leave his wife, but why should he? You could always take the prized status of second wife; the one who insulted you after he released himself inside you; and the one who just had very kind eyes. You looked everywhere your twirling arms could reach. You finally found the man. It was you.

How did it all unravel? One thread pulled, and a life smouldered into indignant tatters. The hopelessly romantic heroines in those black and white movies clawed their way into your carefully put together life. It was a Thursday night, your outfit was black and silver, your earrings were too big and were tugging at your curls, but you were still giving the kind of performance your audience kept coming back for. You felt his gaze before your eyes locked on his defeated frame. Your father, a seasoned drunk, with his pitiful aura still prevailing, was flooding his glass with Red Label. You didn't look at who he was with – it didn't matter.

You knew your face had turned the color of unripened guavas, your insides matching theirs. Your indignation at God's mismanagement simmered. And your success had attracted the evil eye's stare. Resentment battled with gratitude: your father's choices, the outcome for your family, and the road you had taken, that you had loved.

Hijack in Hurghada

A Travelogue

RAZINAT T. MOHAMMED

Somewhere along the serene, long strip of the Red Sea, is an artificial settlement, El Gouna. A carefully tended settlement of splendor thronged with exquisite and homogenous structures that reflect, even in their modernity, the ancient Arabian architecture of near Bronze Age. In its somewhat ambiguous nature, the new seems to constantly hold on to the old as if afraid of drowning in the vibrancy of infringing European civilization. On the faces of things, the battle for supremacy between the old and the new readily captivates the senses in the smoking of the old pipe, Shahshi at musical concerts where American Country music is performed concurrently with a near perfect mimic, of big time Rap music, by 50 Cent. In the symmetry that results, the tenacious dilemma of the old is strung to the new dynamics of the intra-familiar. This is the El Gouna of the Marina, which harbours the rich of Europe, and the fleet of holiday makers that perhaps, not so rich, would work themselves to the bones back home, for a little feel of the real experiences that define the realities of the rich people of this world. Can Doctor Faustus, that ignoble creature of Christopher Marlowe be blamed for wanting the experience with Helen of Troy even if it was short lived?

The El Gouna Marina sprawls at parallel sides like a double-tongued dragon. On the one side, almost at the demarcating gravel stones, stands the Mosiaque; a lovely piece of architecture of modern welfare with Arabian sensibilities. The Mosiaque, only seven months old is the chosen abode for the six visiting writers from around the different Continents of the World; America, Europe, Asia, Australia and good old Africa; however, two writers could not make the program. The one-month Sponsorship program offered by the Oracom Development, a multi-billion-pound organization with huge investments scattered around the world was aimed at providing writers with writing space to help them complete on-going projects.

In Gouna, as the locals refer to the serene holiday spot, is a collection of properties owned by the giant Oracom Development. This company provided the writers with the opportunity to write without having to worry about cooking or the making of their rooms while they were engaged in the tedious activity of recreating the world. They came literally, to be spoilt, by a lover of creativity and a philanthropist they were never opportuned to meet to show appreciation. The four were the favourites of the Mosiaque Hotel and indeed, of the small settlement because, curiously, people got to know they were around; all four of them Anna, Berny, Johnny and Rabia, all very keen chroniclers of the events of the world around their different societies.

Nevertheless, all work and no play, they say, makes Jack a dull boy. Once in a while some of the writers took some time off their lonesome activity and went 'down town' to unwind the stress of their sedentary writing preoccupation. In this sense therefore, a visit to the winery here and another to the coffee shop there, all of which abound in El Gouna, were frequent habits. While all of these were going on, the days were also ticking by and, soon, it was a week to go and a curious visitor joined the writers from Germany. Slim and beautiful with a lovely fairness of the Roman goddess, Venus, Monique brought added sunshine and laughter to the conversations at dinner. One week was dragged like eternity and the bonding amongst the writers and Monique became infectious such that at the end of the one week, parting became almost mournful.

At the Hurghada international Airport to see Monique off, Johnny sat with Rabia sipping fizzy drinks and waited for the arrival of their new friend, Zahir. A 60-year old Egyptian and a passionate lover of African Literature, an Arabic Translator who has done significant work at translating into Arabic some big time writers like Nigeria's Wole Soyinka and South Africa's Nadine Gordimer before each of them became a Nobel Laureate. Tall, slim and properly tanned, Zahir is blessed with a prominent forehead which, perhaps, stores the secret wisdom to his picking on great writers, likely to hit the world in due course. He had a scanty crop of greying hair covering about three quarters of his head; the head nonetheless, was balding from the forehead to the centre. As they waited for his arrival, Rabia remembered their meeting the previous evening, with this exuberant translator and she saw him as a free thinker who could not be bothered about religious philosophy and where faith took one because he readily admonishes the dogmatic and intolerant behaviours of his countrymen, who have sectarianized the Egyptian society halting for months, the country's major foreign currency earner, Tourism. Rabia could not stop wondering if Zahir was a free thinker as he claimed or in fact, he was one just moaning the downturn in his country's economy. Whatever was Zahir's case, he had become their friend and they waited for his arrival after Monique's departure. They were at liberty or so they thought to while away their time since Zahir had offered to return them back to El Gouna, 22 kilometers away from the cosmopolitan city of Hurghada.

The next 30 minutes saw the three of them seated at a restaurant situated within a large shopping Mall. The place belonged to his best friend he told Johnny and Rabia. They sipped at the drinks set before them, Zahir was drinking tea from a glass mug, Rabia sipped her 7 UP from a glass tumbler and Johnny was served a chocolaty pancake roll and a small cup of Turkish coffee. The discussion on the small table, naturally, centred, on writing and translation, because that was the only thing that gave their host the most excitement. In the middle of discussions, Johnny asked Zahir if he was still inclined to drop them at El Gouna and he reacted as though he had never had a discussion that remotely suggested his intention to drop them off.

'In that case, I think we had better start off before we miss our dinner.' it was Rabia who chipped in, because she saw no reason for the continuous tell-tale about African Literature when indeed with her proficiency in the subject she could not care less about the babble of their host.

'Oh! no! I can take you to a very lovely restaurant and you can have your dinner there.'

She looked at Johnny from the corners of her eyes and he got the message that getting out of the coffee shop was the only thing they could handle just then. They had not gone to Hurghada to pay for their dinner. It was clear that their host was about to plunge them into some extra expenses they were not ready for; more so, when their own dinner, a nightly buffet was sprawling on the long white linen tables in El Gouna, waiting graciously for their arrival.

'Ok!'

He shook his head and it was obvious that he was disappointed the two writers did not want to rigmarole in Hurghada with him that night. He adjusted his trousers and quickly excused himself and walked towards the Gents. Just then, the attendant came up with the bill and walked back to his counter. Modestly, Johnny brought out his wallet and placed a 50-pound note in the charge box.

'He is supposed to settle that.' Rabia was referring to Zahir.

'Oh! Well, it's okay,' Johnny's Australian accent re-echoed in her ears as she registered her displeasure at his having to pay for all of them, including the translator, Zahir.

'We came here at his instance Johnny. Okay, please tell me, do people invite their friends out and then share the bill at the end? I may seem foolish to you but where I come from, when someone invites you out, he picks the bill because, you are his guest.'

'Yeaaah, in Australia, well, you could share, but in Spain, and indeed as it seems in Egypt, it is not so.'

'It is alien to me.'

The attendant was already at the table and still their host had not resurfaced from the Gents. Rabia watched as Johnny settled the bill and when his change was kept on the table, Zahir reappeared by which time they were already on their feet. It was a drama well staged. Rabia could swear it was not the first time Zahir and the attendant played out their roles.

As they strolled out of the restaurant, Zahir told them he would take them to a point where they could get a taxi at a reasonable rate and soon, they settled to light discussions about the beauty of Hurghada and its tourist potentials. However, Zahir did not fully participate in their aimless, musing about the town. Rabia stole furtive glances at him in the neon illuminated night.

'I will take you to see the Marina', he proposed suddenly.

'Oh, no Mr Zahir, maybe some other time, we just want to go back before it became too late for us.' It was Rabia again.

'We will not stop or even divert because, it's on the way.'

'In that case, it's okay.' He drove on while the two writers mused on. As for Rabia, her musing at every edifice she saw was her way of faking her interest; actually, she did not want to have any of it. The car took several turns and at each turn, she heard Johnny ask Zahir what the name of the street was and he would say at intervals 'Ashra', 'Misr' and 'Kaana'. The drive seemed long in their own calculation and as they were surrendered to fate, Zahir negotiated yet another bend and brought the car to a stop. Johnny and Rabia quickly opened their doors and stepped out and looked at each other in shock. They looked around and there was no sign of any car, much less, a taxi. In fact, it was an alley of ruins and uncompleted buildings. It was 8.15 p.m.; they waited for their host who began to ensure that each door was properly locked.

'Where are we?' Rabia asked Johnny in a whisper and all he could do was laugh a suppressed kind of laughter which Rabia was forced to join in. what is it they say about situations one is not in the position to change?

'If you cannot change them, join them.'

She too laughed in Johnny's suppressed manner; after all a little laugh cannot harm the soul. They watched Zahir circumvent the car thrice but finally, he came to where they stood and announced that they were to go six floors up the monstrous ruin that stood above them to meet his family.

'What? Mr Zahir, we do not have the time please.' Rabia begged.

'Please, just for 15 minutes, 15 mins.' It was pitiful and he led the way to a red metal door and behold, it was a lift that was fit to be at the ancient and glorious Karnak Temple, in Luxor. They followed him into the piece of antiquity and to start with, it would not lift them up and that made Zahir twist the keys in his hand severally. They watched as he tried every key on the bunch. While he was busy struggling with the keys, Johnny turned and was taking snap-shots of the red walls of the lift. Rabia could no longer bottle the many urges to laugh since they stepped into Zahir's car; so, she let out a little shrilled sound and then she felt her stomach walls ache. She immediately remembered reading somewhere, about ancient monks or Tibetan priests' wise saying: 'Never hold your farts in. They travel up your spine, into your brain, and that's where shitty ideas come from.' That was the feeling that overwhelmed her that evening. Lesson from the two? Laugh and fart when you feel the urge. Suddenly, the ancient machine came to life and up they went to the sixth floor. At the door, Zahir knocked and waited, the curious two also waited, standing behind him. The door opened slightly and he pushed his head through and spoke in whispers to someone whom they could not see. The door closed again and he stood there with his back turned to them. Rabia was certain he was a-flush with shame. A few minutes passed and they were granted entry into a relatively large room filled with a variety of items ranging from bikes to different sizes of tables, a heap of clothes on the floor and all sorts of other odds. A lengthy bookshelf, fully stuffed, hung on the wall. A wooden cabinet also stood against the wall from where a small old fashioned, 14-inch television, was showing a Tom and Jerry cartoon. Zahir asked his guests what they would have; after much drag, they settled for tea for Johnny and water for Rabia, and then he excused himself and went into the interior through a door that was half glass and half wooden.

'Gulp down whatever he brings for you Johnny and let us get out of here.' Johnny only laughed at her. Zahir came out and picked some of his prided translations and showed them. He was particularly elated when he showed his huge Arabic translation of Ben Okri's *The Famished Road* and one would have supposed that he also wrote the English version and not Ben Okri himself.

'I am betting the world of African Literature that in the next five years, Ben Okri will win the Nobel Prize for Literature'.

He enthused enigmatically. While he was still engaged in his predictions, his daughter, a very lovely girl of 19, brought the tea and a pack of juice. The juice was for Rabia. She signaled to Johnny to swallow the drink in a gulp so they could take their leave but poor Johnny, the tea was too hot for him. As he sat there wincing painfully, she felt sorry that he had to be put through all of that.

When they made it to the lift, they were thankful that they were going to breathe the fresh air that was in abundance outside the house. However, they noted with dismay that his wife had refused to see them. As they walked the dark alley, Zahir kept relating the stories of the street which used to be lively and beautiful until its live wire, a billionaire of whatever name, was arrested and his property confiscated by government. He showed them his wife's psychotherapy clinic and he complained that she was not heavily patronized by the people of Hurghada as it was in Cairo before their relocation and, at that, Rabia wondered if charity should not actually begin at home. How could the wife fail to see her very first patient roaming the ruins of the ancient alleys where she herself resides?

Childless

Short Story

KALAPI SEN

As usual, she reached the Princep Ghat railway station for circular rail, overlooking the majestic Ganges. It used to be their regular meeting place since they had met there for the first time. And, as usual, she reached right on time on June 27, 2002. Little did she think that a day like this will ever come in her life! But fate generally has something in store which we never imagine – even in our nightmares. It was undoubtedly their first meeting after their split which had come due to those five words, after a strong relationship of five beautiful springs –

'This kid is not mine!'

A cold chill ran down her spine. She was not prepared – at least for this! After a silence of three seconds, in a shivering voice Sheema said, 'How could you even say that? Is this really what I should get after five long years of commitment to you even by going against my family?'

With tears like two drops of pearl she tried to look up in to the eyes of her love. But as her eyes went up to confront his eyes, Gourav had already moved ten steps away from her. She tried to move towards him and hold his hand. But those ten steps now seemed to be more than ten miles! From a distance Sheema heard him saying, 'Listen, I can't get married to you.'

* * *

After a tumultuous step taken by her to go against her family's decision and the society's rebukes, Sheema was ordained the status of a 'slut' by the person whom she loved more than anyone else in her life. In vain she tried to convince Gourav to get married as soon as possible – not to save herself from being beaten to death by her parents or to save her family's honor and reputation in the society where her own aunt was brutally murdered in the name of 'honor killing'; but only to bring their love-child into this world – a place which she imagined as the 'most beautiful place' till she heard those words which she couldn't believe. Now she began to wonder whether the world was really that beautiful a place as she had imagined it to be, and was Gourav really a partner to be proud of, whose name too meant 'pride'!

Sheema had no further questions left either for Gourav or for her blind faith in love. She had got all the answers to her unasked questions in the very words that Gourav used to project his refusal to accept their baby which was breathing safely inside her, hoping to see the light of the world, very soon. The relationship had to end. And it ended after an extensive quarrel which lasted for three-long-hours, regarding their unborn and perhaps, unwanted baby.

'You know very well, Gourav, that my brother will kill me once the news of my pregnancy is leaked, and maybe in a month or two it will become very explicit! You know I still haven't finished my Higher Secondary Examination! You know very well that in my community girls are not even allowed to go to school after they turn twelve or thirteen! But my father allowed me to continue my education only because he wanted to become the first doctor in our entire community. You very well know that ....'

Cutting her short, he replied, 'That's your problem, not mine!'

With a note of astonishment Sheema gathered courage and asked, 'How can you even say that? Is this my child only? Have you got no responsibility towards it?'

'I told you, I can't do anything about it.'

'It's already passed three and a half months ... maybe I

can keep this as a secret only for another six weeks … But what after that? Where will I go? Who will marry me after knowing that I had conceived without marriage? What will I tell my parents?'

'Listen! Don't drag me into all this! I'm not interested,' he said, very much unperturbed.

'Please don't leave me in this condition, Gourav … You know very well how they killed my *pishi* only because she got married to Ishtiaaq, the Muslim boy in our neighborhood. No one bothered to understand the deep bond of love that *pishi* and *pishemoshai* had for each other, for which they eloped and married … for people like my father, my brother, my uncle only their honor, 'fake honor' mattered![1] Only the conflict between a Hindu and a Muslim mattered to them. *Pishi* and *pishemoshai* were not spared even when they got a legal marriage certificate to live together! But as far as I am concerned, you very well know what my fate will be!'

'So what? What am I supposed to do? You know, I AM GENUINELY NOT BOTHERED!'

Saying this Gourav tried to walk away, but she knew what was going to happen to her and her baby if he didn't marry her at this point of time. In utter desperation, she knelt down on the dusty road and caught Gourav's left leg while he tried to walk away from her.

'Please don't brush me off like this, please! You know my family will be ostracized! You know I will be burnt in broad daylight, ALIVE, along with your child ….'

'Oh please! Don't try that emotional blackmail! Nothing of that sort is going to happen! Stop your melodrama.'

Somewhat suddenly her tears dried up and she spoke with a dry voice:

'You call this melodrama? You don't believe me? You think

---

[1]   *Pishi* and *pishemoshai* – father's sister is called *pishi* and her husband is addressed as *pishemoshai* in Bengali. Bengali is the regional language of West Bengal, India.

that things have changed only because it's the twenty-first century? Imagine, the community which couldn't accept an inter-religion marriage, just seven years back, will it accept my baby out of wedlock? No! The society is much more brutal than you can even imagine! Do you think it was a lie when I told you how Baani jumped off from Howrah Bridge and killed herself only to save her family from a social boycott? She too, you remember, was in a physical union with Birender, *your friend*, and he refused to marry Baani when his family arranged his marriage to a rich girl?'

'Come on! Grow up, Sheema! Pre-marital sex is very common nowadays! Don't fool yourself that Baani committed suicide only because of that! She was a ...'

Before he could finish the sentence, Sheema retorted, 'Yes, she did so, only because of that! You will never understand our community and you can never understand what Baani felt for Birender. It is quite easy for you to call her or me with vulgar names, but the truth is even in the twenty-first century people have a mindset of the twelfth century as far as a girl and her honor is concerned. We haven't moved forward since the days of the Ramayana when a pious lady like Sita was asked by her husband to go through *agni-pariksha* ... Women till date are asked to pass through fire, may be symbolically these days, to prove their virginity and sanctity.'

'All rubbish!' Gourav tried to shut her up.

Sheema burst out with, 'No it's not!'

'Yes, it is!' he said.

But Sheema soon regained her composure and once again tried to convince him into a sacred union thinking that since 'their' baby is concerned, her fate may not be like that of her aunt! In a croaking voice she said, 'Let's not fight, please let's get married ... not for my sake ... for the sake of our baby!'

'Enough is enough! I told you many times don't involve me in this!'

'What do you mean by "don't involve me in this", pointing her finger towards her belly and continued, 'this baby is OUR love-child ... WE both are equally responsible for this pregnancy and WE should do everything WE can to give it a beautiful world!'"

When he couldn't win over Sheema with his arguments, he finally picked his hand up to slap her but ended up saying, 'ENOUGH! This kid is not mine!'

All her dreams of 'living happily ever after' with Gourav and their baby were shattered like a pack of cards in the midst of a fierce *kaal-baishakhi*[2] as soon as these five words reached her ears. She tried to cover her ears with her two shivering hands before they could reach her ears ... but it was of no use. His words travelled faster than her hands could reach her ears. But, was it really that easy for Sheema to believe that everything had come to such a drastic STOP? No, it wasn't! And she had to do something about it. She tried to be brave in front of Gourav, wiped her tears briskly and said with a strong note in her voice: 'O.K. fine, if this kid is not yours, it's better to go for an abortion as soon as possible.'

'Fine ... But Sheema I AM GENUINELY NOT INTEREST-ED in what you do with YOUR child!'

It was very easy for a womanizer like Gourav to shrug off his responsibility and call her a harlot. For him, any woman who has pre-marital sex is a whore! But he didn't seem to remember this before he seduced Sheema when she just turned sixteen.

Months had passed after this and Sheema and Gourav never saw each other's face after the 14th of July 2001, the day she had her pregnancy terminated. But before she could recover from the trauma of abortion, a sudden call on the 22nd of June 2002 gave her another shock. She was

---

[2] *Kaal-baishakhi* – Bengali term for the Nor'westers, fierce thunder-storms accompanied with heavy rain which is generally experienced during the first month of the Bengali New Year, called *Baishakh*. The month of *Baishakh* begins on the 14th or the 15th of April every year and ends around the 14th or the 15th of May.

now trying to recover from the trauma of her frustrated relationship with Gourav.

'Then why did he call up suddenly and said he wanted to meet me?' Sheema thought.

How could it be otherwise than her 'beloved' Gourav trying to blackmail her by saying, 'I have got the papers of your abortion with me, which I may use to ruin the new life – so full of happiness, which you are planning to begin with your Aananda *darling*.' Of course, she had to go. She could not let that happen. After all, Sheema did not want to lose Aananda – whom she met for the first time when she was on the verge of committing suicide by jumping off from the ferry in order to drown herself in the Holy Ganges, only because she was aware of the fact that even if her secret pregnancy was unknown to the world, it is just a matter of time that her family will face severe consequences when she will not be detected as a 'virgin' in her nuptial bed!

* * *

And there she was … once again waiting for Gourav in the Princep Ghat railway station for the circular rail, overlooking the majestic Ganges, their regular meeting place, right on time on June 27, 2002. Now it was past 5:30 p.m. Gourav was late, as usual. 'Some people never change, I guess,' Sheema said to herself and turned around to see if she could munch on to something. Her eyes went on to the same peanut vendor from whom she and Gourav bought peanuts worth Rupees Ten every day for their lunch, as Gourav never had money to treat her in some good restaurant. Eventually, if they went to a good restaurant, Sheema paid for it from her pocket-money. She went to the vendor and asked for peanuts – this time, only for Rupees Five, because she was eating it all alone … no Gourav to give her company! Munching over the roasted peanuts, her eyes went to something written in the paper wrap that contained the roasted nuts so long. She glanced at the printed words on the paper. Half of the print had gone into the folds of the pack. But the legible portion read '… that you cannot get happiness by pursuing it.' Sheema's eyes rolled over these words again and again. She thought about it in terms of her own life.

'How many times have I tried to find happiness in the tears which I used to shed for him … when he hit me with the broken pieces of beer bottles and left me all by myself with a bleeding wrist on Red Road … when he used his boots instead of his hands to slap my face for talking to my school friends who were male … when he abused me left and right only because I was late to pick up his phone calls … so many occasions…'

Suddenly a thought struck her: 'It's not the first time that I have come through these words! … But why can't I remember where I have read them?' Thinking it out for a while, Sheema remembered: 'Of course Bertrand Russell! How can I forget this line?' After a short hollow laugh she said audibly to herself, 'after all this line was the source of inspiration which gave me stamina enough to fight my way out from the clutches of Gourav finally showing me the way to the loving arms of Aananda'.

Trying to hide her tears from public gaze, Sheema looked up towards the blue sky. Few seconds later when her vision moved from the sky, she felt as if someone was sitting beside her and watching her. For a moment, she thought that Gourav must have arrived, but to her surprise she saw a grey-haired man sitting beside her and saying, 'There are a great many people who have all the material conditions of happiness, i.e. health and a sufficient income, and who, nevertheless, are profoundly unhappy.'

Sheema retorted, 'I don't think we know each other, so it will be better if we don't talk.' What was going on in her mind was that perhaps that while she is talking to this man, Gourav arrives and once again abuses her in derogatory terms and his favorite swear-words! Suddenly, a thought came to her and she turned around to ask the man, a thought which was really troubling her: 'Excuse me gentleman. May I ask you something?'

'Young lady, I tried to answer your questions, but I guess you are more interested in what "he" is going to think.'

The old man began to walk towards the jetty. Sheema, very much in a state of hypnosis, also walked behind him and threw a plethora of questions at him. 'How do you know that I was thinking of Gourav? ... O.K. Let that be. How do you know Gourav? Has he sent you to me? Give me the papers ... I can't wait for the entire day for him or his messenger to give me those papers which solely belong to me!'

The man stopped walking and turned towards her. Sheema was taken aback.

'Neither do I know Gourav nor have I come here as his messenger, lady.'

'Then who are you?' asked in utter astonishment.

'You seem to have forgotten me, lady! I was one of your favorite authors when you were trying to "convince" yourself that you are "happy" with him!'

* * *

'What do you mean by my "favorite authors"? ... Listen, I'm seriously not interested in your nonsense!' Sheema roused her eye brows with surprise and anger! But then, with an inquisitive look, she said, 'Let me think! Ummm ... P.B. Shelley, Matthew Arnold, Eliot, Rabindranath Tagore, Bankim Chandra Chattopadhyay ... Athol Fugard, Ruskin Bond ... Ummm ... Bertrand Russell...' With an angry but an anxious face, she looked at the old man and said, 'Is it some kind of a joke? My favorite authors are all DEAD!!!! How can they come back? You know, the dead don't come back. Listen, I am not interested in your crap. Please do not disturb me or else I will ... I will *have* to call the police!'

The old man started walking once again. Sheema thought what sorts of jokes are cracked these days! Her mind once again flew to the thought of Gourav and she began to wander, perhaps Gourav had also cracked a joke and will not come. Her eyes once again went to the empty paper pack for peanut and to her surprise she saw that the man, who was claiming to be one of her favorite authors, was really none other than Bertrand Russell himself! Sheema jerked and started walking fast towards the jetty to try and talk to this man once again. And to her utter disbelief she saw that the man was sitting on a chair, kept for the passengers waiting at the ferry station just adjacent to the railway station. Sheema stopped after moving a few steps towards him. The man said, 'Don't be afraid of me, I am not a living being who can hurt you.'

'I am sorry Mr. Russell ... err ... Sir ... Actually, I was waiting ... But never thought ... No, actually it's you ... I mean ... But you are ... I mean...' Sheema tried to say something sensible, but words won't form into a sentence right now.

* * *

'Yes, my dear, I am Bertrand Arthur William Russell, 3rd Earl Russell of Kingston Russell, Viscount Amberley of Amberley and Ardsalla. Born on May 18, 1872 at Trelleck, Wales. Died on February 2, 1970 at Merioneth, Wales.'

'O my God! I can't believe Sir that YOU are sitting in front of me!'

'So, young lady, times have changed and the world has changed too! I am a misfit perhaps. I am dressed like I used to dress in my days, but things have really changed a lot, and beyond recognition after 32 years of my death!' said the man.

Sheema tried to cover it up by saying, 'No Sir, how can a stalwart like you be a misfit. Your words have relevance even in our days.' Gathering some courage, after trembling with fear and excitement, Sheema said, 'Sir, if we could go and sit somewhere ... perhaps in a nearby café.' The man agreed to her proposal and they both started walking towards the nearest café, on the other side of the road.

* * *

Feeling a bit awkward, walking into a modern day café, with a man dressed in some old fashioned clothes, Sheema entered Café Coffee Day. They took a seat which overlooked the Holy Ganges. Sheema asked him to sit and went to the counter to order for two cups of hazelnut cappuccinos and some sandwiches.

A few moments later, their order arrived at the table and the man was astonished to see the two cups, which actually contained coffee. Dumbfounded, he asked Sheema, 'What is this? I thought you had ordered for some coffee!'

'Yes Sir! This *is* coffee.'

'What? Coffee!! Is it?' He tried to scrutinize the cup of coffee carefully. Then after a few seconds he asked, 'My dear girl, where *is* the coffee? What I can see is nothing more than some creamish-white foam!'

Sheema was at a fix. She is so much used to this sort of a cup, one-third filled with froth and two-third with the liquid. She tried to explain this fact to him. And the man smiled and said,

'I know my dear. But have *you* realized this fact?'

'I am sorry, Sir. Which fact are you talking about?'

'You see, "real" coffee that we like, actually lies deep in the cup, and the froth covers it up. Human beings tend get attracted towards the "froth". However, the real taste of coffee and happiness of sipping it comes only after you have had patience enough to reach the layer of coffee.'

'Sir, I am sorry, but your metaphorical words are not quite comprehensible to me.'

'I'll explain it to you. You see, you had been in love with Gourav for five years. Have you ever thought why?'

Sheema's eyes once again were overflowing with tears. She never thought of her relationship with Gourav in the way this man is saying.

The man continued, 'You were attracted towards him because he was the only guy who showed interest in

you. You must be thinking that this old man is talking all nonsense. But no my dear, it's not utter nonsense. You actually fell in love with the thought of being in love. Your friend, Baani was attractive and had a number of guys falling for her, but you had none. You thought that it was because Baani was beautiful and you are not. You suffered from a very low self-esteem and hence, when Gourav came one day proposing his love for you, you thought, "I shall not get anyone better than this." You thought that if I....'
His words were not even over, when Sheema broke down. Though these thoughts had previously come to her mind, she never thought them to be true.

'Don't cry, my dear. You have done a lot for him. I know how you used to spend all your money to buy him Whisky and Beer, and then tolerated the bruises made by him on your body by those beer bottles and on your mind with his abusive words. I remember you bleeding while you walked through Lindsay Street to Red Road, sat on the bus stop to tend your wound yourself. Time and again you tried to hide your marks of injury from your friends, your parents and most of the times, from yourself. You even thought of coming out of your relationship, but you always thought that it was a part of your life! Moreover, you tried to pacify yourself by saying, "All's fair in love!" and "No one will accept me for marriage because I'm not a virgin anymore!" You thought that was your only "Road to Happiness!"'

It is true that *you* were in love. But have you ever given it a thought as to whether, *he* was in love with you? No! You loved him blindly. And your blindness led you into such a deep trouble! You remember the day when you made love with Gourav, just before you conceived?'

Sheema was speechless so long. Only silent tears rolled down her cheeks, and her body shook tremendously. To this question, she just nodded her head and said 'yes.'

'And do you remember, what did he say, just prior to your intimacy? He called you a whore. Still you agreed to make love! Why? Because you were trying to 'pursue' happiness in Gourav's pleasure. But did you ever think what about you and your happiness?'

It was becoming very difficult for Sheema to take it any longer. She said, 'Can we talk about something else?'

The man, nevertheless, continued: 'What did you get out of your entire effort to make someone happy who only loved your body and your money?'

After being mute for all this while, Sheema cleared her voice and said, 'I tried to come out of that relation a number of times, but … each time I tried to, Gourav said 'Who is going to marry you? You are not a virgin anymore!"

'What? Virginity! In the twenty-first century, who bothers about such things?'

She sobbed heavily, 'Not only that, he also said that whoever I got married to, he will ruin our lives by telling my future husband about my abortion. I had no other option. If my parents would have come to know of it, they would have committed suicide or killed me perhaps like they killed my *pishi* in the name of "honor".'

'But you fell in "real" love with Aananda only after your abortion and it was he who saved you from drowning yourself so that your secret is never revealed. He is such a good companion and a good human being. Why didn't you tell him?'

Sheema cut him short by saying, '… I didn't want to lose him. He is the only man I have met who respects me. He never orders me, never abuses me, never takes away my money, never hits me, never 'rapes' me like Gourav…'

'… and he is always there for you; you know that, don't you?'

'I can't tell him. He will not marry me if he comes to know about my past. Then what about my family and me? We will be ruined!'

'No. Nothing of that sort will happen. You talk to him, at least once.'

'I don't want to cheat a nice and honest person like Aananda. But I can't tell him either … What's more, after my abortion, I don't even know whether I can even give birth to a child. I don't want to cheat him.'

The word 'child' jolted her back from her unconscious state and she opened her misty eyes. She looked around in surprise. She saw that she was lying in a big room with white walls and some yellow tulips in a neat vase beside her beside her bed, and heard the cry of a baby. Sheema was unable to realize where she was. Half in sleep and half-awake a condition she tried to figure out where the child's cry was coming from, but her semi-paralytic state forbade her from getting up and search for the baby. She could not even see where the man had gone, whom she was talking to for so long.

A few seconds later, the door opened and the doctor came in to her room. He helped Sheema to partially rise up from her bed and declared with a smile, 'Congratulations. You have become a proud mother of a sweet little angel.'

Sheema's eyes misted. 'Could this really be true? All these years I only wondered if I could ever give birth to a child!' But as she turned her eyes towards the left of her bed, she saw Aananda standing beside the baby's cot and smiling. He came forward and kissed on her forehead and said, 'I had always told you, my love, you *will* have a baby. And see, here she is.'

'But how is it that I was talking to Bertrand Russell all this while?' Sheema asked.

'You were unconscious for the last two and a half hours,' Aananda replied.

Aananda took their new born in his arms and gave it to Sheema and said, 'Since she has brought so much happiness to our lives, especially you, we should name her Arshika.'

'Arshika? Why Arshika?' Sheema asked.

'... because "Arshika" in Sanskrit means "Happiness".'

Sheema's happiness was clearly visible in the tears of joy that made her vision blurry. Aananda took her in his arms and kissed her once again, but she kept on wondering as to where did Bertrand Russell go; and then her eyes fell on the side table, where lay *The Complete Works of Bertrand Russell* with a photograph of the author. She took the book up only to find that the book had a page mark on the essay, 'The Road to Happiness.' Only then did she remember that after reading a couple of lines from the essay, she had to be rushed to the Operation Theatre, where she was unconscious and woke up to a new world of happiness, joy and love.

The President's Change Agent

AKACHI ADIMORA-EZEIGBO

'There has been a change of "guards" and a new group of officers have assumed office in the Nigerian Police Force. The new Inspector General of Police (IGP) is a relatively young man with a history of uncommon competence, a no-nonsense officer judging from his track record ...'

Rima listened to the voice of the radio announcer droning on, dishing out information about new appointments in the Police Force, as she pressed the accelerator to get the car going faster. The voice was very female; the pretentious drawl and near-perfect foreign intonation irritated Rima. These Nigerians who try to imitate the accent of the owners of the language, who pronounce *dodo* as *dou-dou*, she thought, laughing. 'They are more Oyibo than the Oyibo people sef,' she chuckled aloud.

She switched off the car radio and concentrated on the highway. This road was notorious for accidents – what she always saw as an irony considering that it is in excellent condition, as smooth and flawless as a pebble just retrieved from the Obi-Iyi River, in her home town. For a moment she recalled how excited she was to gather pebbles from the river and used them to decorate her little room in her home. That was long ago. She had been deliriously happy and carefree as a teenager. Pebble hunting was her favourite pastime. She was not alone in this guileless game. Her friends joined in the adventure and they used to fight over the pebbles, especially when two or three people sighted a pebble at the same time and made a dash for it. Sometimes two charging heads knocked together and bodies collapsed in utter agony. It was fun too. Rima sighed wistfully. It was indeed long ago when life was simple, uncomplicated and livable. Now things had changed. Living these days was a nightmare. You felt cheated as though someone had sneaked into your house and robbed you of all your valuables. People were insensitive, cruel. Brutish. Her thought settled briefly on the Uzo-Uwani murderous attack perpetrated by the so-called Fulani Herdsmen. She shuddered. She had lost an uncle and a cousin to the mindless and brutal attack. Where would they strike next? Which village or town was the next target? Who could say?

Rima was quick to observe a massive truck trundling forward at an unearthly speed in front of her, swaying this way and that way like the swollen udder of a very pregnant cow. She pressed the car brake, slowed, watching keenly the mad truck and its antics. Then she steered the car gently to the right, gaining the very edge of the road and rolled completely clear, away from the road. In a moment the truck jolted past just as she looked up at the driver who, to her utter disgust, was grinning at her and shaking his clean-shaven head.

'What's the matter with you?' She screamed, raising her left hand, her five fingers spread as wide as possible. 'Waka!' she yelled, but the driver couldn't have heard the abusive cry.

That was a close shave with death, she thought. The way truck and tanker drivers used the road was unnerving. *Traffic terrorists*, she called them. They were worse than armed robbers, kidnappers and even the Boko Haram group. She wondered why the Federal Road Safety Corps and the Highway Patrol Squad from the Nigerian Police Force allowed these insane drivers to constitute a menace on the highway. These were the offenders they should harass, not innocent and law-abiding citizens or motorists. This was where her role as a columnist in *Daily Gong* newspaper came in handy. She would write about it in her next submission and entitle it 'The Menace of Truck and Tanker Drivers' – to let the people know, to let the world know. The thought gave Rima a measure of comfort. She would not keep quiet. She would air her views through *Daily Gong*.

She pulled on to the road and continued on her way to work. Her course was going to be examined in two hours and she had to move faster if she was to get to the examination venue in good time. Four kilometers later, she sighted a handful of traffic policemen ahead of her on either side of the road. She was not worried, for she had all her vehicle particulars with her. She wondered if they had seen the truck driver and the way he had been driving. They should have stopped and detained him. Could it be that the driver was drunk? That couldn't be ruled out. Driving under the influence of alcohol was a traffic offence. The police should have stopped and interrogated him or tested his breath, she told herself.

One of the policemen who carried a gun moved swiftly to the middle of the road and flagged her down. Stopping, she wound down the glass on the driver's side. 'Good morning,' she said, ready to move on again.

'Where is the permit that allows you to use tinted glass for your car?' He hugged his gun as though he was preparing to use it.

'I have it with me,' Rima said cheerfully, smiling at the policeman. He couldn't have been more than forty years old, she thought. Above his left breast pocket was a name tag. She read it: Sunday Jibril.

'Let me see it,' the man demanded, his face forbidding like an overcast sky.

'Yes, of course.' She pulled out an envelope from the glove compartment and removing the permit, she handed it to him.

He glanced at it and immediately frowned. 'This is the old one.'

'Old one?' she asked. 'I don't understand. Is there a new

one? This is the one I was given three years ago when I bought the car. I'm not aware of a new one.'

'A new one was issued about four months ago and you can get it from the Force Headquarters in Abakaliki. Let me have the rest of your vehicle particulars.'

Rima hesitated. She did not like his countenance.

'Park well,' he said impatiently. 'I say park there.' He was pointing. 'Clear from the road and let me have your particulars.'

She did as he directed. Next she took out all the documents from the envelope and gave them to him, her heart pounding like a piece of ground hit repeatedly by a thousand hoofs. The thought of her examination scheduled for 12 noon came to her mind. She almost panicked, thinking she might be late. Her mind dwelt on the consequence of arriving late or starting the examination late.

Sunday Jibril intruded into her thought and brought her back to the present. 'There is another offence.' He rifled through her vehicle particulars with fingers that looked like spikes. He identified the offending sheet of paper and thrust it forward. 'Why didn't you sign the Allocation of Vehicle Number document?' He looked at her with mean eyes. 'Are you sure you are the one that registered this car? Are you sure this car belongs to you?'

She was about to retort with an uncivil word, but checked herself. 'Of course, I did, officer', she protested. 'This is my car. You can see my name on all the documents.' She was finding it difficult to hide her irritation, her rising anger.

He was to see this as an affront. 'Madam, you talk too much. These are criminal offences.' His voice was aggressive. Intimidating.

'Criminal offences?' Rima was aghast. 'But I was not asked to sign it when the document was given to me after registration.'

'Look at it? Can't you see it? This is where you ought to have signed? Look at the blank space? Can you see it now?' His voice was truly a harangue.

'Please, let me go or I'll be late for my examination. I beg you, let me go. I'll go straight to the Force Headquarters and apply for the permit as soon as the examination is over by two o'clock. I will sign the other document when I get to school...'

Before Rima could finish her appeal, Officer Sunday Jibril had dashed to the passenger side and was pulling the car door. It was locked. He demanded she open the door. 'I'll take you to the Headquarters to pay twenty thousand naira for the offence before you get the permit. Or you can pay five thousand naira here. Unlock the door!'

She observed him stroking his gun. Rima's heart missed a beat, but she wouldn't unlock the door. 'Please, let me go. I'm not a criminal. You can see I have a permit even though you say there is a new one. I didn't know about it but, since you have told me, I'll get it as soon as possible.' Surely this was a reasonable explanation, she thought.

'You didn't know about it? Are you not in this country? You're lying. That's what you all do. You pretend you didn't know. It was announced on Radio and Television and advertised in newspapers and other media...'

She interrupted him. 'Believe me, I never heard about it until now.'

'Madam, you talk too much. It's because you're a woman that I'm being so patient with you. I'll take you to the Headquarters to pay twenty thousand naira or you can give me five thousand naira and go your way. But I advise you to get the new permit. If I see you another day, I'll stop and detain you.' He had a deep frown on his sweaty face.

'I don't have that amount of money with me right now.' Her eyes continued to rest on his face. She noticed how red his eyes were, as though he had not slept well the previous night.

'Park your car over there and go for the money.' He was pointing to where a highway patrol vehicle was parked at a clearing from the road. He had all her vehicle particulars which he proceeded to fold and put in the right pocket of his uniform.

He walked away, leaving Rima to stew in her anger and frustration. She sat motionless for a few minutes. He came back and barked, 'Madam, do something. I say do something.'

'What do you want me to do?' She asked helplessly, looking at his pocket where her vehicle particulars were trapped.

These words infuriated him, it seemed. He glared at her. 'You're asking me what I want you to do, eh? Okay. Stay there.' He ambled away.

'Is this the change we were promised?' Rima mumbled to herself. The police and the military seem more corrupt than they were in the past. Where was the change pontificated about by those in power? Was this man one of the change agents the people should expect? That Mr. President promised the nation? Tears filled Rima's eyes but she fought them fiercely. Grabbing her mobile phone, she dialed a number and waited. She would see if a colleague could stand in for her and conduct the examination.

The policeman returned, smiling mockingly. 'Who are you calling? That will not help you. If you like, call the IGP? You can call the President himself.' He stalked away, a hound torturing its prey.

The call did not go through. 'Network problem,' Rima muttered to herself. What would she do? She had barely one hour to get to the examination venue. She sat rigid, mauling over her predicament, unable to come to a decision on what to do.

In a moment, the man was back. Disdain was written all over his face. His attitude was condescending. Arrogant.

'Officer, I don't have much money with me,' Rima ventured. Would he mellow down if she spoke softly? 'Officer, sir, you are a Christian; please, let me go.'

'I am not a Christian.'

'But your name is Sunday. Only a Christian would answer

such a name.' Her eyes pleaded. In the wake of her thought, decades of police brutalities reared their heads. Horrendous images flitted through her anxious mind – masculine flexing of legal and illegal muscles, a culture of intimidation and impunity. In all this, the helpless citizen was always a victim.

'Officer,' she called, 'What exactly do you want me to do? Please, let me know.'

He drew near again, a sly smile slithering across his face. His black pants stretched across his groin and the vehicle particulars jutted out from the deep pocket. 'How much do you have?' he asked.

Rima grimaced. She longed to have her documents back and safe in the glove compartment of her car. She knew too well that before the end of the day – that was if she extricated herself from the clutches of Sunday Jibril – there were other checkpoints that would require her to show the vehicle particulars. It was a regular routine on this highway of *uniformed robbers*, harassing innocent and hapless commuters and motorists.

'I don't have much money with me.' She took a purse from her handbag and displayed the cash in it – four five-hundred naira notes and three two-hundred naira notes. 'This is all I have, two thousand and six hundred naira.'

The policeman stretched his hand and took all the money.

'Please not all of it. Am I to drive away with not a kobo with me all day?' Rima asked, dismayed. 'That's rather risky. You must not take everything.'

'Okay, take this.' He gave her two hundred naira and put the rest in his pocket. He pulled out the vehicle particulars. 'If you have a black pen in your bag, you can sign the Allocation of Vehicle Number paper or you can sign it as soon as you reach your destination.'

The difference in his voice was clear. Satisfaction. Triumph.

Rima started the car, heading for the school to conduct

her examination. She had thirty minutes and hoped to get there just on time. What a nasty experience, she thought. She felt her humanity diminished. She would definitely write about it – if that was all she could do. This was work to do. At the back of her mind was the sad thought that the encounter with the policeman had dashed any hopes of a change of attitude in the nation's police force. One more betrayal of the change the people voted for and hoped to achieve.

Tribute

In Memoriam
Professor Isidore O. Okpewho
1941–2016

When the news of the passing of Professor Isidore Okpewho – 'Prof', as those of us who came under his tutelage called him in awed deference and fondness – broke, it caused so much sadness at the loss of one of the finest scholars of the oral arts that Africa has produced. But it has also been a personal loss to me as I miss my teacher and mentor of decades.

I was a sophomore at University of Calabar, Nigeria, taking a required course on oral literature, when I first heard of Professor Isidore Okpewho's prominence in the discipline. In the first semester of that year, I had purchased a fat text titled *Oral Literature in Africa* by Ruth Finnegan. It was regarded as the bible of oral literature studies then, and in those days, you knew a student was a second year English major when you saw them proudly sporting a copy of Finnegan's book with its distinct yellowish cover. However, our Oral Lit instructor that year, Ndubuisi Osuagwu, a freshly minted PhD, was giddily telling us about a young Nigerian scholar at University of Ibadan who was busy demolishing one of the controversial claims in Finnegan's book, that Africa didn't possess epic poems. Osuagwu swore by this Ibadan scholar, told us he was bound to become the youngest scholar to be promoted full professor, that he was taking the field in a radically different and exciting direction. He was, of course, referring to Isidore Okpewho, who by then was best known as the author of the novels *The Victims*, starring foolish Obanua and his desperate wives, and *The Last Duty*, where quite a few of us ignored the Nigerian Civil War at the heart of that novel and were enamoured of the servant Odibo's awakened masculinity. I'm not sure my dear Dr Osuagwu even possessed a copy of Okpewho's *The Epic in Africa*, the seminal text in which Prof was basically saying, 'Yes, Ruth, the epic gloriously exists in Africa'. But he had grasped the full significance of Prof's historic feat in that first monograph, which had sprung from his doctoral dissertation at University of Denver, for those of us in that class who would pursue oral literary studies further, we knew that the trajectory of our fieldwork had been irrevocably altered.

When the time came for me to consider graduate school, I knew where I was headed, to the English department at University of Ibadan. I arrived there and Prof Okpewho's course was one of the first classes I enrolled in. I remember the first meeting of the class. We met in Prof's supremely spacious office – he was the chair of the department, after all. He was all business-like. There were theoretical positions to be interrogated, exciting field reports and practices to be emulated, and a vast body of work in the oral arts that was yet to be explored, which he challenged the class to consider. Quickly, he assigned each student a topic to work and present on. He offered an extensive bibliography of texts and, being in Nigeria, where college-level texts are not easy or cheap to come by, he invited us to use his personal library.

I volunteered to go first. Prof lent me a couple of the assigned books and the others I found at the university library. Two weeks later, I made my oral presentation. As we filed out from Prof's office at the end of class, he called me and asked me to stay for a quick chat. I was filled with anxiety. Had I misread the texts so woefully that I needed a royal dressing down? Prof got to the heart of the matter directly: he thought the presentation went well and he had enjoyed the vigour of my performance. If I was interested, he said, he'd be happy to work with me down the road on my thesis. If I was interested! There I was, alone in the office of Isidore Okpewho, award-winning novelist, the Prof who'd blown away my keen undergraduate professor with his ground-breaking work on the African epic, and a few years later, on myth in Africa, being invited by the same to work with him. Of course, I said yes! And right away, he started asking probing questions on my interests, and as I answered, he filled in the gaps on what had been done, what could be redone, and what needed to be done. By the time I left his office that day, we had come up with a research plan for my thesis. It didn't matter that this was my first semester of graduate school and I still had course work to do. With Prof, there was never a good time to waste. There was a sense of urgency with which he pursued research leads, an urgency that wouldn't let a task go until it was completed, a keen attentiveness to trends, but with an unambiguous respect for the fundamentals of scholarship in the best humanistic understanding of that practice.

That was 1989. By 1990, Prof had left Ibadan for Harvard's W.E.B. Du Bois Research Institute as a Visiting Professor and would proceed from there to head the Africana Studies department at Binghamton University. For me, completing the Master's degree at Ibadan only led to three years of meanderings in the treacherous pathways of Nigeria's labour market. It was in that classic Nigerian state of unpaid employment that Prof stepped in again. He had been following my 'progress' and wondered if I'd like to pursue a doctoral program in the US.

As Prof and I began preparations – taking the Graduate Record Examinations, completing graduate admission forms, seeking additional letters of recommendation, applying for a Nigerian passport, etc., friends and family were amazed at the rarity of a Nigerian professor with whom I didn't share ethnic or familial relationship, and whom I had known for less than two years in postgraduate school, showing such extraordinary interest in my education from where he worked in the US. He would call, write letters, send messages through persons visiting Nigeria, all to find out how I was progressing on my own part of the plans and to tell me every step he had taken on my behalf. Those letters became more than bulletins. He would ask after my ailing dad, tell me of conferences he'd attended, and together we'd lament the Nigerian condition under military rule. As the letters came in, I perceived more of Prof, his care, his doggedness, his sincerity and his humour. He was a great letter writer, and I think his choice of the epistolary form for his third novel, *Tides*, stems from that love of the form.

I'll always remember the day I arrived in the US in the fall of 1993 to begin the doctoral program, after securing funding orchestrated by Prof. I had flown from Nigeria into JFK, taken a cab from there to Port Authority Bus Terminal on 42nd Street, as Prof had instructed me weeks earlier. I caught the last bus to Binghamton and it had arrived very late. What a relief it was to see a familiar face at the station after two days of flying across Africa, through Europe, and then the US! Prof had been waiting at the bus station for hours. We shook hands and embraced, and then we got into his Toyota Previa and pulled out of the station, heading to his residence.

We hadn't driven more than two blocks before we came to a red light. Prof pulled to a stop and then we waited. By this time, it was past midnight and downtown Binghamton was deserted. I looked at the four-way intersection and there was no car in sight. I was puzzled; why were we sitting idle at the light when we pretty much had the entire road to ourselves? I think Prof knew what I was thinking; with his hands firmly placed at 10 minutes to 2 o'clock on the steering wheel, he kept his eyes peeled for the light change, and calmly said to me in his deep voice, 'Chiji, this is America; there's no *jaga-jaga* driving here-o', referring to the maddening, haphazard style that defines Nigerian driving.

I have always cherished the memory of that short ride from the station to Prof's house on my first night in America for all it has come to represent to me about Prof. He didn't need to have come to pick me up at the station, but there he was. I was his student, but his robust sense of humour crossed such distinctions effortlessly to a disarming effect. I was the complete beneficiary of his large, generous heart. He had supervised my Master's thesis back at University of Ibadan, Nigeria. Having recently taken up appointment as the new Chair of Africana Studies at Binghamton, he had telephoned me, while I trudged the streets of Lagos doing unpaid jobs, and asked me to apply for the PhD program in English. I had told him that neither I nor my family had the means to pay for graduate education in the US, and he had pulled all stops to secure me a teaching assistantship with tuition scholarship. And when late in the process we found out that the funds had not met the threshold for the International Students Office to issue the required I-20 form, Prof had gone to the Provost's office to plead my case; he had come out with a University Foundation fellowship with a stipend that covered the gap. And what he did for me, I'd find out, he'd do for numerous others, be it in the vast number of theses and dissertations he directed, his crisp editing of drafts of manuscripts for publication, or in writing stellar recommendation letters for jobs or admissions, or in reviewing dossiers for tenure and promotion.

I wish to remember Prof from my vantage point of living through and witnessing his extraordinary kindness and genuine interest in the well-being of people – peers and ordinary folk – with whom he walked this life. There's Isidore Okpewho, Distinguished Professor, phenomenal scholar and award-winning artist. But there's Prof, with whom sometimes I'd walk to campus, in those Binghamton days, and we'd come upon the ubiquitous bushy tailed squirrels; we'd both look at their shiny furs and round cheeks as they preened by the foot path, and we'd both shake our heads at their luck in roaming free at such dangerously close distances in a part of the world where they weren't the main item for a roasted, scrumptious snack!

I remember a loving father, most happy in the company of his children and wife, refereeing the intractable debate between his two sons over who was better – Shaq or Kobe, pouring out praise for every accomplishment of each child, a new book, a new opportunity to memorialize his love in the book's dedication. He reserved his deepest affection for his wife of over 40 years, Ọbiageli. He was crazy about her cooking; they toured the world together; played ping-pong in the basement of their house with hilarious intensity, and made watching tennis appointment TV.

Prof's passing leaves a canyon-sized hole in the fields of African folklore, oral traditional arts – the oral epic and oral performance aesthetics, especially – and African letters, in general, for he was also an astute literary scholar and award-winning novelist. From his debut monograph, *The Epic in Africa* (Columbia UP, 1979), to *African Oral Literature* (Indiana UP, 1992), to *Once Upon A Kingdom: Myth, Hegemony, and Identity* (Indiana UP, 1998), to his final work, *Blood on the Tides: The Ozidi Saga and the Oral Epic Narratology* (U of Rochester P, 2014), it is difficult to imagine any other scholar in our time who has been singularly minded and so influential in championing the cause and steering the course of discourse and research on African oral forms and aesthetics. When he published his fourth novel, *Call Me By My Rightful Name* (AWP, 2004), it was his romantic gesture toward marrying the pleasures of field work, which dominated his intellectual life, with his creative impulses – a point he had first made in *A Portrait of the Artist as a Scholar*, his Inaugural Lecture as Professor of English at University of Ibadan, on 18 May, 1989.

The cultural and political dynamics of our discipline excited him; he pursued it with relentless passion and proved prodigious in his intellectual production, so much so that those of us who sat at his feet and listened to this Iroko tree of a scholar could only marvel at what we were witnessing at close range, while also awed at the size of the shoes we were supposed to step into. But it is a testament to the sagacity of his intellect and generosity of his heart that, throughout his professional life, Prof strove to mentor as many scholars that came into his orbit; no one was too small or insignificant that he couldn't find ways to guide them and lift them up with his praise and encouragement. Today, he is like an ancient baobab tree standing majestic at the centre of the arena, with as many taking shelter under its shade as there are those climbing its trunk and branches (if they would brave it!) to gather leaves, wood and other sustenance.

In gratitude I pay tribute to Prof for sharing his love, intellect, and humanity with us. Far beyond his remarkable intellectual prolificacy, his was a well-lived life given to family, friends and colleagues in equal and full measure.

Chiji Akọma, PhD
Department of Global Interdisciplinary Studies
Villanova University, USA

Reviews

Mohammad Rabie. *Otared*. Translated from Arabic by
Robin Moger.

Cairo, Egypt: Hoopoe, an imprint of the American University in Cairo Press, 2016, £9.99
ISBN 9789774167843, paperback

Otared, a novel by the Egyptian writer Mohammad Rabie
is set in conditions that resemble those in Egypt during the
Arab Spring. The situation depicted in the novel, however,
is exponentially worse than how it was during the Arab
Spring (Or maybe the author is revealing things that were
not apparent to many people about the Arab Spring). The
novel is set in an Egypt that was militarily invaded by the
armed forces of the Republic of the Knights of Malta who
have appointed a new prime minister, and who in his
turn formed a government. The occupation government is
however not much of a government. The country, especially
the city of Cairo is in utter chaos. All semblance of order has
disappeared in large parts of the city. Murder and violence
are rampant. Basic services are non-existent. Mounds of
trash are everywhere. The resistance to the occupation is
led by a shadowy group of former police officers whose
strategy is based on two elements: one, to increase the
suffering of the civilian population to the point they
become convinced that they have no alternative but to side
with the police in their efforts to drive the invaders away,
and perhaps then the killing of civilians would end. Two,
because members of the Egyptian military are potential

competitors for power in the future, the police encouraged military personnel to engage in armed operations in which the latter were very likely to die or be killed. The city of Cairo is divided into two sections. East Cairo where the occupying army is mostly based and West Cairo. All forms of violence whether it is physical, psychological or sexual has been unleashed. There is no credible authority. The morgues are full. Cairo lies in ruins. But this suffering does not result in solidarity and cooperation between the people. Nor does it engender sympathy for the denizens of Cairo. Instead Cairenes are held in contempt for welcoming the invaders instead of resisting them.

This is a predatory world in which many of the characters seem unhinged. Distinctions between right and wrong, truth and lies, kindness and cruelty have disappeared. Hashish and other drugs are part of the daily intake of people. Casual sex and rape are prevalent. Unproven connections between eating raw meat and sex are invented. Even cannibalism is not off-limits. It's a Hobbesian world full of gratuitous violence. The main character, Otared, shows no remorse about killing innocents and dismisses it as collateral damage. He even casually kills a colleague. And it is not just him. This is found throughout the novel. It is a world in which there is a breakdown in normal human interactions and a suspension of basic human values of decency and morality, an anti-heroic world in which neither the corpses strewn on the Corniche nor the woman 'screaming in anguish' mean anything. How can so much suffering and bloodshed be justified? The answer of the perpetrators goes something like this: since they and their victims are living under hellish conditions, by killing people they were sending them to a better world. As one of the characters said, 'Sir. We are in hell. You know it. And what I am currently engaged doing in is of a piece with all our missions.... We really do send people to heaven, and it makes no sense to obstruct me or stop me working.'

Given that one of the fundamental ideas of many religions

is that of death as a release from the troubles and limitations of this world into a much better world, this could be construed as an implicit critique of religion. It is also a critique of the romance of revolution, a point which comes into sharp focus upon Otared's discovery that the invaders did not leave Egypt because the people rose against them but because of other considerations. Sometimes the critique of religion and revolution is done simultaneously and in a single sentence as in Leila's inquiry, 'Can one pray covered in blood?' There is not much difference between those in authority and those who want to topple them and replace them. They both are obsessed with power and deploy ruthless methods to pursue or maintain it. The rest of the population is caught in the struggle between these two forces and do not have much say in the matter.

The novel is replete with people whose personalities had been damaged, which raises the question whether the horrific conditions of the characters and the city are due to the foreign occupation or whether there were pre-existing factors that have been incubating in the country and eventually burst into the open. One of the top leaders of the resistance thinks it is the latter.

Another relevant question is: what is it that sustains the readers' interests in such a novel of victims and executioners? One apparent answer is that since each of the characters mostly dwells in a claustrophobic mental and psychological space and disconnected from others, this creates an urge for the reader to break those barriers and find out what is at the core of those characters. Second, the novel captures possible scenarios for the worse that could take place in many of the world's cities where congestion, pollution, urban decay, rape, terrorism and other crimes are already prevalent. Third, there is the element of loss of self which many people experience in today's global village where the individual is often under the mercy of forces beyond his or her control. This sense of loss and being unable to either understand or be understood by others, is possibly what prompted Otared to declare, 'I didn't care about my fellow snipers, standing around unable to understand what I was up to.' Paradoxically, in that disconnection from others, Otared sees a connection with others. For him and others in the novel, history, language and memory have become a burden, a torment from which they are trying to escape. But then again, aren't we all tormented by one thing or another? Otared actually commends the characters for at least knowing that they are escaping their nightmarish reality, whereas 'Perhaps you and I are both fleeing the same torment without realizing it'.

JAMAL GABOBE, PhD
Instructional Consultant
Center for Teaching and Learning
University of Washington,
Seattle, Washington USA

The Book of Safety. Yasser Abdel Hafez. Translated from Arabic to English by Robin Moger.
Cairo: Hoopoe, an imprint of the American University in Cairo Press, 2017, £9.99
ISBN 9789774168215, paperback

At the heart of Yasser Abdel Hafez's novel *The Book of Safety* is a mystery: what drove Mustafa Ismail, one of the main characters in the novel, to abandon his job as a professor and engage in breaking into the homes of wealthy people. Was he motivated by greed, revenge, some combination thereof or something else? Various theories are presented throughout the novel to explain his motivations which the reader will have to evaluate for himself.

This is a novel of ideas in the vein of Julio Cortazar's *Hopscotch* where most of the characters are of the intellectual type and are trying to make sense of their own thoughts, desires, and the deteriorating situation in their city – Cairo. But despite the preponderance of ideas, the novel is not a mere vehicle for presenting ideas but is populated by characters with distinct and recognizable personalities.

Among these personalities is Nabil Adli (the interrogator of Mustafa Ismail) and Khaled Mamoun (the transcriber of the interrogations). The relationships between these characters as well as others who are less central to the novel are complex and hard to pin down. Many of these relations veer between polar opposites of desire and denial, obedience and defiance, passion and rejection.

The ambiguity is not just in the relations between the characters but extends to attitudes towards history, nationalism, science, the supernatural and other topics. No subject seems to be off limits. The novel, however, is less concerned with descriptions of life in contemporary Cairo than in deconstructing it – a measure of how far the Egyptian novel has come since the days of Naguib Mahfouz's realist novels.

Perhaps as part of the postmodernist urge to avoid linearity, the characters jump from one idea to another, one subject to another, never lingering on one topic for too long, giving a disjointed and incomplete picture of whatever they are discussing and leaving it to the reader to try and complete the picture, if he or she, can.

The novel seems preoccupied with reflections on the nature of art, specifically writing and photography and the boundaries between reality and fiction. It is full of puzzles, paradoxes, and mind-games. As part of this preoccupation with aesthetics, even the places where the novel takes place have eye-catching titles such as the Palace of Confessions, the Cafe of Lunatics, the Lotus House, and Sappho (a bookstore). Appearances however can be misleading, and often there is nothing aesthetically pleasing about what goes on at those locations. One of those locations in particular, the curiously named Palace of Confessions is where confessions are extracted from those accused of crimes against the state – a state that is noticeably absent when it comes to delivering basic services but seems to be everywhere when it comes to spying on citizens and exercising its coercive power.

Besides the power of the state, there is also the power of writing. We get a snippet of this in the case of the transcriber of the Book of Safety who, seduced by the power of writing, at times feels like a 'godling'.

The characters could be almost classified according to their degree of self-consciousness. There are those who subject themselves and everything else to minute inspection and those who exhibit very little consciousness of themselves or the conditions around them. The interactions between some of these opposite types can sometimes lead to engaging yet disastrous results.

The Book of Safety is a book within a book within a book. It is also a book with more than one author. On one level it is was what Mustafa Ismail said during his interrogation. On another level it was what was transcribed by Khaled Mamoun. On a third level it was the combined effort of Khaled Mamoun and Mustafa Ismail's daughter, Hasna. Finally, it was the book written by Yasser Abdel Hafez and published by Hoopoe Press. And that's not all – if we go by the words of the characters in the novel, there are different editions and versions of the book.

The novel, however, is not confined to aesthetic concerns. The author exposes the class, gender and color conflicts that exist in Cairene society. Examples of this are how residents of well-to-do neighborhoods such as Heliopolis see residents of working class districts such as Sayyida Zeinab, al-Hussein as a threat to their well-being; how white color is privileged over brown and black; and how women are often dominated by men. But these depictions are not made in cardboard, stereotypical ways but rather are explored in a complex and nuanced manner.

In conclusion, no matter what aspect of the novel we look at, we will find the enigma of Mustafa Ismail and his transformation from a professor to a thief, casting a long shadow over the characters and the atmosphere of the whole novel. His transformation is not the only one, but it is the most consequential. The novel is in a way an attempt to tell the story of these transformations, for as one of the characters says, 'What are we but a set of stories we tell or hear?'

JAMAL GABOBE, PhD
Instructional Consultant
Center for Teaching and Learning
University of Washington,
Seattle, Washington USA

Sanya Osha. *On a Sad Weather-Beaten Couch*
Mankon, Bamenda: Langaa RPCIG, 2015, 238 pp, np
ISBN 978 9 99567 6 2422

At the beginning of Sanya Osha's *On a Sad Weather-Beaten Couch*, Ade Bantan lies on a sofa 'in his girlfriend's room fanning himself and trying to seize on a measure of coolness. He had nowhere to go.' More than two hundred pages later, at the end of the novel, he finally vacates the couch that he had inhabited throughout most of the narrative and walks out on his girlfriend, Enitan. Interestingly, he is roused out of his inertia by jealousy, among other considerations. When he hears Enitan angrily say or misspeak that she 'didn't mind if she had to sleep with every cop and attorney needed to achieve her aim' (to punish Papa Osaze, who had duped her), Ade 'understood why Enitan confused memories of her other lovers with theirs'. In his thinking, 'every one of her memories of romance was interchangeable to her and it did [not] matter as long as she had a man.' In leaving Enitan, Ade also flees 'from a sinking neighborhood riddled with vigilante gates, orphaned street urchins, and cacophonies that didn't make sense and perhaps weren't ever meant to'. Between these two states of being or consciousness – Ade on the couch and Ade in flight – is a character study that focuses on a thirty-seven-year-old artist who is apparently without prospects, even though everyone had once believed that he was 'destined for impressive things'. But the novel is not simply about Ade's current 'creative cul-de-sac'. Osha manages – by the introduction of related as well as relatable incidents and spatializing tale-tellers – to expand a portrait of an individual crisis into a noirish painting of a neighbourhood's existential dilemma that is also a figuration of a national (or African) dystopia.

The choice of Ade and Enitan as central characters is pivotal to the structural dynamics of *On a Sad Weather-Beaten Couch*. Ade is inclined toward creativity and transcendental essences. He is rather disdainful of the mindless materialism all around him, which in his perception has transformed people into corpses: 'Corpses everywhere. Zombies. Corpses as fathers of the nation. Corpses disguised in robes of laughter and gaiety.' Enitan is initially presented as an opportunist who envisions a relationship with Ade as her passport out of the urban jungle and the daily grind that she is trapped in. But their relationship grows in irony as the narrative progresses. Since Ade lacks the will to apply himself to the translation of his cocoon of ideas into a livelihood, he becomes dependent on Enitan – despite the fact that she also caters for her three sisters and a brother. At some point, Enitan reflects: 'The entire world seemed bent on dragging her down […] She had to do everything by herself. She had a lover who couldn't assist her financially and she even had to push him as well to focus seriously upon his work.' As long as Enitan believes Ade's lie that he is readying for an exhibition in Europe, their relationship remains oriented toward all sorts of possibilities – especially marriage and liberation from economic hardship for Enitan. Considering this premise of their relationship and Ade's inability to rise up to that expectation, their eventual separation seems inevitable. When it happens, it is significant that it is Ade who eventually walks out. That decision is facilitated by the fact that Enitan ultimately becomes a symbol that he finds unsettling. Her life becomes another mirror in which Ade sees not just the beautiful and diligent woman that takes care of him but also the source of unpleasant and somewhat terrifying mental associations. Ade's search, so to speak, is for a line of escape out of the blind alley that he currently is in. Despite her devotion, Enitan registers in his consciousness as possibly a path out of an alley that, at best, simply leads to another sort of dead end: 'Enitan was ready to fight her way out as a good mother hen, but Ade Bantan just couldn't hang around for much longer. [...] Everyone seemed to have an idea of who he could be and not who he actually was. But he knew he would be a disappointment to everyone and the earlier they knew the better.'

The human characters in *On a Sad Weather-Beaten Couch* also function to characterize the neighborhood. In some ways, Osha's novel is more about the urban jungle that these characters inhabit than their particular humdrum or colourless lives. The haunting descriptions of the neighbourhood are among the most poignant aspects of the novel. The insights projected are not about the promise of Africa but its bottomless decline. Consider these representations of the unnamed city at night:

> Apart from the noise, the heat made it difficult to sleep. In the entire area, buildings stood very close to each other; the numerous illegal electric connections caused a mess of wires around buildings; generators grumbled and farted at all hours; interminable traffic jams created a permanent haze of carbon monoxide fumes; commercial motorcycle riders crisscrossed crater-littered streets trying to avoid instant death while they chased after money; cops worried about how they would make up their quota of bribes; mortuaries groaned from the weight of the dead; medical doctors schemed to become

chartered accountants; street urchins held conferences on new ways to extort money; the ocean vomited coins and cowries delivered by innumerable supplicants on the jolting coasts of West Africa; the streams turned brown and fetid with human waste and dead bodies[...]

When the two men emerged onto the streets, many activities were still taking place. Handclapping and drumming was going on at the white garment church. Commercial motorcyclists were making their riotous way across a maze of people, potholes, and paths. Traders had set up their makeshift stalls for a long night of trading and haggling, roadside tea sellers had arranged their tables and benches for worn-out customers who came for tea, bread, butter, and eggs. Peddlers of bootleg gin hailed derelict figures from the fringes and shadows. Masked night-soil men went around the buildings collecting buckets of shit. Those who had a bit of change to spare were laughing noisily, trying to create the impression that things weren't that terrible. Beautiful women who really had nowhere to go were walking up and down the street pretending they had dates to keep.

This is a dystopic universe with oversized signposts highlighting both deprivation and downheartedness. In this world mapped by gloom and failed aspirations, almost everything that can go wrong actually does. In this elegiac interrogation of both the inner city and the city center, armed robbers run amok; a young boy sleeps with his sister; a father uses his baby daughter as a sex object; Enitan's sanctimonious neighbour defrauds her and then prays for her death; churches lucratively peddle false promises; children gather to egg on street brawlers; families fight to use putrid toilets in overcrowded houses; hospitals are ill-equipped to function as health facilities. And as if all these are not enough, the heat and mosquitoes – referenced again and again in the novel – foreground the sort of everyday apocalypse that is the life of the ordinary person in a system created or corrupted by 'corpses as fathers of the nation'. Death is quite alive in *On a Sad Weather-Beaten Couch* and it is sometimes even more a death of the spirit. The novel seems in fact to pose several questions about the resilience or inclination of human character in a season of anomie. While the novel is concerned with how extreme poverty can (and does) disfigure human capability and imagination, it ultimately translates into a cautionary tale about the consequences of mindlessness at various levels of society.

Strategically, *On a Sad Weather-Beaten Couch* is more a novel of character than of plot, a distinction that can be as illuminating as it is sometimes problematic. The plot is rather thin and static, which is not altogether surprising considering that the principal character is mostly in a state of inertia. Somewhat comparable to Vladimir and Estragon waiting for Godot, not knowing whether he even exists, Ade sits or lies on Enitan's couch waiting for a resolution that he can sometimes almost conceive but is nevertheless unsure of. 'Nothing happens, nobody comes, nobody goes, it's awful!' says Estragon in Samuel Beckett's *Waiting for Godot*. There is a discernible existentialist strain in *On a Sad Weather-Beaten Couch*, but the plot is also rather dynamic in that people keep arriving and departing – regardless of Ade's inertia – with tales that further narrative spatialization. One instance is Ulmanmadu, Enitan's distant relative, who shows up twice to try to talk Ade into speedily marrying Enitan. The most significant talebearer is Chidi, whose ambition is to become 'a rude boy'. As he tells Ade, 'I'm prepared to do anything to survive. This country is fucked. The criminals are in charge and so the rules of the game have changed. If you sit there thinking that the good shall inherit the earth then you're totally fucked.' One of his tales is about Benjamin Pancho, a con artist and get-rich-quick ritualist who seemingly reforms himself with the help of the church. In the public imagination conditioned by rumor mongers, he is 'the ultimate monarch of the future'. But Benjamin Pancho is a compulsive cheater who wants to sleep with all his wife's sisters and also a paedophile who is sexually attracted to his baby daughter. Even though he is the richest man in the area, he also ranks among the most tormented and immoral. When he dies in a car crash 'three months after he was caught molesting his baby', intriguing and vaulting stories about him become part of the neighborhood's storytelling mosaic. Chidi describes him as 'a great man'. Ade is unsurprisingly not impressed. The comings and goings in the novel make Ade less isolated, but in reality, he is unable to strike a bond with any of the other characters. He remains more like a spectator in a figurative blind alley witnessing a gory feast of dystopian spectacles that deepen the overall noirish aatmosphere of the narrative.

The world of Osha's novel is extremely bleak and suffocatingly claustrophobic, reminding the reader in various ways of the calisthenics of the cage in Franz Kafka, boundless desperation in Ben Okri (without the magical realism), and scatological realism in Ayi Kwei Armah. It is a world from which escape seems impossible but in which struggle is inevitable. Whatever other literary voices or strains exist or appear to exist in Osha's novel, however, his own voice and vision are unimpeded. There is often a starkness in the use of language that enhances the narrative texture in a way that aligns with thematic direction. When Ade met Enitan, for instance, he was said to be 'blind to the fact that no one was exempt from the plunder, murder, and hypocritical complicity; no one was free from the cycle of eating shit for breakfast, lunch, and dinner and then sitting on the throne of shit at night. Everyone was running on the treadmill of shit production either as a consumer or as a producer.' Regardless of this tendency, many parts of *On a Sad Weather-Beaten Couch* read like a poet's novel, producing in effect a nuanced narrative that often sparkles with nuggets of language. Thinking about his way of life or predilections as a misunderstood dialect, Ade reflects that 'for language to accomplish full form, for it to become fully defined and find a worthy place among the living, it had to be shared within at least a small community of outcasts.' His thoughts embed a theory of semiosis, including the relationship between langue and parole, that provide psychological insights about him and the general orientation of the novel. Several other instances include a reflection on 'the seductive power of patriarchy'; a haunting description of the neighbourhood as a place where 'hope went around in robes of resplendent colors murdering those who offered prayers to it' and 'the laughter of the dead created earthquakes across the land'; an extended metaphor on space as sunlight; a conditional projection of what would have happened if Ade had 'remained in the purgatory of compromise'. The laughter of the dead, in a metaphoric sense, haunts many corners of *On a Sad Weather-Beaten Couch*, and Osha's language and philosophical fragments highlight this strikingly. In one instance – out of several examples of rhythmic repetition – a single word 'die' is chanted by Papa Osaze, as he prays for the death of someone that he has wronged, over two pages. While the novel focuses on a world of waste and wantonness, corruption and bestiality, Osha's language and vision often encompass as well as gesture beyond that world. Osha's novel is also in some respects an experimental novel without chapters and some other novelistic conventions but with a lot of feeling and aesthetic dexterity.

Some parts of *On a Sad Weather-Beaten Couch* – such as the shifts in point of view and some of the transitions from one narrative strand to another – could arguably have been better integrated. But, overall, Osha accomplishes a perceptive, often poetic, texturization of a single narrative that is also several stories and multiple stories that are ultimately a singular narrative.

MAIK NWOSU, PhD
English Department
University of Denver, Denver,
Colorado, USA

Adam Mayer. *Naija Marxism: Revolutionary Thought in Nigeria.*
London: Pluto Press, 2016, 241 pp, np
ISBN 978 0 7453 3657 6 paperback

In 2005, the National Intelligence Council of the US published predictions that African countries, especially Nigeria, would disintegrate by the year 2015. Edwin Madunagu called that 'wishful thinking' in his column for *The Guardian* and theorized that the Nigerian state was still strong enough to withstand disintegration pressures. In 2010, the former US Ambassador to Nigeria, John Campbell, followed up with a book that called Nigeria a 'bastard child of colonialism' and said that the country was 'Dancing on the Brink' of collapse unless resources were made available to fight poverty in the Northeast, without mentioning the lack of educational opportunities as a major cause of poverty. Why did Nigeria manage to survive the predicted collapse in 2015?

Naija Marxisms by Adam Mayer reads like an intelligence report of the sort that British colonial administrators commissioned from 200 colonial anthropologists, following the Women's War of 1929, to figure out why the Igbo were difficult to subject to colonial rule. Mayer is obviously aware of this implicit meaning of his book because he cited Ikenna Nzimiro (110) on this point as if pre-empting any suspicions that he was conducting counter-insurgency style surveillance on the state of revolutionary thought in Nigeria today. The suspicion that the book is, knowingly or unknowingly, a spy story was raised in the preliminary pages where the author thanked one of his doctoral thesis advisers, a 'Professor Colonel' in Hungary, for pointing him in the direction of the security implications of his topic. The suspicion was thickened by the fact that the author used the assertions of John Campbell as the theoretical framework for the book from beginning to end. Campbell is positioned by the author as the 'foremost expert on Nigeria' and his prediction that 'Nigeria may well produce a Fidel Castro' is the 'problematique' that the Hungarian author tried to investigate with the admission that the emergence of a Castro in Nigeria would be 'a very unwelcome idea' from the point of view of the US (3).

In answer to the security query raised by Campbell, the author observed that '... there was no violent Marxist group in Nigeria that would have advocated terrorist methods, nor do we find any Nigerian Marxist thinkers who embraced left communism and its theories' (37). This was a missed chance for the author to explore non-violence as a core part of African philosophy but the preferred approach of Mayer was to see how European Marxism influenced Nigerian thinkers. There was no attempt by the author to see how Africans influenced the theories of Karl Marx himself or how the philosophy of non-violence from Africa may have influenced the relatively peaceful collapse of the Soviet Union and Eastern European Marxist states. Thus, the book is deliberately Eurocentric as if the author had all the answers and was looking for the 'problematique' to apply his ready-made cookie-cutters rather than humbly seek for new knowledge from Africa with which to challenge the taken-for-granted beliefs about the nature of Marxism in Europe. Elsewhere, I took the Africa-centered approach by identifying the hundreds of references in *Capital* where Marx acknowledged that he was learning from people of African descent (Agozino, 2014).

Had the author been less ethnocentric in his approach to the history of ideas, he would have recognized immediately that his reference to 1968 (i.e., at the height of the genocide in Biafra) and to the New Left demanded references to the Cultural Studies of Stuart Hall (2016) who was the founding editor of *New Left Review* and who borrowed from South Africa and from the *Capital* of Marx, the theory of the articulation of race-class-gender relations in societies structured in dominance such as the UK under Thatcherism, and by extension, genocidist

Nigeria. According to Hall (and to Du Bois, Cabral, Rodney or Fanon), it would be ignorant for any crude economist to assert that what was going on in South Africa was exclusively class struggles when it was obvious that the struggles against racism and sexism were articulated, disarticulated and rearticulated with the class struggles in Africa, Europe and in North America as well. Race-class-gender were different struggles but they were never separate struggles. Mayer attempted different ways of emphasizing to Nigerian Marxists that the struggles in the country did not involve only class struggles as they would like to believe in a country where millions of people were subjected to genocide simply because of their ethnicity, where women remained second-class citizens and where history was banned as a high school subject probably to conceal the bloody history of the country from the youth.

The most original contribution to the history of ideas, in the centre of the book, is the section on Ikenna Nzimiro with his counter-intuitive theory that the Biafra struggle was a class struggle and not an ethnic conflict. Mayer could have pointed out that it was always intersectionally ethnic-class-gender struggles in articulation, disarticulation and rearticulation. According to Nzimiro, the Marxists in Biafra saw themselves as being engaged in an ideological struggle with the dictatorial Biafra ruling class as part of the resistance against genocide that arose from the class conflict of the First Republic. The Marxists in Nigeria rallied around the genocidal state out of a sense of patriotic duty but Lenin would have dismissed such nationalism as 'national defencism'. The Ahiara Declaration of socialism as the ideology for Biafra, though too little too late, remains an indication that the Marxists in Biafra relatively won the ideological struggle while the Marxists who supported Nigeria had nothing to show for it other than the crass opportunism that Niyi Oniororo and Edwin Madunagu railed against. Madunagu earned himself the slur from Balarabe Musa that he must be an 'ethnicist' perhaps because he called on the Left to address the opportunistic roles they played during the civil war. With the ongoing proclamation of the right to self-determination by the supporters of Biafra in the Southeast and their violent repression by the state (not mentioned in the book), it is not surprising that the author indirectly indicted Nigerian Marxists for their refusal to examine their scandalous roles in the most violent episode of the history of Marxist ideas in Nigeria. Indirectly, the book asks if Naija Marxists are among the genocidist intellectuals identified by Herbert Ekwe-Ekwe (2006).

Mayer distracted readers by accusing Nzimiro of 'entirely reactionary line of historical analysis coming from a Marxist author' due to his finding that some Igbo communities supported their traditional kings. Rather than address the genocide that Nzimiro stated as a fact that 'indeed' occurred against the Igbo (113), two ethnically Yoruba Marxists, Tajudeen Abdul Raheem and Bayo Olukoshi (both of whom later became UN bureaucrats; Olukoshi may no longer want to be identified as a Marxist, the author noted), criticized Nzimiro for not mentioning the 'clandestine Biafra Communist Party' (163), for later serving as an adviser to the dictatorship of Ibrahim Babangida (without crediting Nzimiro with persuading the dictator to set up the Political Bureau that recommended socialism as the ideology preferred by Nigerian masses), and for not saying that the Igbo Marxists who supported the federal government during the war were acting out of principle and not out of political expediency. But Abdul Raheem and Olukoshi did not extend such principles to the non-Igbo officers in the Biafra government the way that Bassey Ekpo Bassey praised Colonel Phillip Effiong for his principled leadership of the Biafran army. As a foreigner, the author must have been wondering what sorts of Marxists would continue to support a neocolonial genocidal war that claimed millions of lives long after the crimes against humanity had been documented? Leading

Naija Marxists simply wrote excellent textbooks on the political economy of underdevelopment and corruption or about fictional works but without a word of condemnation about the killing of more than three million fellow citizens by the bourgeois ruling classes with the support of both British imperialism and the Soviet Union?

The author had a habit of indicating that the Igbo Marxists were 'ethnically Igbo' every time they were mentioned but did not always disclose the ethnicity of all the other characters in the book. For instance, Madunagu was repeatedly called ethnically Igbo even though his first language was Yoruba, he organized a village commune in Yoruba forests during the war, and he was quoted to say that he gave a television interview in Calabar to journalists, who probably did not speak Yoruba, but chose to give the interview in 'fluent Yoruba'. The author concluded that Madunagu remains today the foremost Marxist intellectual in Nigeria but the author also took Madunagu to tasks for serving as an adviser to the Political Bureau of the Babangida dictatorship. This is misleading since the Bureau members were not advisers but moderators of a national debate on national ideology. Moreover, other Marxist intellectuals who worked in government-controlled universities or in foreign-funded NGOs frequently offered unsolicited advice in the form of newspaper opinion editorials and other policy publications or consultancy reports.

Mayer carried the methodology of 'quotism', that Madunagu derided in Oniororo's work, too far by reproducing verbatim, without analysis, a newspaper column by Madunagu, which took up five pages of the book, just to assert that 1989 was a tragic year for Marxism (74-8). The author also highlighted the ideas of other 'ethnically Igbo' Marxists whom he apparently admired – Mokwugo Okoye and his wife, Ifeoma Okoye, Chinua Achebe, Samuel Ikoku, and Okwudiba Nnoli (who was better known for his work on ethnicity as a tool for class domination). The Zikist Movement was said to have helped to advance

Marxist ideas in the 1950s (52-4), drawing from the militant organizing in the Nigeria labour movement in the 1940s by Nduka Eze and Michael Imoudu. The Zikists rallied around the 'ethnically Igbo' leader of the struggle for the restoration of independence, Dr Nnamdi Azikiwe (who was born in the North and spoke Hausa first before learning to speak Igbo, Yoruba and Efik fluently) but Zik repudiated their 'youthful exuberance' and many of the Zikist were jailed for sedition.

The Northern Elements Progressive Union was noted as an anti-feudalist party in the North that was led by Aminu Kano who formed an alliance with Azikiwe's National Council for Nigerian Citizens. The party tendency continues in Nigeria today in the form of Peoples Redemption Party as the oldest existing party in the country that was founded by Aminu Kano, Chinua Achebe, Michael Imoudu, Eskor Toyo, Wole Soyinka, Samuel Ikoku, Bala Usman, Bala Mohamad, Abubakar Rimi, Balarabe Musa, Arthur Nwankwo, Edwin Madunagu, etc. By contrast, the author stated that it would be a stretch to call Obafemi Awolowo a Marxist (maybe because Awo defended 'starvation as a legitimate weapon of war', not mentioned in the book) despite his free education and free health programs or his 'lukewarm pro-Soviet stance' as Leader of the Opposition (94). Mayer also lost respect for the Marxist credentials of Yusuf Bala Usman who was accused in the book of 'habitual lack of internationalism' and of sounding increasingly like a 'fascist' in the closing years of his life (117). Bala had started claiming that the Yoruba and the Igbo were scheming to deprive the North of access to the oil that must have formed from the flora of Northern ancestors (though Mayer did not provide this detail in his book). Mayer included the Agbekoya peasant uprising as a Marxist organization because of the class character of their struggles and the fact that they did not launch ethnic violence directly against any ethnic group. However, according to the firsthand memoirs of Toyin

Falola, unknown to Mayer, the members of the Agbekoya revolt prepared magical charms and sent them to the genocidal troops fighting in Biafra to embolden them and when one of the most notorious genocidist commanders, Benjamin Adekunle, returned from the war front on leave, they celebrated him as a national hero (Falola, 2014). Readers who are not familiar with the historical background that Mayer omitted may like to know that Nigerian intellectuals continue to justify the genocide against the Igbo with the false propaganda that the first military coup in the country was carried out by Igbo officers who killed Northern and Western Nigerian leaders and spared Igbo ones. On the contrary, the coup that Mayer wrongly called the 'Ironsi coup' was carried out by officers of the Nigerian Army with the aim of releasing Obafemi Awolowo from prison and making him Prime Minister. Ironsi quelled the coup and arrested the culprits. The Igbo officers among them were from the old Western region too. As a result of ethnic propaganda, most Nigerians were made to believe that the genocide against the Igbo was committed by Northern Muslims in vengeance. Quite the contrary, Christian Yoruba and Christian Middle Belt officers led the genocide against Igbo people in Nigeria and Naija Marxists are yet to publish a book explaining their roles in such crimes against humanity nor do they join the Igbo to call for reparations (Achebe, 2012; Ekwe-Ekwe, 2006; Jacobs, 1987).

The book is very well written and professionally copyedited with the high standards for which Pluto Press is known. It kicked off with unflattering truths about the Nigerian condition that readers of *The Trouble With Nigeria* by Chinua Achebe (1983) or of *Nigeria: The Challenge of Biafra* by Arthur Nwankwo (1972) will be familiar with (see also, Agozino, 2016). No one in the country knows exactly how many people live in the country due to the politicization of the national census since colonial days. Rubbish is left to pile up on the streets and people are forced to ease themselves in public without any privacy because the oil-rich state provides no public toilets, nor electricity, nor pipe-borne water, nor good schools, nor safe roads, nor healthcare, nor employment opportunities, while the bourgeoisie robs the people blind. None of this is news to Nigerians or close observers of the country. What is new and original to the book is the contention that Nigerian Marxists have remained consistent in providing alternative ideas that are capable of rescuing the country from the plundering ruling classes and yet no book has been written exclusively on the history of Marxist thought in Nigeria until now. For this feat, the author deserves all the praises that the book has attracted from established scholars around the world. Nigerian professors should take the cue and encourage their doctoral students to do similar work in the sociology of knowledge in the country.

Eurocentrism weakened the originality of the book by always looking for European models into which to fit original African thinkers particularly when the Soviet Union and Eastern Europe were exaggerated as 'the precondition for the emergence' of Marxism in Nigeria (191). Eskor Toyo was repeatedly called a Trotskyist and Maoist whereas he was known as an original thinker (86-7). The author concluded by asserting that 'Eskor Toyo has been proved blatantly wrong' for stating that dependency theories overemphasized external determinants of agency (191). Mayer apparently misunderstood what Toyo was saying – that Nigerians, as social agents, were primarily responsible for the underdevelopment of their country today, though imperialism shares the blames. It is factually wrong for the author to claim that Eskor Toyo, Edwin Madunagu, Ola Oni, Sylvester Ejiofor and other Marxists joined a Social Democratic labour party created by the Babangida dictatorship (74). The author was confusing the Labour Party (that was banned by Babangida) with the Social Democratic Party that Babangida imposed as 'a little to my left' along with the Republican Party that he decreed to be 'a little to my right'.

Nigerian 'Marxist Feminists' were being forced into a debate about the pleasures of sex in Lenin's Russia when they may never have identified themselves as either feminists or Marxists with the exception of activist-intellectuals like Ifeoma Okoye, Molara Ogundipe-Leslie, Bene Madunagu and Amina Mama. The African preference for unity in the struggles by African women for the rights of both women and men should have been held up as the model for gender-separatist European feminism itself. Parity has been inscribed in the constitution of the African Union Parliament and in the country of Senegal with the expectation of the equal representation of men and women. The author also missed the opportunity to reflect the debates around the campaign for the Peoples Republic of Africa or for a United States of Africa as one possible solution to the problems with Nigeria – a country rich in natural resources but ran into the ground by elite compradors.

REFERENCES

Achebe, Chinua (1983) *The Trouble With Nigeria*, Enugu, Fourth Dimension Publishing Company.

Achebe, Chinua (2012) *There Was A Country: A Personal History of Biafra*, New York, Penguin.

Agozino, Biko (2014) 'The Africana paradigm in Capital: the debts of Karl Marx to people of African descent', *Review of African Political Economy*, 41:140, 172-84.

Agozino, Biko (2016) *Critical, Creative and Centred Scholar-Activism: The Fourth Dimensionalism of Agwuncha Arthur Nwankwo*, Enugu, Fourth Dimension Publishing Co.

Ekwe-Ekwe, Herbert (2006) *Biafra Revisited*, Dakar, African Renaissance.

Falola, Toyin (2014) *Counting the Tiger's Teeth: An African Teenager's Story*, Ann Arbor, University of Michigan Press.

Hall, Stuart (2016) *Cultural Studies 1983: A Theoretical History*,

Durham, Duke University Press.

Jacobs, Dan (1987) *The Brutality of Nations*, New York, Alfred A. Knopf.

Nwankwo, Agwuncha Arthur (1972) *Nigeria: The Challenge of Biafra*, Enugu, Fourth Dimension Publishing Co.

BIKO AGOZINO, PhD
Virginia Tech University, Blacksburg
Virginia, USA

NoViolet Bulawayo. *We Need New Names*
Vintage Books, London, 2014, 294pp, £8.99
ISBN 978-0-099-58188-8 paperback

NoViolet Bulawayo's debut novel is a deeply and freshly cut story that excites and startles at the same time. It is contemporary in temper and like many other African novels is committed to drawing attention to the myriad troubles besetting Africa in contemporary times. It is in two parts: the first part explores Darling's and her friends' lives of poverty and hardship in Paradise (Africa) due to colonial invasion. The destruction of their former system affects every family such that the children become guava hunters in a forbidden area (Budapest, white settlement). Hunger emboldens them and they regularly trespass into the white area in search of food (guava). The harsh experiences of being forced to cater for themselves at a tender age and abject poverty push the children to always dream of escaping to other countries. Somebody like Darling does not have the protection and love of either of her parents. Her Father abandons them: 'Now Father is in South Africa, working, but he never writes, never sends us money never nothing. It makes me angry thinking about him so most of the time I just pretend he doesn't exist; it's better this way' (22-3). Her mother on the other hand is so busy with trading and herself that Darling is left to the care of her not-loving grandmother. Darling's only true family is her circle of friends. This explains her always feeling out of place, inadequate and sad whenever circumstances force her to be away from them. An instance of her frustration is seen when her sick Father returns from South Africa, and she is forced to not only stay away from them, but to lie to them in order to prevent the fact that her Father has HIV from spreading in the vicinity. 'It's not the lying itself that makes me feel bad but the fact that I'm here lying to my friends. I don't like not playing with them because they are the most important thing to me and when I'm not with them I feel like I'm not even me' (94).

In the second part of the novel which is set in America, the text explores the different world views that will appear strange in Darling's country and culture but are very acceptable in America. There, Darling wonders at the various modernist and post modernist ideologies that inform the attitude and behavior of people. Parents have no real control over their children like in her country for they cannot flog a naughty child, people smile at situations that they should frown at. An example of this is seen when rather than scold the disobedient son of the bride at a wedding for his naughtiness, the child is applauded, 'when Mandla gets the ball, he throws it and it hits an old lady in a pink dress on the breast. I stop breathing, but the old lady just smiles like nothing's happened, picks up the ball from her lap, and holds it out to Mandla. Isn't he a sweetheart? She says to Dumi with an old lady's pointless smile, and Dumi smiles back' (181-2). Also whenever people are tired of their sex and wish to transform to something else, they do it through medical surgery, and people just accept it, old parents are taken to old peoples' homes by their children who do not see anything wrong in that. The narrator's attitude towards these strange ways is skeptical.

The novel also explores the sad and demeaning experiences of illegal immigrants in America. The fact that a lot is sacrificed by them to get into America compels the immigrants to want to justify all the sacrifices and expectations of people at home by remaining in America at all costs. They hide their true situations from the people back home by sending money home for the training of their younger ones and the upkeep of their ageing parents. Their illegal status makes visiting their home countries an impossibility since they will not be allowed to re-enter America. Thus they find themselves trying to survive in a place where they are not wanted. Their illegal status also makes it impossible for them to get good jobs, so they are left with back-breaking and disgusting jobs which they keep changing in order to escape being captured and deported. The great measure of their insecurity is such that they take on new names in order to hide their true identities. The children born to them are also given meaningless names so they can be accepted in America. The sad thing about their new identities is that they long for the old ones and really would prefer to raise their children according to African traditions, but are unable to do so because they are in an environment that does not recognize their own life values. One very disturbing thing about the situation of these immigrants is that they long for home while obviously they will not be able to fit in again, if given the opportunity. Even though it is difficult for some of the characters to accept this truth, it is very clear in the text:

> When are you coming back? Stina says after a long silence. I open my mouth and hear Aunt Fostalina's voice inside my head. I don't know how to tell Stina that I don't know when I'm coming home. Through the window, I can see the tall mailman walking up the driveway, towards the house. I wait for him to ring the door before I put the phone down after telling Stina to hold on, knowing I will not be picking up the phone. It's hard to explain, this feeling; it's like there's two of me. One part is yearning for my friends; the other doesn't know how to connect with them anymore, as if they

are people I've never met. I feel a little guilty but I brush the feeling away. (210)

From this excerpt, it is obvious that profound alienation and a sense of the disconnections of exile breeds disarticulation. It becomes increasingly difficult for Darling to connect with the people she earlier describes as 'the most important thing' (94) in her life, because, increasingly, she no longer fits into the routine of their lives anymore, and by extension, into the demands of her African tradition or past. On the other hand, though her friends ask when she will return home, their action of naming Chipo's child after her, shows they already replaced her. 'Darling is Chipo's daughter; they claimed they decided to name her after me so there would be another Darling in case something happened to me in America. It's kind of cute, but I don't know how to feel about it, somebody being named after me like I'm dead or something' (210). Their action of replacing her resonates with Stina's words that Darling remembers while in America, '... Leaving your country is like dying, and when you come back, you are like a ghost returning to earth...' (160). Thus, Darling will be like a ghost (a stranger) that they cannot truly relate to, if she eventually comes back. This then is the fate of many African immigrants. They are on self-imposed exile. The narrator describes it thus: 'We stayed, like prisoners, only we chose to be prisoners and we loved our prison; it was not a bad prison' (247). One very significant aspect of the Bulawayo's novel that most readers will fall in love with at once, is Bulawayo's narrative technique – the first person voice of a child-narrator. The story told incorporates the experiences of Darling, the child-narrator and her friends. This is made evident by the narrator's constant use of the first person plural pronoun 'we'. This use of the collective 'we' persists throughout the novel, and lends it is powerful sense of intimacy, and of the shared experience. Even in America, the stories of other illegal immigrants are put in the same context with Darling's stories, in such a way that at every point in time the collective experiences of the people is the point of the narrative experience and not so much that of an individual. This resonates with the title of the novel: 'We Need New Names', and not 'I Need a New Name'.

The child-narrator's blending of innocence, sadness, indifference, and joy in the narration heightens the narrative mood altogether. There is a tragi-comic quality to it. In an important moment in the story, halfway through running away from the dangling corpse of a dead woman, the children decide to make the woman's loss their gain. Their leader says, 'Look, did you notice that woman's shoes were almost new? If we can get them then we can sell them and buy a loaf, or maybe even one and a half. We all turn around and follow Bastard back into the bush, the dizzying smell of Lobels bread all around us now, and then we are rushing, then we are running, then we are running and laughing and laughing and laughing' (18). It becomes a situation of survival of the fittest. The most important thing is to survive in a jungle. Thus the end justifies the means. The child-narrator's way of telling the story wipes away any moral question that might be raised.

Again, the narrator, even though still a child, is very self-aware. She is able to see through the hypocrisy of some white people who pretend to love Africans. She pays them back in their own coins. When in America a woman gives her a patronizing attention, she gets even with her by giving her a bleached smile: 'I look in the mirror, and this woman in a blue dress is standing there smiling at me. I notice the smell of her sweet perfume is all over, like a living thing. I smile back. It's not exactly a smile-smile, just the brief baring of teeth' (174).

In subtle ways, the narrator also laughs at some of the excesses that the American world endorses. This is revealed in Darling's tone in describing the shock of the people at the wedding reception where she beats the naughty boy who has been throwing his ball at adults: 'It's only when I sit down and look around that I realize what I have done. The white people have already gasped, and a shocked voice has already said, oh my God. Heads have been shaken and eyes have widened in disbelief. A few hands have already flown over mouths, and the silence has already descended. It stays in the air like a stain, until this booming voice, which I quickly recognize as Tshaka Zulu's, shouts from near the door, where he is seated' (183). She captures the disapproval of people in the hall, and the precise detail of her description underscores her own attitude, decidedly alien, to the values she satirizes. Instead of applauding her, they reproach her for disciplining the child. The American moral condition is reflective of her excess, much like her crisis of obesity, which mirrors, in Bulawayo's story, the American excess. In fact, the obese American is clearly synecdochal, because it is an image redolent with significance, that captures both the situation of waste and moral indolence in America's psychic and physical health in a parabolic way in this novel: The narrator's description is very strong and clear such that her attitude towards any subject is made evident. In her natal country, people feed well and get robust in a way that is appealing to the eyes, but 'fatness' in America is different: 'American fatness takes it to a whole another level: the body is turned into something else- the neck becomes a thigh, the stomach an anthill, an arm a thing, a buttock a I don't even know what' (171). America is both morally and physically distorted, a caricature in fact, which in the perceptive and eloquent observations of the novelist telegraphs her moral condition or crisis.

In conclusion, *We Need New Names* is very original and fresh in the way it captures the experiences of the African in the American world. The telling is fluent, there are no hitches; no boring moments in its development. It is a story which should be read by all who struggle daily to make sense of their societies, and especially by Africans who still think that their only best option is to leave Africa and go in search of some mythical el-dorado in America. If Bulawayo's novel teaches us anything, it must be the cliché, that nothing often seems as it is painted, or plainly, that not all that glitters is gold. Those Africans who escape to America and the west come eventually to understand this in the long run, and by which time, they would have developed complex relationships with their past and their homeland in ways that can only best be described as that search for 'new names' that comes with exile and alienation.

NONYE CHINYERE AHUMIBE
Department of English,
Imo State University, Owerri, Nigeria

Okey Ndibe. *Never Look an American in the Eye: Flying Turtles, Colonial Ghosts, and the Making of a Nigerian American*
New York, Soho Press, Inc., 2016, 210 pages. $25.00
ISBN 978-1-61695-760-5 hardback

'Never look an American in the Eye', warned Ochendu, Okey Ndibe's uncle at his farewell family gathering in Nigeria before the young Okey sets off to the United States to edit a new magazine *African Commentary*. Although the uncle had never travelled outside of Nigeria, Okey took the advice to heart and assiduously avoided eye contact with any Americans he met until that fateful day while standing waiting for a bus in Amherst, MA. He looked up straight into the eyes of a police officer waiting in his cruiser. The light changed and the officer drove off around the corner. The next minute Ndibe felt a hand on his shoulder, 'Sir, do you mind stepping out to the back of the bus stop?' (72). Only 13 days in the country and he was mistaken for a bank robber! With no identification on him, the officer asked that he put his hands over his head while he was frisked. What was frisking Ndibe wondered? And what must the others at the bus stop think was happening to him? The officer then drove him back to his residence where he produced his passport and was cleared of any suspicion. In retrospect, the writer was able to recreate the terror he felt, the embarrassment, and the mental agony as he thought about what the police were like and could do in Nigeria under similar circumstances,

> What if the Amherst police officer drove me to an isolated spot in town and, with nobody to witness the dastardly act, simply 'wasted' me...I contemplated my next move. A part of me wanted to sprint away. I had been a notable track athlete in high school. I was confident of outrunning the police officer. But the sight of the officer's gun froze me... (76-7)

Okey Ndibe's memories of the early clashes in etiquette are equally amusing and penetrating. An American woman invited him to lunch so they could continue their discussion on her desire to trace her Nigerian father whom she had never met. Assuming this to be a case of free lunch, it turns into an embarrassing lesson in going Dutch:

> In an instant, my first meal with a 'generous' American turned into a moment of profound cultural disorientation... To compound the problem, as a Nigerian, I didn't know what a 'tip' meant.

With no money on him he had to ask the woman to pay and he would reimburse her. He quickly returned to host, Prof. Nnaji's office, on campus where they had met so he could retrieve his wallet and refund her. She paid reluctantly.

Despite these initial confusions, Okey Ndibe's humour and love of a good story prevail throughout his gripping tale of adventure. His chapter on the play between his name and the expression 'okey' is hilarious. 'Are you Okey?' was often misinterpreted to mean, 'Are you okey/all right?' Always in a precarious financial state due to the inadequate funding of *African Commentary* which collapsed after only 3 years, Ndibe remains in Amherst and is able to start an MFA program at the University of Massachusetts. Of course, his admission into the university was not without its own chequered story. He met an author while browsing in a used bookstore in town who knew he had been editor of the now defunct magazine. The man, an author himself, asked Ndibe if he was then working on a novel. Quickly, Ndibe lied that he was. Suggesting that he send him a sample as he could possibly help him gain admission to the writing program, Ndibe went home and began what later became *Arrows of Rain,* Ndibe's first novel.

Ndibe did not set out to become an American. His memoir is grounded in a warm childhood in his village of Amawbia in southeastern Nigeria (present day Anambra State) where he often dreamed of Britain, then the USSR, and then after a vacation in Enugu where he watched American wrestling and other exports, America. 'It was the swashbuckling drama and flair for evocative names that compelled my attention [to America].' Later he would connect to such authors as Martin Luther King, Jr., Richard Wright, Ralph Ellison, John Steinbeck, Ernest Hemingway, and James Baldwin. Reading fueled his desire to write, but ironically he had graduated from Yaba College of Technology in Lagos and the Institute of Management and Technology (IMT) at Enugu where he majored in business administration. But his first job was as a staff correspondent with the Lagos-based, *African Concord* and later at the weekly newsmagazine *African Guardian* as assistant editor. Ndibe had formed a personal relationship with Chinua Achebe by this time and it was at his (Achebe's) invitation that he agreed to leave Nigeria for Massachusetts to edit the nascent magazine *African Commentary.*

If Nigerians had stereotypical images of America, it was equally true that Americans had stereotypical images of Africa and Ndibe is particularly good at sharing these stories. A graduate student named Chris with whom he had a casual, joking relationship asked him one day, 'I've been wondering about something. I see a lot of Africans around town [Amherst, MA]. How are you guys able to come to America when there are no airports in Africa?'

> Thinking Chris was just pulling his leg, Okey replied, 'Why, we ride on the backs of crocodiles across the Atlantic.'
>   'Crocodiles? Don't they eat you?'
>   'Oh no,' I assured. 'African languages make crocodiles docile. If you speak an African language a crocodile would give you a hug...' (96)

It turned out that Chris had shockingly not been joking at all and had even shared Okey's story with his roommates who wanted confirmation from the source of the story.

In 1993 while on a visit to Nigeria, Ndibe finds that his father's health is rapidly deteriorating. In June he was diagnosed with renal disease. Realizing how little he knew of his father's early life, Ndibe begins to delve more deeply into family history. He knew his parents married out of love, a very unusual situation among this Igbo community since his father was 36 at the time and his mother 33 – considered well past the marriageable age. He had served in Burma during the Second World War and became a postal clerk on return. She had trained as a teacher. They had four sons, Okey being the second, and a daughter. Though not rich – certainly no car or TV – they were well off in character, dignity, and intelligence. His father was a simple but remarkable man who was never afraid to speak his mind. It was as a soldier under a British officer that his frank remark that Tucker, the officer, has his rank because he was British, not because he knew signaling as well as some of the African soldiers, got him noticed. Such comments alarmed his fellow Africans, but Tucker soon went out of his way to befriend Ndibe's father. The two began to hold long discussions and their friendship through correspondence lasted a lifetime.

Ndibe describes himself as a Nigerian American. He does not hate his place of birth, but as he says, Nigeria is 'a heartbreak nation full of promise and prospect but short on achievement' (147). More specifically,

> Sadly, Nigeria is also a country conceived in hope but nurtured – primarily by its gluttonous leaders and their global corporate partners in crime – into hopelessness. If Nigerian scams had made themselves felt around the world, it was largely because the country's leaders had respected no bounds or limits in the egregious grasping, in their culture of self-aggrandizement and illicit enrichment. (148)

Okey Ndibe's candour and his journalist's dauntless sagacity, both enrich the memoir and give it integrity. It is a memoir with a difference. Ordinarily, an immigrant's, sojourner's 'arrivistes story', with all the known features of travails and vicissitudes, the ever constant insecurity of troubled existence, *Never Look an American in the Eye*... transforms into a metaphor for refugee-survival across borders. What could be more topical today? It could be anybody's story. What gives it a befitting space on every reader's shelf are the author's impeccable skills as a storyteller, his inimitable blending of a journalist's daring in the face of odds with an unflinching determination to stick to the path of truth through thick and thin. It goes beyond a Nigerian immigrant's tale of 'a path to citizenship in America'. It is a story of the rites of passage – what it takes to survive in the midst of uncertainties, failed expectations, and lost hopes regained. Okey Ndibe's memoir is in the end, a validation of the truism that 'where there is a will, there's always a way.'

PATRICIA T. EMENYONU, PhD
Department of Africana Studies/English
University of Michigan-Flint, USA

Reviews of Nigerian Poetry

Obari Gomba. *For Every Homeland.*
Lagos: Narrative Landscape Press. 2017, 165 pp., N800
ISBN 978-978-958-831-2 paperback

Obari Gomba has often deployed his poetry to illuminate the material realities of the Niger Delta; nowhere in his corpus is this more particularly evident than in *Pearls of the Mangroves* (1999), a volume trenchant in its denunciation of the despoliation of the oil-rich region by transnational oil corporations. However, the Niger Delta makes a passing appearance in his latest poetry collection, *For Every Homeland*. In this volume, the world is the lens through which he casts a sweeping eye across our shared (at times contested/ negated) humanity. The themes explored are familiar, and even resonate more than ever, in this era of neo-fascism and ultra-nationalism.

Gomba has so far authored seven poetry collections, and *For Every Homeland* is his seventh. He teaches Literature and Creative Writing at the University of Port Harcourt, Nigeria, and was longlisted for the 2017 LNG Nigeria Prize for Literature, an award for which a previous collection of his, *Length of Eyes,* was earlier longlisted in 2013. Taken together, his poetry has earned him critical acclaim from notable Nigerian poets such as JP Clark-Bekederemo, Tanure Ojaide, and Lindsay Barrett. Odia Ofeimum, another renowned Nigeria poet, has praised his poetic vision for having 'the freshness of an insurrection'.

For Every Homeland is composed of forty-three poems grouped under three sections. Most of the poems run into three or four pages; the longest is 'The Wood Revolt', an eight-page long poem. Poems such as 'To Firefly', 'I Speak Niglish', 'To See or not to See', 'A Few Words', 'Is it Your Fingerprint', etcetera, barely span two pages. The poems deal with death and genocide, terror and terrorism, racism and American supremacy. Family, sex, travel, and nostalgia are also touched upon. The moods evoked oscillate between the solemn and the satiric, mediated in a way that never undercuts the urgency of the personal and the political. The poet's diction is precise and unencumbered, his imagery devoid of opacity. Myth is utilised in a few poems to heighten narrative resonance, and much of the poetry is marked by musicality, thus attesting to the poet's fidelity to lyricism.

The volume opens with 'Unfinished Ballad', a poem narrating the communal killing of a child and the tragedies that follow. Dark and haunting, it foreshadows the motif of death addressed in some poems. The stanza below illustrates the 'the folly of the living':

> They bury the child alive at the riverbank.
> The child's cry follows them back to town.
> The child's cry haunts the whole town. (4)

The *pièce de resistance*, for me, is 'She Reminds Me of Hecuba'. Drawing on classical, biblical, historical, and contemporary events, this powerful poem documents in lucid details the slaughtering that occurred during the precolonial, colonial, and postcolonial periods, all in the name of varied 'isms' and ideologies. Atrocities suffered by women and children in Greece, Bethlehem, Carthage, the Americas, Congo, Sudan, Afghanistan, Somali, Iraq, Syria, Libya, and Yemen, as well as by the Jews in Nazi Germany, Palestinians in Zionist Israel, Biafran and Tutsi women in Nigeria and Rwanda are likewise portrayed. The poet recalls that 'She reminds me of the women/Of the world/ Of women everywhere.../Of deaths, of deaths and of deaths' (83). The tragedy of being a child in conflict-ridden nations finds accent in 'Save the Children', another equally funereal poem, which echoes, if obliquely, the opening poem. It reads as a paean to childhood innocence, wherein the poet declares that 'Evil is neither Jew nor Arab/Neither male nor female/Evil denies children a decent foothold' (100).

The poems are not grim altogether, for there are also sprinklings of erotic playfulness. In 'Is a Pun Risky or Risqué,' the poet employs a *double entendre* such as 'The prick went deeper than we expected…/The prick is deep' (35-8). Another instance of this is in 'Redefinitions', where the poet recounts: 'You muse over all thighs you/ Have uncovered in the past, their shades and fires' (9). Frankfurt, one of the cities the poet visits, is personified as a 'graceful coquette' whose 'thighs are too tight/No penetration – she says' (133). The poem 'Getting Home' is all but confessional and autobiographical, reflecting a subject many poets practicing their art in Nigeria are familiar with: the penurious rewards of poetry. The poet bemoans this fact: 'It's a pity how I bring more books home/Always more books than money' (25).

In 2016, Gomba participated in the International Writers' Program at the University of Iowa, and his peregrinations are evoked in the following poems: 'In a City with Hawk-Eyes', 'First Night in Seattle', 'On Starbucks and its Mermaid' and 'At Pike Market Place'. In fact, he devotes the third section of the collection to ruminating on his travels. 'Different Stations of the Alchemy' traces his itinerary from Nigeria through Germany and finally to the United States. Arriving in Iowa, he enthuses

> I have dipped my navel's cord into the earth
> I have come – child of the Tropics. I am here
> I hear icy footfalls close by, coming over.
> It is the year-god: decked in snowflakes. (137)

However, the eponymous poem 'For Every Homeland' charts his climatic journey from the US back to Nigeria, thus bringing the collection to a close. As the poet declaims, on stepping foot in his homeland,

> I shouted my father's words
> Into the air and I asked the birds
> To take them to troubled folks
> In all afflicted homelands. (165)

'What Does Live Matter', and 'After the Shootings' draw attention to the spectre of police violence and racialized killings in the US. The poet comments on 'the black in America' and the 'apostles of hate', highlighting the Black Lives Matter movement. He laments, 'For everyone who can aim a shot/Black folks are always under fire' (146), then goes on to ask: 'What does live matter in a country/ Where everyone claims to be colour-blind/Because everyone knows the colour of death?' (146). In 'Chicago Diary,' the city, which the poet had hoped to revel in, is troubled by 'The peal of police sirens/[that]fills the air with foreboding' (151). It is this terror, common to every African American, that chips away some elation the poet felt while in the US.

'Electile Erection' and 'Build the Wall' speak tellingly to the American recent electoral experiences. In these poems, the poet lampoons the 'United States of Trumpica' and its 'beatification of that Yellow Donut' (159), at the same time reminding us that 'Walls are as old/As time is old/Power loves to cling to Folly' (163). Written with an unforced aesthetic sensibility, Gomba interrogates various subjectivities in a world much authorized by violence, precarity, and an inveterate phobia for otherness. He demonstrates nonpareil confidence and mastery in this volume, which consolidates his position as an important poet among his peers in Nigeria. Here is a poet who lends his voice, resolute, unstinting, yet cadenced, to our postcolonial and global failings without once sounding neither contemptuous nor maudlin.

At the end of the collection, Obari Gomba leaves us contemplating human folly and individual complicity in the world's manifold tragedy. As he wonders in 'Is it Your Fingerprint':

Look at the fingerprint on
The tragedies of the world
Does it look like yours? (120)

Musa Idris Okpanachi. *Music of the Dead*
Lagos: Origami Books. 2016, 126 pp, np
ISBN 978-978-540-794-5 paperback

Musa Idris Okpanachi, an Associate Professor of English
at the Department of English, Federal University, Dutse,
Jigawa state, has authored three collections of poems: *The
Eaters of the Living* (2007), *From the Margins of Paradise*
(2012), and *Music of the Dead* (2016). Dark, haunting
images of blood, corpses, and cemetery recur in his poetry,
apparently depicting the regularity of death in his country.
By utilizing satiric and hyperbolic elements, limpid diction
interspersed with sepulchral images, Okpanachi uncovers
the degeneration usually indicative of postcolonial failure.
It is this persistent degeneration in Nigeria that animates
Okpanachi's preoccupation with funereal imagery.

His latest poetry collection, *Music of the Dead*, is made up of
72 poems. It opens with 'A Long Silence', a prose poem which
presents in dense rhythm a montage of uncanny scenes of
'an age stranger than time and chameleon' (1). In this strange
age, the news of people dying is so common, but the causes
of their deaths might seem ludicrous were it not strange. Due
to the commonness of death in the land, the poet laments
that 'the graveyards are full; the country is a cemetery in
the hands of the dead' (2). The poem prefaces the kind of
grim imagery one will mainly come across in the collection
– imagery that induces anything but hope and cheer.

The sequence of poems in 'Dogs and Angels 1-111'
narrate the manifestations of 'gallows', 'nooses', 'graves',
'houses ablaze', 'cemetery' etc., (9-12). 'The Forerunner'
portrays the ruler's perversity which leaves behind a trail
of death (18), while the poem 'Sharks' is shot through with
grisly images:

> Death is a million
> Magic numbers
> In democratic coffins
> We have dug 150 million graves. (26)

The theme of death finds more resonance in 'Black Flower', a poem recounting the 'seasons of massacre' (28). In 'The Hawkers of Blood', the poet comments on the sense of vile triumphalism exhibited by killers who boast that they are heirs of the 'primitive gods of war' and delight 'in celebration of death' (76). The scenes depicted in this poem evoke the devastation wrought in certain parts of Nigeria by Boko Haram, an Islamist terrorist group.

Irony and satire are strong features of Okpanachi's poems, and he deploys them quite effectively in 'You the People's Choice'; a poem satirizing the ruler as Pharaoh whose reign heralds 'the season of madness' (85). He is a poet invested in the political discourse of nationhood, and so he articulates the social concerns of the people as well as deprecates the political elite for their treachery that has spawned widespread dispossession and death in the nation. 'My Father's House' parodies *Our Lord's Prayer* or the Pater Noster, one of the most spoken prayers in the world. In the poem, the poet brings the atrocities of the 'new butchers' – newly elected politicians – who have transformed the country into 'the slaughter house of the high priests' (92) to God's attention. Implicated in this carnage are the following 'professional murderers':

> The judge who miscarries justice
> The hangman who unfurls the noose
> The tailor who sews the shroud
> The butcher who stitches the flesh
> ...
> The carpenter who makes the coffins
> The undertaker who closes the graves
> The executioners of mourners of the beloved
> The priest who lies against God
> The poet whose tears are the streams of treason (92)

In 'King of Cemetery', the atrocities of the butchers are set in relief. The poem's depiction of events may as well be the most bizarre in the collection. The butchers ensure that those 'they bury alive' do not leave the cemetery, and beyond this, they also ensure 'they rape the dead in their graves' (96).

Okpanachi's *Music of the Dead* signals the extent to which Nigeria has foundered in its democratic journey: the civilian government seems even more exploitative than its military counterpart. The citizens may have only succeeded in replacing one set of oppressors with another. Okpanachi's poetry demonstrates that the democratic rule in Nigeria has been no less horrifying than military despotism. By using images both dark and haunting in his poetry, Okpanachi effectively draws the reader's attention to the currency of anomalies in Nigeria, all the while denouncing the political class and its penchant for power abuse. Though the nation is no longer brutalized by military junta, it appears stricken altogether – 'a country of cemetery'.

Musa Idris Okpanachi's fascination with funereal imagery is not that he delights in it, but because he is attempting to represent the gruesome times Nigerians live in under democratic rule, a time where death seems to have become so banal that 'it is so easy [for people] to die'.

UCHECHUKWU PETER UMEZURIKE
Department of English and Film Studies,
University of Alberta, Canada